Rob J Hyndman and George Athanasopoulos

Forecasting
Principles and Practice

ONLINE, OPEN-ACCESS TEXTBOOKS

Forecasting: Principles and Practice

ISBN 978-0-9875071-0-5

Copyright © 2014.
Rob J Hyndman and George Athanasopoulos

Available online at *http://otexts.com/fpp/*

Print edition, April 2014

PUBLISHED BY OTEXTS.COM

Contents

Preface

This textbook is intended to provide a comprehensive introduction to forecasting methods and present enough information about each method for readers to use them sensibly. We don't attempt to give a thorough discussion of the theoretical details behind each method, although the references at the end of each chapter will fill in many of those details.

The book is written for three audiences: (1) people finding themselves doing forecasting in business when they may not have had any formal training in the area; (2) undergraduate students studying business; (3) MBA students doing a forecasting elective. We use it ourselves for a second-year subject for students undertaking a Bachelor of Commerce degree at Monash University, Australia.

For most sections, we only assume that readers are familiar with algebra, and high school mathematics should be sufficient background. Readers who have completed an introductory course in statistics will probably want to skip some of Chapters 2 and 4. There are a couple of sections which also require knowledge of matrices, but these are flagged.

At the end of each chapter we provide a list of "further reading". In general, these lists comprise suggested textbooks that provide a more advanced or detailed treatment of the subject. Where there is no suitable textbook, we suggest journal articles that provide more information.

We use R throughout the book and we intend students to learn how to forecast with R. R is free and available on almost every operating system. It is a wonderful tool for all statistical analysis, not just for forecasting. See http://otexts.com/fpp/using-r for instructions on installing and using R.

The book is different from other forecasting textbooks in several ways.

- It is free and online, making it accessible to a wide audience.
- It uses R, which is free, open-source, and extremely powerful software.
- The online version is continuously updated. You don't have to wait until the next edition for errors to be removed or new methods to be discussed. We will update the book frequently.
- There are dozens of real data examples taken from our own consulting practice. We have worked with hundreds of businesses and organizations helping them with forecasting issues, and this experience has contributed directly to many of the examples given here, as well as guiding our general philosophy of forecasting.
- We emphasise graphical methods more than most forecasters. We use graphs to explore the data, analyse the validity of the models fitted and present the forecasting results.

Happy forecasting!

Rob J Hyndman
George Athanasopoulos
April 2014.

1
Getting started

Forecasting has fascinated people for thousands of years, sometimes being considered a sign of divine inspiration, and sometimes being seen as a criminal activity. The Jewish prophet Isaiah wrote in about 700 BC

> *Tell us what the future holds, so we may know that you are gods.*
> (Isaiah 41:23)

One hundred years later, in ancient Babylon, forecasters would foretell the future based on the distribution of maggots in a rotten sheep's liver. By 300 BC, people wanting forecasts would journey to Delphi in Greece to consult the Oracle, who would provide her predictions while intoxicated by ethylene vapours. Forecasters had a tougher time under the emperor Constantine, who issued a decree in AD357 forbidding anyone "to consult a soothsayer, a mathematician, or a forecaster ... May curiosity to foretell the future be silenced forever." A similar ban on forecasting occurred in England in 1736 when it became an offence to defraud by charging money for predictions. The punishment was three months' imprisonment with hard labour!

The varying fortunes of forecasters arise because good forecasts can seem almost magical, while bad forecasts may be dangerous. Consider the following famous predictions about computing.

- *I think there is a world market for maybe five computers.*
  (Chairman of IBM, 1943)

- *Computers in the future may weigh no more than 1.5 tons.*
  (Popular Mechanics, 1949)

- *There is no reason anyone would want a computer in their home.* (President, DEC, 1977)

The last of these was made only three years before IBM produced the first personal computer. Not surprisingly, you can no longer buy a DEC computer. Forecasting is obviously a difficult activity, and businesses that do it well have a big advantage over those whose forecasts fail.

In this book, we will explore the most reliable methods for producing forecasts. The emphasis will be on methods that are replicable and testable, and have been shown to work.

1/1   What can be forecast?

Forecasting is required in many situations: deciding whether to build another power generation plant in the next five years requires forecasts of future demand; scheduling staff in a call centre next week requires forecasts of call volumes; stocking an inventory requires forecasts of stock requirements. Forecasts can be required several years in advance (for the case of capital investments), or only a few minutes beforehand (for telecommunication routing). Whatever the circumstances or time horizons involved, forecasting is an important aid to effective and efficient planning.

Some things are easier to forecast than others. The time of the sunrise tomorrow morning can be forecast very precisely. On the other hand, tomorrow's lotto numbers cannot be forecast with any accuracy. The predictability of an event or a quantity depends on several factors including:

1. how well we understand the factors that contribute to it;
2. how much data are available;
3. whether the forecasts can affect the thing we are trying to forecast.

For example, forecasts of electricity demand can be highly accurate because all three conditions are usually satisfied. We have a good idea on the contributing factors: electricity demand is driven largely by temperatures, with smaller effects for calendar variation such as holidays, and economic conditions. Provided there is a sufficient history of data on electricity demand and weather conditions, and we have the skills to develop a good model linking electricity demand and the key driver variables, the forecasts can be remarkably accurate.

On the other hand, when forecasting currency exchange rates, only one of the conditions is satisfied: there is plenty of available data. However, we have a very limited understanding of the factors that affect exchange rates, and forecasts of the exchange rate have a direct effect on the rates themselves. If there are well-publicised forecasts that the exchange rate will increase, then people will immediately adjust the price they are willing to pay and so the forecasts are self-fulfilling. In a sense the exchange rates become their own forecasts. This is an example of the "efficient market hypothesis". Consequently, forecasting whether the exchange rate will rise or fall tomorrow is about as predictable as forecasting whether a tossed coin will come down as a head or a tail. In both situations, you will be correct about 50% of the time whatever you forecast. In situations like this, forecasters need to be aware of their own limitations, and not claim more than is possible.

Often in forecasting, a key step is knowing when something can be forecast accurately, and when forecasts will be no better than tossing a coin. Good forecasts capture the genuine patterns and relationships which exist in the historical data, but do not replicate past events that will not occur again. In this book, we will learn how to tell the difference between a random fluctuation in the past data that should be ignored, and a genuine pattern that should be modelled and extrapolated.

Many people wrongly assume that forecasts are not possible in a changing environment. Every environment is changing, and a good forecasting model captures the way in which things are changing. Forecasts rarely assume that the environment is unchanging. What is normally assumed is that *the way in which the environment is changing* will continue into the future. That is, a highly volatile environment will continue to be highly volatile; a business with fluctuating sales will continue to have fluctuating sales; and an economy that has gone through booms and busts will continue to go through booms and busts. A forecasting model is intended to capture the way things move, not just where things are. As Abraham Lincoln said, "If we could first know where we are and whither we are tending, we could better judge what to do and how to do it".

Forecasting situations vary widely in their time horizons, factors determining actual outcomes, types of data patterns, and many other aspects. Forecasting methods can be very simple such as using the most recent observation as a forecast (which is called the "naïve method"), or highly complex such as neural nets and econometric systems of simultaneous equations. Sometimes, there will be no data available at all. For example, we may wish to forecast the sales of a new product in its first year, but there are obviously no data to work with. In situations like this, we use judgmental forecasting, discussed in Chapter 3. The choice of method depends on what data are available and the predictability of the quantity to be forecast.

1/2 *Forecasting, planning and goals*

Forecasting is a common statistical task in business, where it helps to inform decisions about the scheduling of production, transportation and personnel, and provides a guide to long-term strategic planning. However, business forecasting is often done poorly, and is frequently confused with planning and goals. They are three different things.

Forecasting is about predicting the future as accurately as possible, given all of the information available, including historical data and knowledge of any future events that might impact the forecasts.

Goals are what you would like to have happen. Goals should be linked to forecasts and plans, but this does not always occur. Too often, goals are set without any plan for how to achieve them, and no forecasts for whether they are realistic.

Planning is a response to forecasts and goals. Planning involves determining the appropriate actions that are required to make your forecasts match your goals.

Forecasting should be an integral part of the decision-making activities of management, as it can play an important role in many areas of a company. Modern organizations require short-term, medium-term and long-term forecasts, depending on the specific application.

Short-term forecasts are needed for the scheduling of personnel, production and transportation. As part of the scheduling process, forecasts of demand are often also required.

Medium-term forecasts are needed to determine future resource requirements, in order to purchase raw materials, hire personnel, or buy machinery and equipment.

Long-term forecasts are used in strategic planning. Such decisions must take account of market opportunities, environmental factors and internal resources.

An organization needs to develop a forecasting system that involves several approaches to predicting uncertain events. Such forecasting systems require the development of expertise in identifying forecasting problems, applying a range of forecasting methods, selecting appropriate methods for each problem, and evaluating and refining forecasting methods over time. It is also important to have strong organizational support for the use of formal forecasting methods if they are to be used successfully.

1/3   Determining what to forecast

In the early stages of a forecasting project, decisions need to be made about what should be forecast.

For example, if forecasts are required for items in a manufacturing environment, it is necessary to ask whether forecasts are needed for:

1. every product line, or for groups of products?
2. every sales outlet, or for outlets grouped by region, or only for total sales?
3. weekly data, monthly data or annual data?

It is also necessary to consider the forecasting horizon. Will forecasts be required for one month in advance, for 6 months, or for ten years? Different types of models will be necessary depending on what forecast horizon is most important.

How frequently are forecasts required? Forecasts that need to be produced frequently are better done using an automated system than with methods that require careful manual work.

It is worth spending time talking to the people who will use the forecasts to ensure that you understand their needs, and how the forecasts are to be used, before embarking on extensive work in producing the forecasts.

Once it has been determined what forecasts are required, it is then necessary to find or collect the data on which the forecasts will be based. The data required for forecasting may already exist. These days, a lot of data are recorded, and the forecaster's task is often to identify where and how the required data are stored. The data may include sales records of a company, the historical demand for a product, or the unemployment rate for a geographical region. A large part of a forecaster's time can be spent in locating and collating the available data prior to developing suitable forecasting methods.

1/4   Forecasting data and methods

The appropriate forecasting methods depend largely on what data are available.

If there are no data available, or if the data available are not relevant to the forecasts, then *qualitative forecasting* methods must be used. These methods are not purely guesswork—there are well-developed structured approaches to obtaining good forecasts without using historical data. These methods are discussed in Chapter 3.

Quantitative forecasting can be applied when two conditions are satisfied:
1. numerical information about the past is available;
2. it is reasonable to assume that some aspects of the past patterns will continue into the future.

There is a wide range of quantitative forecasting methods, often developed within specific disciplines for specific purposes. Each method has its own properties, accuracies, and costs that must be considered when choosing a specific method.

Most quantitative forecasting problems use either time series data (collected at regular intervals over time) or cross-sectional data (collected at a single point in time).

Cross-sectional forecasting

With cross-sectional data, we are wanting to predict the value of something we have not observed, using the information on the cases that we have observed. Examples of cross-sectional data include:

- House prices for all houses sold in 2011 in a particular area. We are interested in predicting the price of a house not in our data set using various house characteristics: position, number of bedrooms, age, etc.

- Fuel economy data for a range of 2009 model cars. We are interested in predicting the carbon footprint of a vehicle not in our data set using information such as the size of the engine and the fuel efficiency of the car.

Example 1.1   Car emissions

Table 1.1 gives some data on 2009 model cars, each of which has an automatic transmission and an engine size under 2 liters.

Model	Litres (litres)	City (mpg)	Highway (mpg)	Carbon (tons CO_2)
Chevrolet Aveo	1.6	25	34	6.6
Chevrolet Aveo 5	1.6	25	34	6.6
Honda Civic	1.8	25	36	6.3
Honda Civic Hybrid	1.3	40	45	4.4
Honda Fit	1.5	27	33	6.1
Honda Fit	1.5	28	35	5.9
Hyundai Accent	1.6	26	35	6.3
Kia Rio	1.6	26	35	6.1
Nissan Versa	1.8	27	33	6.3
Nissan Versa	1.8	24	32	6.8
Pontiac G3 Wave	1.6	25	34	6.6
Pontiac G3 Wave 5	1.6	25	34	6.6
Pontiac Vibe	1.8	26	31	6.6
Saturn Astra 2DR Hatchback	1.8	24	30	6.8
Saturn Astra 4DR Hatchback	1.8	24	30	6.8
Scion xD	1.8	26	32	6.6
Toyota Corolla	1.8	27	35	6.1
Toyota Matrix	1.8	25	31	6.6
Toyota Prius	1.5	48	45	4.0
Toyota Yaris	1.5	29	35	5.9

Table 1.1: Fuel economy and carbon footprints for 2009 model cars with automatic transmissions and small engines. City and Highway represent fuel economy while driving in the city and on the highway.

A forecaster may wish to predict the carbon footprint (tons of CO_2 per year) for other similar vehicles that are not included in the above table. It is necessary to first estimate the effects of the predictors (number of cylinders, size of engine, and fuel economy) on the variable to be forecast (carbon footprint). Then, provided that we know the predictors for a car not in the table, we can forecast its carbon footprint.

Cross-sectional models are used when the variable to be forecast exhibits a relationship with one or more other predictor variables. The purpose of the cross-sectional model is to describe the form of the relationship and use it to forecast values of the forecast variable that have not been observed. Under this model, any change in predictors will affect the output of the system in a predictable way, assuming that the relationship does not change. Models in this class include regression models, additive models, and some kinds of neural networks. These models are discussed in Chapters 4, 5 and 9.

Some people use the term "predict" for cross-sectional data and "forecast" for time series data (see below). In this book, we will not make this distinction—we will use the words interchangeably.

Time series forecasting

Time series data are useful when you are forecasting something that is changing over time (e.g., stock prices, sales figures, profits, etc.). Examples of time series data include:
- Daily IBM stock prices
- Monthly rainfall
- Quarterly sales results for Amazon
- Annual Google profits

Anything that is observed sequentially over time is a time series. In this book, we will only consider time series that are observed at regular intervals of time (e.g., hourly, daily, weekly, monthly, quarterly, annually). Irregularly spaced time series can also occur, but are beyond the scope of this book.

When forecasting time series data, the aim is to estimate how the sequence of observations will continue into the future. Figure 1.1 shows the quarterly Australian beer production from 1992 to the third quarter of 2008.

The blue lines show forecasts for the next two years. Notice how the forecasts have captured the seasonal pattern seen in the historical data and replicated it for the next two years. The dark shaded region shows 80% prediction intervals. That is, each future value is expected to lie in the dark shaded region with a probability of 80%. The light shaded region shows 95% prediction intervals. These prediction intervals are a very useful way of displaying the uncertainty in forecasts. In this case, the

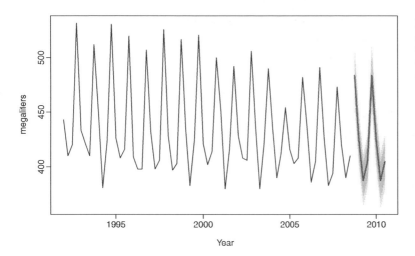

Figure 1.1: Australian quarterly beer production: 1992Q1–2008Q3, with two years of forecasts.

forecasts are expected to be very accurate, hence the prediction intervals are quite narrow.

Time series forecasting uses only information on the variable to be forecast, and makes no attempt to discover the factors which affect its behavior. Therefore it will extrapolate trend and seasonal patterns, but it ignores all other information such as marketing initiatives, competitor activity, changes in economic conditions, and so on.

Time series models used for forecasting include ARIMA models, exponential smoothing and structural models. These models are discussed in Chapters 6, 7 and 8.

Predictor variables and time series forecasting

Predictor variables can also be used in time series forecasting. For example, suppose we wish to forecast the hourly electricity demand (ED) of a hot region during the summer period. A model with predictor variables might be of the form

$$ED = f(\text{current temperature, strength of economy, population,}$$
$$\text{time of day, day of week, error}).$$

The relationship is not exact—there will always be changes in electricity demand that cannot be accounted for by the predictor variables. The "error" term on the right allows for random variation and the effects of relevant variables that not included in the model. We call this an "explanatory model" because it helps explain what causes the variation in electricity demand.

Because the electricity demand data form a time series, we could also use a time series model for forecasting. In this case, a suitable time series forecasting equation is of the form

$$\text{ED}_{t+1} = f(\text{ED}_t, \text{ED}_{t-1}, \text{ED}_{t-2}, \text{ED}_{t-3}, \ldots, \text{error}),$$

where t is the present hour, $t + 1$ is the next hour, $t - 1$ is the previous hour, $t - 2$ is two hours ago, and so on. Here, prediction of the future is based on past values of a variable, but not on external variables which may affect the system. Again, the "error" term on the right allows for random variation and the effects of relevant variables that are not included in the model.

There is also a third type of model which combines the features of the above two models. For example, it might be given by

$$\text{ED}_{t+1} = f(\text{ED}_t, \text{current temperature}, \text{time of day}, \text{day of week}, \text{error}).$$

These types of mixed models have been given various names in different disciplines. They are known as dynamic regression models, panel data models, longitudinal models, transfer function models, and linear system models (assuming f is linear). These models are discussed in Chapter 9.

An explanatory model is very useful because it incorporates information about other variables, rather than only historical values of the variable to be forecast. However, there are several reasons a forecaster might select a time series model rather than an explanatory model. First, the system may not be understood, and even if it was understood it may be extremely difficult to measure the relationships that are assumed to govern its behavior. Second, it is necessary to know or forecast the future values of the various predictors in order to be able to forecast the variable of interest, and this may be too difficult. Third, the main concern may be only to predict what will happen, not to know why it happens. Finally, the time series model may give more accurate forecasts than an explanatory or mixed model.

The model to be used in forecasting depends on the resources and data available, the accuracy of the competing models, and how the forecasting model is to be used.

Notation

For cross-sectional data, we will use the subscript i to indicate a specific observation. For example, y_i will denote the ith observation in a data set. We will also use N to denote the total number of observations in the data set.

For time series data, we will use the subscript t instead of i. For example, y_t will denote the observation at time t. We will use T to denote the number of observations in a time series.

When we are making general comments that could be applicable to either cross-sectional or time series data, we will tend to use i and N.

1/5 Some case studies

The following four cases are from our consulting practice and demonstrate different types of forecasting situations and the associated problems that often arise.

Case 1 The client was a large company manufacturing disposable tableware such as napkins and paper plates. They needed forecasts of each of hundreds of items every month. The time series data showed a range of patterns, some with trends, some seasonal, and some with neither. At the time, they were using their own software, written in-house, but it often produced forecasts that did not seem sensible. The methods that were being used were the following:

1. average of the last 12 months data;
2. average of the last 6 months data;
3. prediction from a straight line regression over the last 12 months;
4. prediction from a straight line regression over the last 6 months;
5. prediction obtained by a straight line through the last observation with slope equal to the average slope of the lines connecting last year's and this year's values;
6. prediction obtained by a straight line through the last observation with slope equal to the average slope of the lines connecting last year's and this year's values, where the average is taken only over the last 6 months.

They required us to tell them what was going wrong and to modify the software to provide more accurate forecasts. The software was written in COBOL making it difficult to do any sophisticated numerical computation.

Case 2   In this case, the client was the Australian federal government who needed to forecast the annual budget for the Pharmaceutical Benefit Scheme (PBS). The PBS provides a subsidy for many pharmaceutical products sold in Australia, and the expenditure depends on what people purchase during the year. The total expenditure was around A\$7 billion in 2009 and had been underestimated by nearly \$1 billion in each of the two years before we were asked to assist with developing a more accurate forecasting approach.

In order to forecast the total expenditure, it is necessary to forecast the sales volumes of hundreds of groups of pharmaceutical products using monthly data. Almost all of the groups have trends and seasonal patterns. The sales volumes for many groups have sudden jumps up or down due to changes in what drugs are subsidised. The expenditures for many groups also have sudden changes due to cheaper competitor drugs becoming available.

Thus we needed to find a forecasting method that allowed for trend and seasonality if they were present, and at hte same time was robust to sudden changes in the underlying patterns. It also needed to be able to be applied automatically to a large number of time series.

Case 3   A large car fleet company asked us to help them forecast vehicle re-sale values. They purchase new vehicles, lease them out for three years, and then sell them. Better forecasts of vehicle sales values would mean better control of profits; understanding what affects resale values may allow leasing and sales policies to be developed in order to maximize profits.

At the time, the resale values were being forecast by a group of specialists. Unfortunately, they saw any statistical model as a threat to their jobs and were uncooperative in providing information. Nevertheless, the company provided a large amount of data on previous vehicles and their eventual resale values.

Case 4 In this project, we needed to develop a model for fore-casting weekly air passenger traffic on major domestic routes for one of Australia's leading airlines. The company required forecasts of passenger numbers for each major domestic route and for each class of passenger (economy class, business class and first class). The company provided weekly traffic data from the previous six years.

Air passenger numbers are affected by school holidays, major sporting events, advertising campaigns, competition behaviour, etc. School holidays often do not coincide in different Australian cities, and sporting events sometimes move from one city to another. During the period of the historical data, there was a major pilots' strike during which there was no traffic for several months. A new cut-price airline also launched and folded. Towards the end of the historical data, the airline had trialled a redistribution of some economy class seats to business class, and some business class seats to first class. After several months, however, the seat classifications reverted to the original distribution.

1/6 The basic steps in a forecasting task

A forecasting task usually involves five basic steps.

Step 1: Problem definition. Often this is the most difficult part of forecasting. Defining the problem carefully requires an understanding of the way the forecasts will be used, who requires the forecasts, and how the forecasting function fits within the organization requiring the forecasts. A forecaster needs to spend time talking to everyone who will be involved in collecting data, maintaining databases, and using the forecasts for future planning.

Step 2: Gathering information. There are always at least two kinds of information required: (a) statistical data, and (b) the accumulated expertise of the people who collect the data and use the forecasts. Often, it will be difficult to obtain enough historical data to be able to fit a good statistical model. However, occasionally, very old data will be less useful due to changes in the system being forecast.

Step 3: Preliminary (exploratory) analysis. Always start by graphing the data. Are there consistent patterns? Is there a significant trend? Is seasonality important? Is there evidence of the presence of business cycles? Are there any outliers in the data that need to be explained by those with expert knowledge? How strong are the relationships among the variables available for analysis? Various tools have been developed to help with this analysis. These are discussed in Chapters 2 and 6.

Step 4: Choosing and fitting models. The best model to use depends on the availability of historical data, the strength of relationships between the forecast variable and any explanatory variables, and the way the forecasts are to be used. It is common to compare two or three potential models. Each model is itself an artificial construct that is based on a set of assumptions (explicit and implicit) and usually involves one or more parameters which must be "fitted" using the known historical data. We will discuss regression models (Chapters 4 and 5), exponential smoothing methods (Chapter 7), Box-Jenkins ARIMA models (Chapter 8), and a variety of other topics including dynamic regression models, neural networks and vector autoregression in Chapter 9.

Step 5: Using and evaluating a forecasting model. Once a model has been selected and its parameters estimated, the model is used to make forecasts. The performance of the model can only be properly evaluated after the data for the forecast period have become available. A number of methods have been developed to help in assessing the accuracy of forecasts. There are also organizational issues in using and acting on the forecasts. A brief discussion of some of these issues is in Chapter 2.

1/7 *The statistical forecasting perspective*

The thing we are trying to forecast is unknown (or we wouldn't be forecasting it), and so we can think of it as a *random variable*. For example, the total sales for next month could take a range of possible values, and until we add up the actual sales at the end of the month we don't know what the value will be. So, until we know the sales for next month, it is a random quantity.

Because next month is relatively close, we usually have a good idea what the likely sales values could be. On the other hand, if we are forecasting the sales for the same month next year, the possible values it could take are much more variable. In most forecasting situations, the variation associated with the thing we are forecasting will shrink as the event approaches. In other words, the further ahead we forecast, the more uncertain we are.

When we obtain a forecast, we are estimating the *middle* of the range of possible values the random variable could take. Very often, a forecast is accompanied by a prediction interval giving a *range* of values the random variable could take with relatively high probability. For example, a 95% prediction interval contains a range of values which should include the actual future value with probability 95%.

A forecast is always based on some observations. Suppose we denote all the information we have observed as $\mathcal{I}$ and we want to forecast y_i. We then write $y_i|\mathcal{I}$ meaning "the random variable y_i given what we know in $\mathcal{I}$". The set of values that this random variable could take, along with their relative probabilities, is known as the "probability distribution" of $y_i|\mathcal{I}$. In forecasting, we call this the "forecast distribution".

When we talk about the "forecast", we usually mean the average value of the forecast distribution, and we put a "hat" over y to show this. Thus, we write the forecast of y_t as $\hat{y}_t$, meaning the average of the possible values that y_i could take given everything we know. Occasionally, we will use $\hat{y}_i$ to refer to the *median* (or middle value) of the forecast distribution instead.

With time series forecasting, it is often useful to specify exactly what information we have used in calculating the forecast. Then we will write, for example, $\hat{y}_{t|t-1}$ to mean the forecast of y_t taking account of all previous observations $(y_1,\ldots,y_{t-1})$. Similarly, $\hat{y}_{T+h|T}$ means the forecast of y_{T+h} taking account of $y_1,\ldots,y_T$ (i.e., an h-step forecast taking account of all observations up to time T).

1/8 Exercises

1.1 For each of the four case studies in Section 1/5, what sort of data is involved: time series or cross-sectional data?

1.2 For cases 3 and 4 in Section 1/5, list the possible predictor variables that might be useful, assuming that the relevant data are available.

1.3 For case 3 in Section 1/5, describe the five steps of forecasting in the context of this project.

1/9 Further reading

- Armstrong, J. S., ed. (2001). *Principles of forecasting: a handbook for researchers and practitioners.* Boston, MA: Kluwer Academic Publishers.
- Ord, J. K. and R. Fildes (2012). *Principles of business forecasting.* South-Western College Pub.

2
The forecaster's toolbox

Before we discuss any forecasting methods, it is necessary
to build a toolbox of techniques that will be useful for many
different forecasting situations. Each of the tools discussed in
this chapter will be used repeatedly in subsequent chapters as
we develop and explore a range of forecasting methods.

2/1   Graphics

The first thing to do in any data analysis task is to plot the
data. Graphs enable many features of the data to be visualized
including patterns, unusual observations, changes over time,
and relationships between variables. The features that are seen
in plots of the data must then be incorporated, as far as possible,
into the forecasting methods to be used.

Just as the type of data determines what forecasting method
to use, it also determines what graphs are appropriate.

Time plots

For time series data, the obvious graph to start with is a time
plot. That is, the observations are plotted against the time of
observation, with consecutive observations joined by straight
lines. Figure 2.1 below shows the weekly economy passenger
load on Ansett Airlines between Australia's two largest cities.

Figure 2.1: Weekly economy passenger load on Ansett Airlines.

─────────────── R code ───────────────
```
plot(melsyd[,"Economy.Class"],
  main="Economy class passengers: Melbourne-Sydney",
  xlab="Year", ylab="Thousands")
```

The time plot immediately reveals some interesting features.

- There was a period in 1989 when no passengers were carried — this was due to an industrial dispute.
- There was a period of reduced load in 1992. This was due to a trial in which some economy class seats were replaced by business class seats.
- A large increase in passenger load occurred in the second half of 1991.
- There are some large dips in load around the start of each year. These are due to holiday effects.
- There is a long-term fluctuation in the level of the series which increases during 1987, decreases in 1989 and increases again through 1990 and 1991.
- There are some periods of missing observations.

Any model will need to take account of all these features in order to effectively forecast the passenger load into the future.

A simpler time series is shown in Figure 2.2. Here there is a clear and increasing trend. There is also a strong seasonal pattern that increases in size as the level of the series increases. The sudden drop at the end of each year is caused by a government subsidisation scheme that makes it cost-effective for

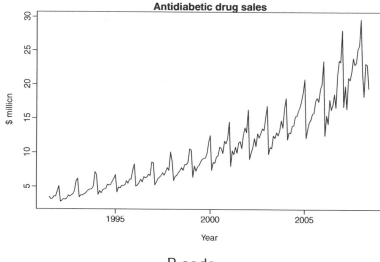

Figure 2.2: Monthly sales of antidiabetic drugs in Australia.

─────────────────── R code ───────────────────
```
plot(a10, ylab="$ million", xlab="Year",
  main="Antidiabetic drug sales")
```

patients to stockpile drugs at the end of the calendar year. Any forecasts of this series would need to capture the seasonal pattern, and the fact that the trend is changing slowly.

Time series patterns

In describing these time series, we have used words such as "trend" and "seasonal" which need to be more carefully defined.

- A *trend* exists when there is a long-term increase or decrease in the data. There is a trend in the antidiabetic drug sales data shown above.
- A *seasonal* pattern occurs when a time series is affected by seasonal factors such as the time of the year or the day of the week. The monthly sales of antidiabetic drugs above show seasonality partly induced by the change in cost of the drugs at the end of the calendar year.
- A *cycle* occurs when the data exhibit rises and falls that are not of a fixed period. These fluctuations are usually due to economic conditions and are often related to

the "business cycle". The economy class passenger data above showed some indications of cyclic effects.

It is important to distinguish cyclic patterns and seasonal patterns. Seasonal patterns have a fixed and known length, while cyclic patterns have variable and unknown length. The average length of a cycle is usually longer than that of seasonality, and the magnitude of cyclic variation is usually more variable than that of seasonal variation. Cycles and seasonality are discussed further in Section 6/1.

Many time series include trend, cycles and seasonality. When choosing a forecasting method, we will first need to identify the time series patterns in the data, and then choose a method that is able to capture the patterns properly.

Seasonal plots

A seasonal plot is similar to a time plot except that the data are plotted against the individual "seasons" in which the data were observed. An example is given below showing the antidiabetic drug sales.

These are exactly the same data shown earlier, but now the data from each season are overlapped. A seasonal plot allows the underlying seasonal pattern to be seen more clearly, and is especially useful in identifying years in which the pattern changes.

In this case, it is clear that there is a large jump in sales in January each year. Actually, these are probably sales in late December as customers stockpile before the end of the calendar year, but the sales are not registered with the government until a week or two later. The graph also shows that there was an unusually low number of sales in March 2008 (most other years show an increase between February and March). The small number of sales in June 2008 is probably due to incomplete counting of sales at the time the data were collected.

Seasonal subseries plots

An alternative plot that emphasises the seasonal patterns is where the data for each season are collected together in separate mini time plots.

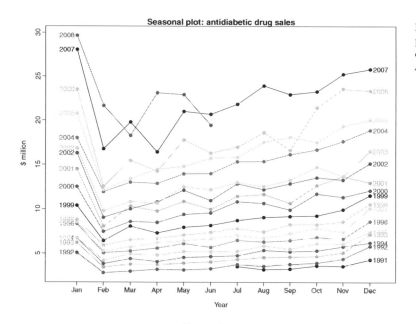

Figure 2.3: Seasonal plot of monthly anti-diabetic drug sales in Australia.

─────────────────── R code ───────────────────
```
seasonplot(a10,ylab="$ million", xlab="Year",
   main="Seasonal plot: antidiabetic drug sales",
   year.labels=TRUE, year.labels.left=TRUE, col=1:20, pch=19)
```

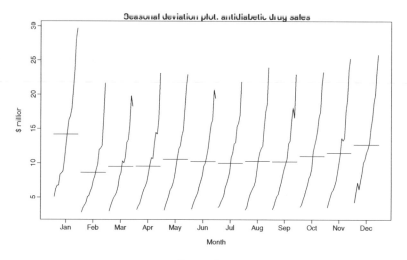

Figure 2.4: Seasonal plot of monthly anti-diabetic drug sales in Australia.

─────────────────── R code ───────────────────
```
monthplot(a10,ylab="$ million",xlab="Month",xaxt="n",
   main="Seasonal deviation plot: antidiabetic drug sales")
axis(1,at=1:12,labels=month.abb,cex=0.8)
```

The horizontal lines indicate the means for each month. This form of plot enables the underlying seasonal pattern to be seen clearly, and also shows the changes in seasonality over time. It is especially useful in identifying changes within particular seasons. In this example, the plot is not particularly revealing; but in some cases, this is the most useful way of viewing seasonal changes over time.

Scatterplots

The graphs discussed so far are useful for time series data. Scatterplots are most useful for exploring relationships between variables in cross-sectional data.

The figure below shows the relationship between the carbon footprint and fuel economy for small cars (using an extension of the data set shown in Section 1/4). Each point on the graph shows one type of vehicle.

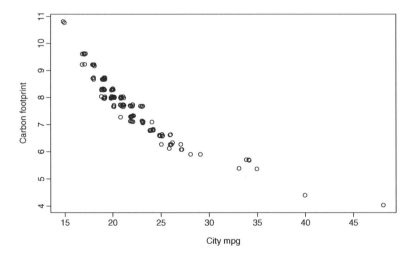

Figure 2.5: Carbon footprint and fuel economy for cars made in 2009.

──────── R code ────────
```
plot(jitter(fuel[,5]), jitter(fuel[,8]),
  xlab="City mpg", ylab="Carbon footprint")
# The use of jitter is to add a small random value
# to each point to prevent overlapping points.
```

There is a strong non-linear relationship between the size of a car's carbon footprint and its city-based fuel economy. Vehicles with better fuel-economy have a smaller carbon-footprint than vehicles that use a lot of fuel. However, the relationship is not linear — there is much less benefit in improving fuel-economy from 30 to 40 mpg than there was in moving from 20 to 30 mpg. The strength of the relationship is good news for forecasting: for any cars not in this database, knowing the fuel economy of the car will allow a relatively accurate forecast of its carbon footprint.

The scatterplot helps us visualize the relationship between the variables, and suggests that a forecasting model must include fuel-economy as a predictor variable. Some of the other information we know about these cars may also be helpful in improving the forecasts.

Scatterplot matrices

When there are several potential predictor variables, it is useful to plot each variable against each other variable. These plots can be arranged in a scatterplot matrix, as shown in Figure 2.6. For each panel, the variable on the vertical axis is given by the variable name in that row, and the variable on the horizontal axis is given by the variable name in that column. For example, the graph of carbon-footprint against city mpg is shown on the bottom row, second from the left.

The value of the scatterplot matrix is that it enables a quick view of the relationships between all pairs of variables. Outliers can also be seen. In this example, there are two vehicles that have very high highway mileage, small engines and low carbon footprints. These are hybrid vehicles: Honda Civic and Toyota Prius.

2/2   Numerical data summaries

Numerical summaries of data sets are widely used to capture some essential features of the data with a few numbers. A summary number calculated from the data is called a *statistic*.

Univariate statistics

For a single data set, the most widely used statistics are the *average* and *median*.

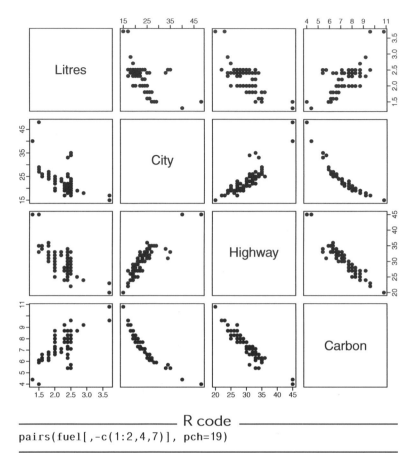

Figure 2.6: Scatterplot matrix of measurements on 2009 model cars.

──────────────── R code ────────────────
```
pairs(fuel[,-c(1:2,4,7)], pch=19)
```

Suppose N denotes the total number of observations and x_i denotes the ith observation. Then the average can be written as[1]

$$\bar{x} = \frac{1}{N} \sum_{i=1}^{N} x_i = (x_1 + x_2 + x_3 + \cdots + x_N)/N.$$

[1] The $\sum$ indicates that the values of x_i are to be summed from $i = 1$ to $i = N$.

The average is also called the *sample mean*.

By way of illustration, consider the carbon footprint from the 20 vehicles listed in Section 1/4. The data listed in order are

4.0	4.4	5.9	5.9	6.1	6.1	6.1	6.3	6.3	6.3
6.6	6.6	6.6	6.6	6.6	6.6	6.6	6.8	6.8	6.8

In this example, $N = 20$ and x_i denotes the carbon footprint of vehicle i. Then the average carbon footprint is

$$\bar{x} = \frac{1}{20} \sum_{i=1}^{20} x_i$$

$$= (x_1 + x_2 + x_3 + \cdots + x_{20})/20$$

$$= (4.0 + 4.4 + 5.9 + \cdots + 6.8 + 6.8 + 6.8)/20$$

$$= 124/20 = 6.2 \text{ tons } CO_2.$$

The *median*, on the other hand, is the middle observation when the data are placed in order. In this case, there are 20 observations and so the median is the average of the 10th and 11th largest observations. That is

$$\text{median} = (6.3 + 6.6)/2 = 6.45.$$

Percentiles are useful for describing the distribution of data. For example, 90% of the data are no larger than the 90th percentile. In the carbon footprint example, the 90th percentile is 6.8 because 90% of the data (18 observations) are less than or equal to 6.8. Similarly, the 75th percentile is 6.6 and the 25th percentile is 6.1. The median is the 50th percentile.

A useful measure of how spread out the data are is the *interquartile range* or IQR. This is simply the difference between the 75th and 25th percentiles. Thus it contains the middle 50% of the data. For the example,

$$\text{IQR} = (6.6 - 6.1) = 0.5.$$

An alternative and more common measure of spread is the *standard deviation*. This is given by the formula

$$s = \sqrt{\frac{1}{N-1} \sum_{i=1}^{N} (x_i - \bar{x})^2}.$$

In the example, the standard deviation is

$$s = \sqrt{\frac{1}{19} [(4.0 - 6.2)^2 + (4.4 - 6.2)^2 + \cdots + (6.8 - 6.2)^2]} = 0.74.$$

————————————— R code —————————————
```
fuel2 <- fuel[fuel[,"Litres"]<2,]
summary(fuel2[,"Carbon"])
sd(fuel2[,"Carbon"])
```

Bivariate statistics

The most commonly used bivariate statistic is the *correlation coefficient*. It measures the strength of the relationship between two variables and can be written as

$$r = \frac{\sum(x_i - \bar{x})(y_i - \bar{y})}{\sqrt{\sum(x_i - \bar{x})^2}\sqrt{\sum(y_i - \bar{y})^2}},$$

where the first variable is denoted by x and the second variable by y. The correlation coefficient only measures the strength of the *linear* relationship; it is possible for two variables to have a strong non-linear relationship but low correlation coefficient. The value of r always lies between -1 and 1 with negative values indicating a negative relationship and positive values indicating a postive relationship.

For example, the correlation between the carbon footprint and city mpg variables shown in Figure 2.5 (in the previous section) is -0.97. The value is negative because the carbon footprint decreases as the city mpg increases. While a value of -0.97 is very high, the relationship is even stronger than that number suggests due to its nonlinear nature.

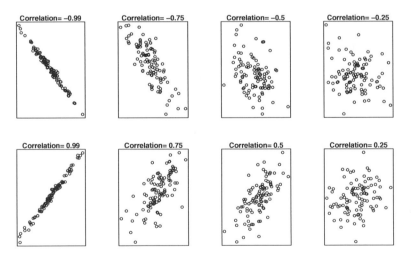

Figure 2.7: Examples of data sets with different levels of correlation.

The graphs in Figure 2.7 show examples of data sets with varying levels of correlation. Those in Figure 2.8 all have correlation coefficients of 0.82, but they have very different shaped relationships. This shows how important it is not to rely only on correlation coefficients but also to look at the plots of the data.

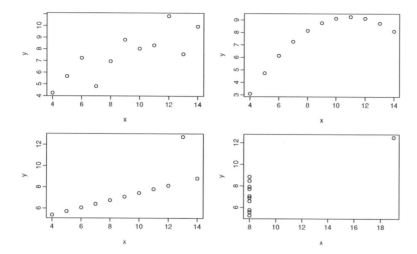

Figure 2.8: Each of these plots has a correlation coefficient of 0.82. Data from Anscombe F. J. (1973) Graphs in statistical analysis. *American Statistician*, **27**, 17–21.

Autocorrelation

Just as correlation measures the extent of a linear relationship between two variables, autocorrelation measures the linear relationship between *lagged values* of a time series. There are several autocorrelation coefficients, depending on the lag length. For example, r_1 measures the relationship between y_t and y_{t-1}, r_2 measures the relationship between y_t and y_{t-2}, and so on.

Figure 2.9 displays scatterplots of the beer production time series where the horizontal axis shows lagged values of the time series. Each graph shows y_t plotted against y_{t-k} for different values of k. The autocorrelations are the correlations associated with these scatterplots.

The value of r_k can be written as

$$r_k = \frac{\sum_{t=k+1}^{T} (y_t - \bar{y})(y_{t-k} - \bar{y})}{\sum_{t=1}^{T} (y_t - \bar{y})^2},$$

where T is the length of the time series.

The first nine autocorrelation coefficients for the beer production data are given in the following table.

r_1	r_2	r_3	r_4	r_5	r_6	r_7	r_8	r_9
-0.126	-0.650	-0.094	0.863	-0.099	-0.642	-0.098	0.834	-0.116

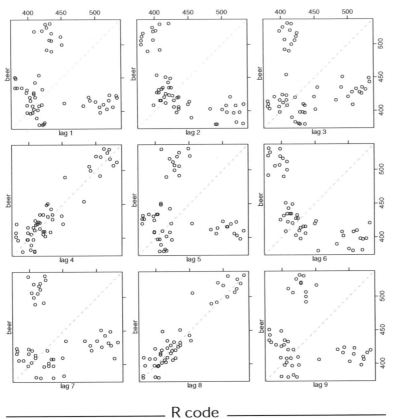

Figure 2.9: Lagged scatterplots for quarterly beer production.

R code

```
beer2 <- window(ausbeer, start=1992, end=2006-.1)
lag.plot(beer2, lags=9, do.lines=FALSE)
```

These correspond to the nine scatterplots in Figure 2.9. The autocorrelation coefficients are normally plotted to form the *autocorrelation function* or ACF, shown in Figure 2.10. The plot is also known as a *correlogram*.

In this graph:

- r_4 is higher than for the other lags. This is due to the seasonal pattern in the data: the peaks tend to be four quarters apart and the troughs tend to be four quarters apart.

- r_2 is more negative than for the other lags because troughs tend to be two quarters behind peaks.

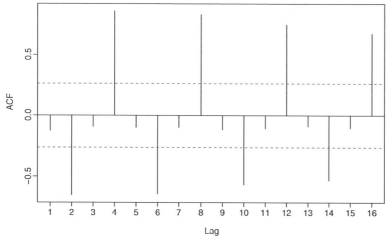

Figure 2.10: Autocorrelation function of quarterly beer production.

─────────── R code ───────────

```
Acf(beer2)
```

White noise

Time series that show no autocorrelation are called "white noise". Figure 2.11 gives an example of a white noise series.

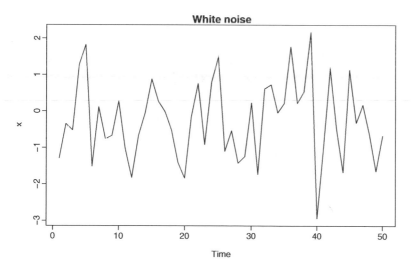

Figure 2.11: A white noise time series.

─────────── R code ───────────

```
set.seed(30)
x <- ts(rnorm(50))
plot(x, main="White noise")
```

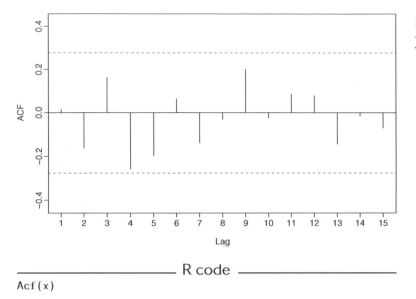

Figure 2.12: Autocorrelation function for the white noise series.

─────────── R code ───────────

```
Acf(x)
```

For white noise series, we expect each autocorrelation to be close to zero. They are not exactly zero as there is some random variation. For a white noise series, we expect 95% of the spikes in the ACF to lie within $\pm 2/\sqrt{T}$, where T is the length of the time series. It is common to plot these bounds on a graph of the ACF. If there are one or more large spikes outside these bounds, or if more than 5% of spikes are outside these bounds, then the series is probably not white noise.

In this example, $T = 50$ and so the bounds are at $\pm 2/\sqrt{50} = \pm 0.28$. All autocorrelation coefficients lie within these limits, confirming that the data are white noise.

2/3 Some simple forecasting methods

Some forecasting methods are very simple and surprisingly effective. Here are four methods that we will use as benchmarks for other forecasting methods.

Average method

Here, the forecasts of all future values are equal to the mean of the historical data. If we let the historical data be denoted by $y_1, \ldots, y_T$, then we can write the forecasts as

$$\hat{y}_{T+h|T} = \bar{y} = (y_1 + \cdots + y_T)/T.$$

The notation $\hat{y}_{T+h|T}$ is a short-hand for the estimate of y_{T+h} based on the data $y_1, \ldots, y_T$.

Although we have used time series notation here, this method can also be used for cross-sectional data (when we are predicting a value not included in the data set). Then the prediction for values not observed is the average of those values that have been observed. The remaining methods in this section are only applicable to time series data.

```
──────────────── R code ────────────────
meanf(y, h)
# y contains the time series, h is the forecast horizon
```

Naïve method

All forecasts are simply set to be the value of the last observation. That is, the forecasts of all future values are set to be y_T, where y_T is the last observed value. This method works remarkably well for many economic and financial time series.

```
──────────────── R code ────────────────
naive(y, h)
rwf(y, h) # Alternative
```

Seasonal naïve method

A similar method is useful for highly seasonal data. In this case, we set each forecast to be equal to the last observed value from the same season of the year (e.g., the same month of the previous year). Formally, the forecast for time $T + h$ is written as

$$y_{T+h-km} \text{ where } m = \text{seasonal period}, k = \lfloor (h-1)/m \rfloor + 1,$$

and $\lfloor u \rfloor$ denotes the integer part of u. That looks more complicated than it really is. For example, with monthly data, the forecast for all future February values is equal to the last observed February value. With quarterly data, the forecast of all future Q2 values is equal to the last observed Q2 value (where Q2 means the second quarter). Similar rules apply for other months and quarters, and for other seasonal periods.

```
──────────────── R code ────────────────
snaive(y, h)
```

Drift method

A variation on the naïve method is to allow the forecasts to increase or decrease over time, where the amount of change over time (called the drift) is set to be the average change seen in the historical data. So the forecast for time $T + h$ is given by

$$y_T + \frac{h}{T-1} \sum_{t=2}^{T} (y_t - y_{t-1}) = y_T + h\left(\frac{y_T - y_1}{T-1}\right).$$

This is equivalent to drawing a line between the first and last observation, and extrapolating it into the future.

———————————— R code ————————————

```
rwf(y, h, drift=TRUE)
```

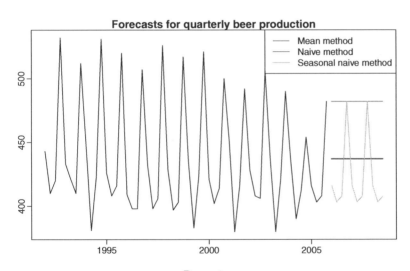

Figure 2.13: Forecasts of Australian quarterly beer production.

———————————— R code ————————————

```
beer2 <- window(ausbeer,start=1992,end=2006-.1)
beerfit1 <- meanf(beer2, h=11)
beerfit2 <- naive(beer2, h=11)
beerfit3 <- snaive(beer2, h=11)

plot(beerfit1, plot.conf=FALSE,
  main="Forecasts for quarterly beer production")
lines(beerfit2$mean,col=2)
lines(beerfit3$mean,col=3)
legend("topright",lty=1,col=c(4,2,3),
  legend=c("Mean method","Naive method","Seasonal naive method"))
```

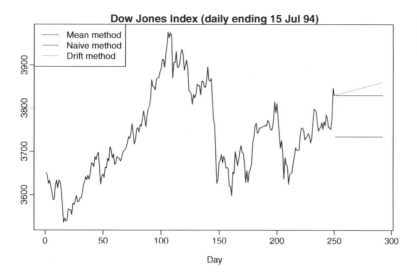

Figure 2.14: Forecasts based on 250 days of the Dow Jones Index.

─────────── R code ───────────

```
dj2 <- window(dj,end=250)
plot(dj2,main="Dow Jones Index (daily ending 15 Jul 94)",
  ylab="",xlab="Day",xlim=c(2,290))
lines(meanf(dj2,h=42)$mean,col=4)
lines(rwf(dj2,h=42)$mean,col=2)
lines(rwf(dj2,drift=TRUE,h=42)$mean,col=3)
legend("topleft",lty=1,col=c(4,2,3),
  legend=c("Mean method","Naive method","Drift method"))
```

Examples

Figure 2.13 shows the first three methods applied to the quarterly beer production data.

In Figure 2.14, the non-seasonal methods were applied to a series of 250 days of the Dow Jones Index.

Sometimes one of these simple methods will be the best forecasting method available. But in many cases, these methods will serve as benchmarks rather than the method of choice. That is, whatever forecasting methods we develop, they will be compared to these simple methods to ensure that the new method is better than these simple alternatives. If not, the new method is not worth considering.

2/4   *Transformations and adjustments*

Adjusting the historical data can often lead to a simpler fore-casting model. Here we deal with four kinds of adjustments: mathematical transformations, calendar adjustments, popu-lation adjustments and inflation adjustments. The purpose of all these transformations and adjustments is to simplify the patterns in the historical data by removing known sources of variation or by making the pattern more consistent across the whole data set. Simpler patterns usually lead to more accurate forecasts.

Mathematical transformations

If the data show variation that increases or decreases with the level of the series, then a transformation can be useful. For example, a logarithmic transformation is often useful. If we de-note the original observations as $y_1, \ldots, y_T$ and the transformed observations as $w_1, \ldots, w_T$, then $w_t = \log(y_t)$. Logarithms are useful because they are interpretable: changes in a log value are relative (or percentage) changes on the original scale. So if log base 10 is used, then an increase of 1 on the log scale corres-ponds to a multiplication of 10 on the original scale. Another useful feature of log transformations is that they constrain the forecasts to stay positive on the original scale.

Sometimes other transformations are also used (although they are not so interpretable). For example, square roots and cube roots can be used. These are called *power transformations* because they can be written in the form $w_t = y_t^p$.

A useful family of transformations that includes logarithms and power transformations is the family of "Box-Cox transform-ations", which depend on the parameter λ and are defined as follows:

$$w_t = \begin{cases} \log(y_t) & \text{if } \lambda = 0; \\ (y_t^\lambda - 1)/\lambda & \text{otherwise.} \end{cases}$$

The logarithm in a Box-Cox transformation is always a natural logarithm (i.e., to base e). So if $\lambda = 0$, natural logarithms are used, but if $\lambda \neq 0$, a power transformation is used followed by some simple scaling.

Figure 2.15 shows a logarithmic transformation of the monthly electricity demand data.

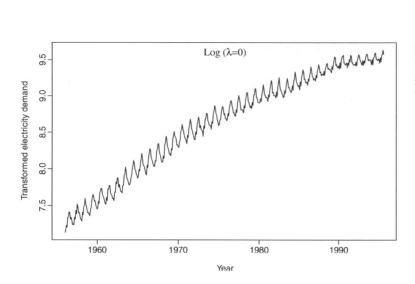

Figure 2.15: Power transformations of Australian monthly electricity data.

R code

```
plot(log(elec), ylab="Transformed electricity demand",
 xlab="Year", main="Transformed monthly electricity demand")
title(main="Log",line= 1)
```

A good value of λ is one that makes the size of the seasonal variation about the same across the whole series, as that makes the forecasting model simpler. In this case, $\lambda = 0.30$ works quite well, although any value of λ between 0 and 0.5 would give similar results.

R code

```
# The BoxCox.lambda() function will choose a value of lambda for you.
lambda <- BoxCox.lambda(elec) # = 0.27
plot(BoxCox(elec,lambda))
```

Having chosen a transformation, we need to forecast the transformed data. Then, we need to reverse the transformation (or *back-transform*) to obtain forecasts on the original scale. The reverse Box-Cox transformation is given by

$$y_t = \begin{cases} \exp(w_t) & \lambda = 0; \\ (\lambda w_t + 1)^{1/\lambda} & \text{otherwise.} \end{cases}$$

Features of power transformations

- If some $y_t < 0$, no transformation is possible unless all observations are adjusted by adding a constant to all values.

- Choose a simple value of λ. It makes explanations easier.

- Forecasting results are relatively insensitive to the value of λ.

- Often no transformation is needed.

- Transformations sometimes make little difference to the forecasts but have a large effect on prediction intervals.

Calendar adjustments

Some variation seen in seasonal data may be due to simple calendar effects. In such cases, it is usually much easier to remove the variation before fitting a forecasting model.

For example, if you are studying monthly milk production on a farm, then there will be variation between the months simply because of the different numbers of days in each month in addition to seasonal variation across the year.

Notice how much simpler the seasonal pattern is in the average daily production plot compared to the average monthly production plot. By looking at average daily production instead of average monthly production, we effectively remove the variation due to the different month lengths. Simpler patterns are usually easier to model and lead to more accurate forecasts.

A similar adjustment can be done for sales data when the number of trading days in each month will vary. In this case, the sales per trading day can be modelled instead of the total sales for each month.

Population adjustments

Any data that are affected by population changes can be adjusted to give per-capita data. That is, consider the data per person (or per thousand people, or per million people) rather than the total. For example, if you are studying the number of hospital beds in a particular region over time, the results are much easier to interpret if you remove the effect of population changes by considering number of beds per thousand people. Then you can see if there have been real increases in the number of beds, or whether the increases are entirely due to population increases. It is possible for the total number of beds to increase, but the number of beds per thousand people to decrease. This occurs when the population is increasing faster than the number of

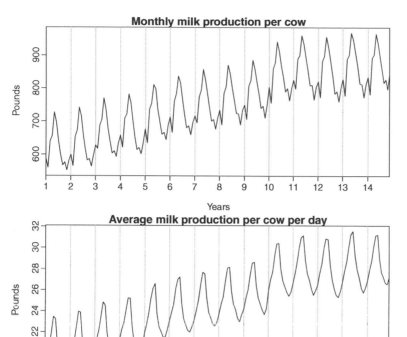

Figure 2.16: Monthly milk production per cow. Source: Cryer (1986).

---------- R code ----------

```
monthdays <- rep(c(31,28,31,30,31,30,31,31,30,31,30,31),14)
monthdays[26 + (4*12)*(0:2)] <- 29
par(mfrow=c(2,1))
plot(milk, main="Monthly milk production per cow",
  ylab="Pounds",xlab="Years")
plot(milk/monthdays, main="Average milk production per cow per day",
  ylab="Pounds", xlab="Years")
```

hospital beds. For most data that are affected by population changes, it is best to use per-capita data rather than the totals.

Inflation adjustments

Data that are affected by the value of money are best adjusted before modelling. For example, data on the average cost of a new house will have increased over the last few decades due to inflation. A $200,000 house this year is not the same as a

$200,000 house twenty years ago. For this reason, financial time series are usually adjusted so all values are stated in dollar values from a particular year. For example, the house price data may be stated in year 2000 dollars.

To make these adjustments a price index is used. If z_t denotes the price index and y_t denotes the original house price in year t, then $x_t = y_t/z_t * z_{2000}$ gives the adjusted house price at year 2000 dollar values. Price indexes are often constructed by government agencies. For consumer goods, a common price index is the Consumer Price Index (or CPI).

2/5   Evaluating forecast accuracy

Forecast accuracy measures

Let y_i denote the ith observation and $\hat{y}_i$ denote a forecast of y_i.

Scale-dependent errors   The forecast error is simply $e_i = y_i - \hat{y}_i$, which is on the same scale as the data. Accuracy measures that are based on e_i are therefore scale-dependent and cannot be used to make comparisons between series that are on different scales.

The two most commonly used scale-dependent measures are based on the absolute errors or squared errors:

$$\text{Mean absolute error: MAE} = \text{mean}(|e_i|),$$

$$\text{Root mean squared error: RMSE} = \sqrt{\text{mean}(e_i^2)}.$$

When comparing forecast methods on a single data set, the MAE is popular as it is easy to understand and compute.

Percentage errors   The percentage error is given by $p_i = 100e_i/y_i$. Percentage errors have the advantage of being scale-independent, and so are frequently used to compare forecast performance between different data sets. The most commonly used measure is:

$$\text{Mean absolute percentage error: MAPE} = \text{mean}(|p_i|).$$

Measures based on percentage errors have the disadvantage of being infinite or undefined if $y_i = 0$ for any i in the period of interest, and having extreme values when any y_i is close to zero. Another problem with percentage errors that is often over-looked is that they assume a meaningful zero. For example, a percentage error makes no sense when measuring the accuracy of temperature forecasts on the Fahrenheit or Celsius scales.

They also have the disadvantage that they put a heavier pen-alty on negative errors than on positive errors. This observation led to the use of the so-called "symmetric" MAPE (sMAPE) proposed by Armstrong (1985, p.348), which was used in the M3 forecasting competition. It is defined by

$$\text{sMAPE} = \text{mean}\left(200|y_i - \hat{y}_i|/(y_i + \hat{y}_i)\right).$$

However, if y_i is zero, $\hat{y}_i$ is also likely to be close to zero. Thus, the measure still involves division by a number close to zero. Also, the value of sMAPE can be negative, so it is not really a measure of "absolute percentage errors" at all.

Hyndman and Koehler (2006) recommend that the sMAPE not be used. It is included here only because it is widely used, although we will not use it in this book.

Scaled errors   Scaled errors were proposed by Hyndman and Koehler (2006) as an alternative to using percentage errors when comparing forecast accuracy across series on different scales. They proposed scaling the errors based on the *training* MAE from a simple forecast method. For a non-seasonal time series, a useful way to define a scaled error uses naïve forecasts:

$$q_j = \frac{e_j}{\dfrac{1}{T-1}\displaystyle\sum_{t=2}^{T}|y_t - y_{t-1}|}.$$

Because the numerator and denominator both involve values on the scale of the original data, q_j is independent of the scale of the data. A scaled error is less than one if it arises from a better forecast than the average naïve forecast computed on the training data. Conversely, it is greater than one if the forecast is worse than the average naïve forecast computed on the training data. For seasonal time series, a scaled error can be defined using seasonal naïve forecasts:

$$q_j = \frac{e_j}{\dfrac{1}{T-m}\displaystyle\sum_{t=m+1}^{T}|y_t - y_{t-m}|}.$$

For cross-sectional data, a scaled error can be defined as

$$q_j = \frac{e_j}{\dfrac{1}{N}\displaystyle\sum_{i=1}^{N} |y_i - \bar{y}|}.$$

In this case, the comparison is with the mean forecast. (This doesn't work so well for time series data as there may be trends and other patterns in the data, making the mean a poor comparison. Hence, the naïve forecast is recommended when using time series data.)

The *mean absolute scaled error* is simply

$$\text{MASE} = \text{mean}(|q_j|).$$

Similarly, *mean squared scaled errors* (MSSE) can be defined where the errors (on the training data and test data) are squared instead of using absolute values.

Examples

Figure 2.17 shows three forecast methods applied to the quarterly Australian beer production using data only to the end of 2005. The actual values for the period 2006–2008 are also shown.

We compute the forecast accuracy measures for this period.

Method	RMSE	MAE	MAPE	MASE
Mean method	38.01	33.78	8.17	2.30
naïve method	70.91	63.91	15.88	4.35
Seasonal naïve method	12.97	11.27	2.73	0.77

—————————————— R code ——————————————
```
beer3 <- window(ausbeer, start=2006)
accuracy(beerfit1, beer3)
accuracy(beerfit2, beer3)
accuracy(beerfit3, beer3)
```

It is obvious from the graph that the seasonal naïve method is best for these data, although it can still be improved, as we will discover later. Sometimes, different accuracy measures will lead to different results as to which forecast method is best. However, in this case, all the results point to the seasonal naïve method as the best of these three methods for this data set.

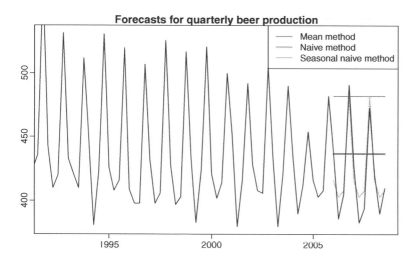

Figure 2.17: Forecasts of Australian quarterly beer production using data up to the end of 2005.

─────────── R code ───────────

```
beer2 <- window(ausbeer,start=1992,end=2006-.1)
beerfit1 <- meanf(beer2,h=11)
beerfit2 <- rwf(beer2,h=11)
beerfit3 <- snaive(beer2,h=11)
plot(beerfit1, plot.conf=FALSE,
  main="Forecasts for quarterly beer production")
lines(beerfit2$mean,col=2)
lines(beerfit3$mean,col=3)
lines(ausbeer)
legend("topright", lty=1, col=c(4,2,3),
  legend=c("Mean method","Naive method","Seasonal naive method"))
```

To take a non-seasonal example, consider the Dow Jones Index. The following graph shows the 250 observations ending on 15 July 1994, along with forecasts of the next 42 days obtained from three different methods.

Method	RMSE	MAE	MAPE	MASE
Mean method	148.24	142.42	3.66	8.70
Naïve method	62.03	54.44	1.40	3.32
Drift method	53.70	45.73	1.18	2.79

─────────── R code ───────────

```
dj3 <- window(dj, start=251)
accuracy(meanf(dj2,h=42), dj3)
accuracy(rwf(dj2,h=42), dj3)
accuracy(rwf(dj2,drift=TRUE,h=42), dj3)
```

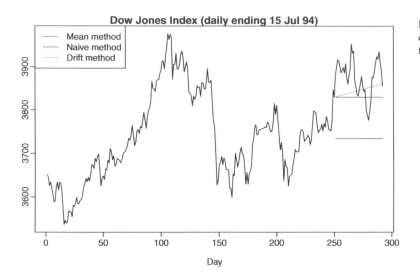

Figure 2.18: Forecasts of the Dow Jones Index from 16 July 1994.

———————— R code ————————

```
dj2 <- window(dj, end=250)
plot(dj2, main="Dow Jones Index (daily ending 15 Jul 94)",
  ylab="", xlab="Day", xlim=c(2,290))
lines(meanf(dj2,h=42)$mean, col=4)
lines(rwf(dj2,h=42)$mean, col=2)
lines(rwf(dj2,drift=TRUE,h=42)$mean, col=3)
legend("topleft", lty=1, col=c(4,2,3),
  legend=c("Mean method","Naive method","Drift method"))
lines(dj)
```

Here, the best method is the drift method (regardless of which accuracy measure is used).

Training and test sets

It is important to evaluate forecast accuracy using genuine forecasts. That is, it is invalid to look at how well a model fits the historical data; the accuracy of forecasts can only be determined by considering how well a model performs on new data that were not used when fitting the model. When choosing models, it is common to use a portion of the available data for testing, and use the rest of the data for fitting the model, as was done in the above examples. Then the testing data can be used to measure how well the model is likely to forecast on new data.

The size of the test set is typically about 20% of the total sample, although this value depends on how long the sample is and how far ahead you want to forecast. The size of the test set should ideally be at least as large as the maximum forecast horizon required.

The following points should be noted.

- A model which fits the data well does not necessarily forecast well.
- A perfect fit can always be obtained by using a model with enough parameters.
- Over-fitting a model to data is as bad as failing to identify the systematic pattern in the data.

Some references describe the test set as the "hold-out set" because these data are "held out" of the data used for fitting. Other references call the training set the "in-sample data" and the test set the "out-of-sample data". We prefer to use "training set" and "test set" in this book.

Cross-validation

A more sophisticated version of training/test sets is cross-validation.

For cross-sectional data, cross-validation works as follows.

1. Select observation i for the test set, and use the remaining observations in the training set. Compute the error on the test observation.

2. Repeat the above step for $i = 1, 2, \ldots, N$ where N is the total number of observations.

3. Compute the forecast accuracy measures based on the errors obtained.

This is a much more efficient use of the available data, as you only omit one observation at each step. However, it can be very time consuming to implement.

For time series data, the procedure is similar but the training set consists only of observations that occurred *prior* to the observation that forms the test set. Thus, no future observations can be used in constructing the forecast. However, it is not possible to get a reliable forecast based on a very small training set, so the earliest observations are not considered as test sets.

Suppose k observations are required to produce a reliable forecast. Then the process works as follows.

1. Select the observation at time $k + i$ for the test set, and use the observations at times $1, 2, \ldots, k+i-1$ to estimate the forecasting model. Compute the error on the forecast for time $k + i$.

2. Repeat the above step for $i = 1, 2, \ldots, T - k$ where T is the total number of observations.

3. Compute the forecast accuracy measures based on the errors obtained.

This procedure is sometimes known as a "rolling forecasting origin" because the "origin" $(k + i - 1)$ at which the forecast is based rolls forward in time.

With time series forecasting, one-step forecasts may not be as relevant as multi-step forecasts. In this case, the cross-validation procedure based on a rolling forecasting origin can be modified to allow multi-step errors to be used. Suppose we are interested in models that produce good h-step-ahead forecasts.

1. Select the observation at time $k + h + i - 1$ for the test set, and use the observations at times $1, 2, \ldots, k + i - 1$ to estimate the forecasting model. Compute the h-step error on the forecast for time $k + h + i - 1$.

2. Repeat the above step for $i = 1, 2, \ldots, T - k - h + 1$ where T is the total number of observations.

3. Compute the forecast accuracy measures based on the errors obtained.

When $h = 1$, this gives the same procedure as outlined above.

2/6   Residual diagnostics

A residual in forecasting is the difference between an observed value and its forecast based on other observations: $e_i = y_i - \hat{y}_i$. For time series forecasting, a residual is based on one-step forecasts; that is $\hat{y}_t$ is the forecast of y_t based on observations $y_1, \ldots, y_{t-1}$. For cross-sectional forecasting, a residual is based on all other observations; that is $\hat{y}_i$ is the prediction of y_i based on all observations *except* y_i.

A good forecasting method will yield residuals with the following properties:

- The residuals are uncorrelated. If there are correlations between residuals, then there is information left in the residuals which should be used in computing forecasts.
- The residuals have zero mean. If the residuals have a mean other than zero, then the forecasts are biased.

Any forecasting method that does not satisfy these properties can be improved. That does not mean that forecasting methods that satisfy these properties can not be improved. It is possible to have several forecasting methods for the same data set, all of which satisfy these properties. Checking these properties is important to see if a method is using all available information well, but it is not a good way for selecting a forecasting method.

If either of these two properties is not satisfied, then the forecasting method can be modified to give better forecasts. Adjusting for bias is easy: if the residuals have mean m, then simply add m to all forecasts and the bias problem is solved. Fixing the correlation problem is harder and we will not address it until Chapter 8.

In addition to these essential properties, it is useful (but not necessary) for the residuals to also have the following two properties.

- The residuals have constant variance.
- The residuals are normally distributed.

These two properties make the calculation of prediction intervals easier (see the next section for an example). However, a forecasting method that does not satisfy these properties cannot necessarily be improved. Sometimes applying a transformation such as a logarithm or a square root may assist with these properties, but otherwise there is usually little you can do to ensure your residuals have constant variance and have a normal distribution. Instead, an alternative approach to finding prediction intervals is necessary. Again, we will not address how to do this until later in the book.

Example: Forecasting the Dow-Jones Index

For stock market indexes, the best forecasting method is often the naïve method. That is each forecast is simply equal to the last observed value, or $\hat{y}_t = y_{t-1}$. Hence, the residuals are simply equal to the difference between consecutive observations:

$$e_t = y_t - \hat{y}_t = y_t - y_{t-1}.$$

The following graphs show the Dow Jones Index (DJI), and the residuals obtained from forecasting the DJI with the naïve method.

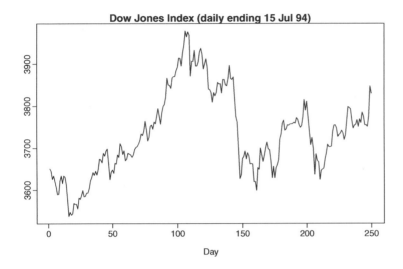

Figure 2.19: The Dow Jones Index measured daily to 15 July 1994.

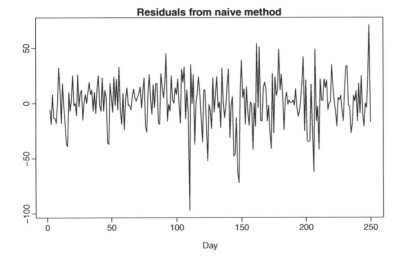

Figure 2.20: Residuals from forecasting the Dow Jones Index with the naïve method.

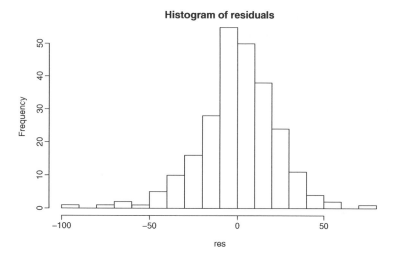

Histogram of residuals

Figure 2.21: Histogram of the residuals from the naïve method applied to the Dow Jones Index. The left tail is a little too long for a normal distribution.

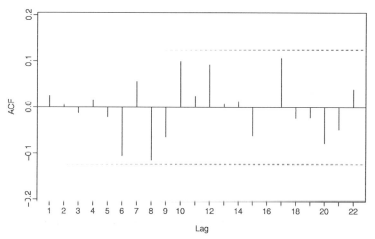

Figure 2.22: ACF of the residuals from the naïve method applied to the Dow Jones Index. The lack of correlation suggests the forecasts are good.

─────────── R code ───────────
```
dj2 <- window(dj, end=250)
plot(dj2, main="Dow Jones Index (daily ending 15 Jul 94)",
  ylab="", xlab="Day")
res <- residuals(naive(dj2))
plot(res, main="Residuals from naive method",
  ylab="", xlab="Day")
Acf(res,main="ACF of residuals")
hist(res, nclass="FD", main="Histogram of residuals")
```

These graphs show that the naïve method produces forecasts that appear to account for all available information. The mean of the residuals is very close to zero and there is no significant correlation in the residuals series. The time plot of the residuals shows that the variation of the residuals stays much the same across the historical data, so the residual variance can be treated as constant. However, the histogram suggests that the residuals may not follow a normal distribution — the left tail looks a little too long. Consequently, forecasts from this method will probably be quite good but prediction intervals computed assuming a normal distribution may be inaccurate.

Portmanteau tests for autocorrelation

In addition to looking at the ACF plot, we can do a more formal test for autocorrelation by considering a whole set of r_k values as a group, rather than treat each one separately.

Recall that r_k is the autocorrelation for lag k. When we look at the ACF plot to see if each spike is within the required limits, we are implicitly carrying out multiple hypothesis tests, each one with a small probability of giving a false positive. When enough of these tests are done, it is likely that at least one will give a false positive and so we may conclude that the residuals have some remaining autocorrelation, when in fact they do not.

In order to overcome this problem, we test whether the first h autocorrelations are significantly different from what would be expected from a white noise process. A test for a group of autocorrelations is called a *portmanteau test*, from a French word describing a suitcase containing a number of items.

One such test is the *Box-Pierce test* based on the following statistic

$$Q = T \sum_{k=1}^{h} r_k^2,$$

where h is the maximum lag being considered and T is number of observations. If each r_k is close to zero, then Q will be small. If some r_k values are large (positive or negative), then Q will be large. We suggest using $h = 10$ for non-seasonal data and $h = 2m$ for seasonal data (where m is the period of seasonality). However, the test is not good when h is large, so if these values are larger than $T/5$, then use $h = T/5$.

A related (and more accurate) test is the *Ljung-Box test* based on

$$Q^* = T(T+2) \sum_{k=1}^{h} (T-k)^{-1} r_k^2.$$

Again, large values of Q^* suggest that the autocorrelations do not come from a white noise series.

How large is too large? If the autocorrelations did come from a white noise series, then both Q and Q^* would have a χ^2 distribution with $(h - K)$ degrees of freedom where K is the number of parameters in the model. If they are calculated from raw data (rather than the residuals from a model), then set $K = 0$.

For the Dow-Jones example, the naive model has no parameters, so $K = 0$ in that case also. For both Q and Q^*, the results are not significant (i.e., the p-values are relatively large). So we can conclude that the residuals are not distinguishable from a white noise series.

—————————————— R code ——————————————

```
# lag=h and fitdf=K
> Box.test(res, lag=10, fitdf=0)
        Box-Pierce test
X-squared = 10.6548, df = 10, p-value = 0.385
> Box.test(res,lag=10, fitdf=0, type="Lj")
        Box-Ljung test
X-squared = 11.0879, df = 10, p-value = 0.3507
```

2/7 Prediction intervals

As discussed in Section 1/7, a prediction interval gives an interval within which we expect y_i to lie with a specified probability. For example, assuming the forecast errors are uncorrelated and normally distributed, then a simple 95% prediction interval for the next observation in a time series is

$$\hat{y}_i \pm 1.96\hat{\sigma},$$

where $\hat{\sigma}$ is an estimate of the standard deviation of the forecast distribution. In forecasting, it is common to calculate 80% intervals and 95% intervals, although any percentage may be used.

When forecasting one-step ahead, the standard deviation of the forecast distribution is almost the same as the standard deviation of the residuals. (In fact, the two standard deviations are identical if there are no parameters to be estimated such as with the naïve method. For forecasting methods involving parameters to be estimated, the standard deviation of the forecast distribution is slightly larger than the residual standard deviation, although this difference is often ignored.)

For example, consider a naïve forecast for the Dow-Jones Index. The last value of the observed series is 3830, so the forecast of the next value of the DJI is 3830. The standard deviation of the residuals from the naïve method is 21.99. Hence, a 95% prediction interval for the next value of the DJI is

$$3830 \pm 1.96(21.99) = [3787, 3873].$$

Similarly, an 80% prediction interval is given by

$$3830 \pm 1.28(21.99) = [3802, 3858].$$

The value of the multiplier (1.96 or 1.28) determines the percentage of the prediction interval. Table 2.1 gives the values to be used for different percentages.

Percentage	Multiplier
50	0.67
55	0.76
60	0.84
65	0.93
70	1.04
75	1.15
80	1.28
85	1.44
90	1.64
95	1.96
96	2.05
97	2.17
98	2.33
99	2.58

Table 2.1: Multipliers to be used for prediction intervals.

The use of this table and the formula $\hat{y}_i \pm k\hat{\sigma}$ (where k is the multiplier) assumes that the residuals are normally distributed and uncorrelated. If either of these conditions does not hold, then this method of producing a prediction interval cannot be used.

The value of prediction intervals is that they express the uncertainty in the forecasts. If we only produce point forecasts, there is no way of telling how accurate the forecasts are. But if we also produce prediction intervals, then it is clear how much uncertainty is associated with each forecast. For this reason, point forecasts can be of almost no value without accompanying prediction intervals.

To produce a prediction interval, it is necessary to have an estimate of the standard deviation of the forecast distribution. For one-step forecasts for time series, the residual standard deviation provides a good estimate of the forecast standard deviation. But for all other situations, including multi-step forecasts for time series, a more complicated method of calculation is required. These calculations are usually done with standard forecasting software and need not trouble the forecaster (unless he or she is writing the software!).

A common feature of prediction intervals is that they increase in length as the forecast horizon increases. The further ahead we forecast, the more uncertainty is associated with the forecast, and so the prediction intervals grow wider. However, there are some (non-linear) forecasting methods that do not have this attribute.

If a transformation has been used, then the prediction interval should be computed on the transformed scale, and the end points back-transformed to give a prediction interval on the original scale. This approach preserves the probability coverage of the prediction interval, although it will no longer be symmetric around the point forecast.

2/8   Exercises

2.1 For each of the following series (from the **fma** package), make a graph of the data. If transforming seems appropriate, do so and describe the effect.

   (a) Monthly total of people on unemployed bene-fits in Australia (January 1956–July 1992).
   (b) Monthly total of accidental deaths in the United States (January 1973–December 1978).
   (c) Quarterly production of bricks (in millions of units) at Portland, Australia (March 1956–September 1994).

Hints:

- data(package="fma") will give a list of the available data.

- To plot a transformed data set, use plot(BoxCox(x,0.5)) where x is the name of the data set and 0.5 is the Box-Cox parameter.

2.2 Use the Dow Jones index (data set dowjones) to do the following:

   (a) Produce a time plot of the series.
   (b) Produce forecasts using the drift method and plot them.
   (c) Show that the graphed forecasts are identical to extending the line drawn between the first and last observations.
   (d) Try some of the other benchmark functions to forecast the same data set. Which do you think is best? Why?

2.3 Consider the daily closing IBM stock prices (data set ibmclose).

   (a) Produce some plots of the data in order to become familiar with it.
   (b) Split the data into a training set of 300 observations and a test set of 69 observations.
   (c) Try various benchmark methods to forecast the training set and compare the results on the test set. Which method did best?

2.4 Consider the sales of new one-family houses in the USA, Jan 1973 – Nov 1995 (data set hsales).

   (a) Produce some plots of the data in order to become familiar with it.
   (b) Split the hsales data set into a training set and a test set, where the test set is the last two years of data.
   (c) Try various benchmark methods to forecast the training set and compare the results on the test set. Which method did best?

2.5 Why is a Box-Cox transformation unhelpful for the cangas data?

2/9   Further reading

Graphics and data summary

- Cleveland, W. S. (1993). *Visualizing Data*. Hobart Press.
- Maindonald, J. and H. Braun (2010). *Data analysis and graphics using R: an example-based approach*. 3rd ed. Cambridge, UK: Cambridge University Press.

Simple forecasting methods

- Ord, J. K. and R. Fildes (2012). *Principles of business forecasting*. South-Western College Pub.

Evaluating forecast accuracy

- Hyndman, R. J. and A. B. Koehler (2006). Another look at measures of forecast accuracy. *International Journal of Forecasting* 22(4), 679–688.

2/A The forecast package in R

This book uses the facilities in the forecast package in R (which is automatically loaded whenever you load the fpp package). This appendix briefly summarizes some of the features of the package. Please refer to the help files for individual functions to learn more, and to see some examples of their use.

Functions that output a forecast object:

- meanf()
- naive(), snaive()
- rwf()
- croston()
- stlf()
- ses()
- holt(), hw()
- splinef
- thetaf
- forecast()

The forecast class contains

- Original series
- Point forecasts
- Prediction interval
- Forecasting method used
- Residuals and in-sample (training) one-step forecasts

forecast() function

- Takes a time series or time series model as its main argument
- If first argument is of class ts, it returns forecasts from automatic ETS algorithm.
- Methods are available for objects of class Arima, ar, HoltWinters, StructTS, etc.
- Output as class forecast.

———————————— R output ————————————

```
> forecast(beer)

         Point Forecast Lo 80 Hi 80 Lo 95 Hi 95
2008 Q4          480.8 458.7 503.7 446.5 515.7
2009 Q1          423.3 403.0 442.9 392.3 452.5
2009 Q2          386.1 367.4 404.6 357.6 414.8
2009 Q3          402.7 382.5 423.2 371.8 433.9
2009 Q4          481.0 455.0 508.3 441.1 522.5
2010 Q1          423.5 398.8 448.7 386.2 461.8
2010 Q2          386.3 362.8 411.3 350.5 423.1
2010 Q3          402.9 377.5 429.5 363.7 444.8
```

3
Judgmental forecasts

3/1 *Introduction*

Forecasting using judgement is very common in practice. There
are many cases where judgmental forecasting is the only option,
such as when there is a complete lack of historical data, or when
a new product is being launched, or when a new competitor
enters the market, or during completely new and unique market conditions. For example, in December 2012 the Australian
government was the first in the world to pass legislation that
banned the use of company logos on cigarette packets, and required all cigarette packets to be a dark green color. Judgement
must be applied in order to forecast the effect of such a drastic
policy as there are no historical precedents.

There are also situations where the data are incomplete or
only become available after some delay. For example central
banks include judgement when forecasting the current level of
economic activity, a procedure known as nowcasting, as GDP
only becomes available on a quarterly basis.

What has been learned from research in this area[1] is that
the accuracy of judgmental forecasting improves when the
forecaster has (i) important domain knowledge, and (ii) more
timely up-to-date information. A judgmental approach can be
quick to adjust to such changes, information or events.

Over the years the acceptance of judgmental forecasting as
a science has increased and so has the recognition for its need.
More importantly the quality of judgmental forecasts has also
improved as a direct result of recognising that improvements
in judgmental forecasting can be achieved by implementing

[1] M. Lawrence, P.
Goodwin, M. O'Connor
and D. Önkal (2006).
Judgmental forecasting:
A review of progress
over the last 25 years.
*International Journal
of Forecasting* 22(3),
493–518.

well-structured and systematic approaches. It is important to recognise that judgmental forecasting is subjective and comes with limitations. However, implementing systematic and well-structured approaches can confine these limitations and markedly improve forecast accuracy.

There are three general settings where judgmental forecasting is used: (i) there are no available data so that statistical methods are not applicable and judgmental forecasting is the only feasible approach; (ii) data are available, statistical forecasts are generated and these are then adjusted using judgement; and (iii) data are available and statistical and judgmental forecasts are independently generated and then combined. We should clarify that when data are available, applying statistical methods (such as those discussed in other chapters of this book), is preferable and should, at the very least, be used as a starting point. Statistical forecasts are in general superior to generating forecasts using only judgement and this is commonly observed in the literature. For the majority of the chapter we focus on the first setting where no data are available, and in the very last section we discuss judgmentally adjusting statistical forecasts. We leave combining forecasts for a later edition of this book.

3/2 Beware of limitations

Judgmental forecasts are subjective and therefore do not come free of bias or limitations.

Judgmental forecasts can be inconsistent. Unlike statistical forecasts which can be generated by the same mathematical formulae every time, judgmental forecasts depend heavily on human cognition and are vulnerable to its limitations. For example, a limited memory may render recent events more important than they actually are and may ignore momentous events from the more distant past; or a limited attention span may result in important information being missed; or a mis-understanding of causal relationships may lead to erroneous inference. Furthermore, human judgement can vary due to the effect of psychological factors. We can think of a manager who is in a positive frame of mind one day, generating forecasts that may tend to be somewhat optimistic, and in a negative frame of mind another day, generating somewhat less optimistic forecasts.

Judgement can be clouded by personal or political agendas, where targets and forecasts (as defined in Chapter 1) are not segregated. For example if a sales manager knows that the forecasts she generates will be used to set the expectation of sales (targets), she may have the tendency to set these low in order to show a good performance (i.e., exceed the expected targets). Even in cases where targets and forecasts are well segregated, judgement may be plagued with optimism or wishful thinking. For example, it would be highly unlikely that a team working towards launching a new product would forecast its failure. As we will discuss later, this optimism can be accentuated in a group meeting setting. "Beware of the enthusiasm of your marketing and sales colleagues"[2].

Another undesirable property commonly seen in judgmental forecasting is the effect of anchoring. In this case, subsequent forecasts tend to converge or be very close to an initial familiar reference point. For example, it is common to take the last observed value as a reference point. The forecaster is unduly influenced by prior information and therefore gives this more weight in the forecasting process. Anchoring may lead to conservatism and undervaluing new and more current information and thereby create a systematic bias.

[2] R. Fildes and P. Goodwin (2007b). Good and bad judgment in forecasting: lessons from four companies. *Foresight: The International Journal of Applied Forecasting* (8), 5–10.

3/3 Key principles

Using a systematic and well structured approach in judgmental forecasting helps to reduce the adverse effects of the limitations of judgmental forecasting, some of which we listed in the previous section. Whether this approach involves one or many individuals, the following principles should be followed.

Set the forecasting task clearly and concisely

Care is needed when setting the forecasting challenges and expressing the forecasting tasks. It is important that everyone is clear about what the task is. All definitions should be clear and comprehensive, avoiding ambiguous and vague expressions. Also it is important to avoid incorporating emotive terms and irrelevant information that may distract the forecaster. In the

Delphi method that follows (see Section 3/4), it may be sometimes useful to conduct a preliminary round of information gathering before setting the forecasting task.

Implement a systematic approach

Forecast accuracy and consistency can be improved by using a systematic approach to judgmental forecasting involving checklists of categories of information relevant to the forecasting task. For example, it is helpful to identify what information is important and how this information is to be weighted. When forecasting the demand of a new product, what factors should we account for and how should we account for them? Should it be the price, the quality and/or quantity of the competition, the economic environment at the time, the target population of the product? It is worth while devoting significant effort and resources in putting together decision rules that lead to the best possible systematic approach.

Document and justify

Formalising and documenting the decision rules and assumptions implemented in the systematic approach can promote consistency as the same rules can be implemented repeatedly. Also, requesting a forecaster to document and justify forecasts leads to accountability which can lead to a reduced bias. Furthermore, formal documentation significantly aids in the systematic evaluation process that is suggested next.

Systematically evaluate forecasts

Systematically monitoring the forecasting process can identify unforeseen irregularities. In particular, keep records of forecasts and use them to obtain feedback as the forecasted period becomes observed. Although you can do your best as a forecaster, the environment you operate in is dynamic. Changes occur and you need to monitor these in order to evaluate the decision rules and assumptions. Feedback and evaluation helps forecasters learn and improve forecast accuracy.

Segregate forecasters and users

Forecast accuracy may be impeded if the forecasting task is carried out by users of the forecasts, such as those responsible for implementing plans of action about which the forecast is concerned. We should clarify again here (as in Section 1/2), forecasting is about predicting the future as accurately as possible, given all the information available including historical data and knowledge of any future events that might impact the forecasts. Forecasters and users should be clearly segregated. A classic case is that of a new product being launched. The forecast should be a reasonable estimate of the sales volume of a new product, which may be very different to what management expects or hopes the sales will be in order to meet company financial objectives. A forecaster in this case may be delivering a reality check to the user.

It is important that forecasters thoroughly communicate forecasts to potential users. As we will see in Section 3/8, users may feel distant and disconnected from forecasts and may not have full confidence in them. Explaining and clarifying the process and justifying basic assumptions that led to forecasts will provide some assurance to users.

How forecasts may then be used and implemented will clearly depend on managerial decision making. For example, management may decide to adjust a forecast upwards (be over-optimistic) as the forecast may be used to guide purchasing and stock keeping levels. Such a decision may have been taken after cost-benefit analysis reveals that the cost of holding excess stock is much lower than that of lost sales. This type of adjustment should be part of setting goals or planning supply rather than part of the forecasting process. In contrast, if forecasts are used as targets, they may be set low so that these can be exceeded more easily. Again, setting targets is different from producing forecasts, and the two should not be confused.

The example that follows comes from our experience in industry. It exemplifies two contrasting styles of judgmental forecasting — one that adheres to the principles we have just presented and one that does not.

Example 3.1   *Pharmaceutical Benefits Scheme (PBS)*

The Australian government subsidises the cost of a wide range of prescription medicines as part of the PBS. Each subsidised medicine falls into one of four categories: concession copayments, concession safety net, general copayments, and general safety net. Each person with a concession card makes a concession copayment per PBS medicine ($5.80)[3] until they reach a set threshold amount labelled the concession safety net ($348). For the rest of the financial year all PBS listed medicines are free. Each general patient makes a general copayment per PBS medicine ($35.40) until the general safety net amount is reached ($1,363.30). For the rest of the financial year they contribute a small amount per PBS listed medicine ($5.80). The PBS forecasting process uses 84 groups of PBS listed medicines, and produces forecasts of the medicine volume and the total expenditure for each group and for each of the four PBS categories, a total of 672 series. This forecasting process aids in setting the government budget allocated to the PBS which is over $7 billion per year or approximately 1% of GDP.

[3] These are Australian dollar amounts published by the Australian government for 2012.

Figure 3.1 summarises the forecasting process. Judgmental forecasts are generated for new listings of medicines and for estimating the impact of new policies. These are shown by the green items. The pink items indicate the data used obtained from various government departments and associated authorites. The blue items show things that are calculated from the data provided. There were judgmental adjustments to the data to take account of new listings and new policies, and there were judgmental adjustments to the forecasts also. Because of the changing size of the concession population and the total population, forecasts are produced on a per capita basis, and then multiplied for the forecast population to obtain forecasts of total volume and expenditure per month.

One of us (Hyndman) was asked to evaluate the forecasting process a few years ago. We found that using judgement for new listings and new policy impacts gave better forecasts than using a statistical model alone. However, we also found that forecasting accuracy and consistency could be improved through a more structured and systematic process, especially for policy impacts.

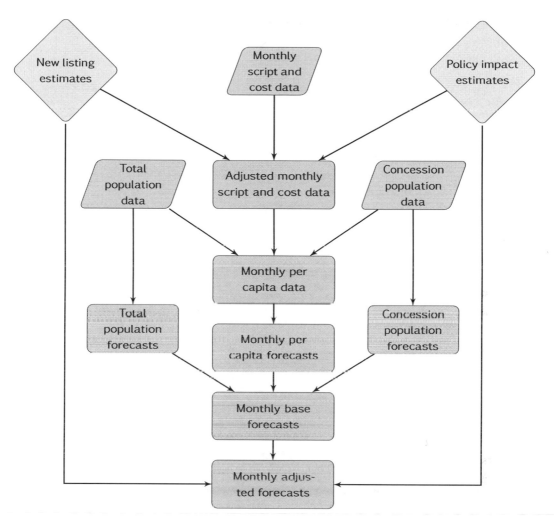

Figure 3.1: Process for producing PBS forecasts.

Forecasting new listings: Companies who are applying for their medicine to be added to the PBS are asked to submit detailed forecasts for various aspects of the medicine, such as projected patient numbers, market share of the new medicine, substitution effects, etc. The Pharmaceutical Benefits Advisory Committee provides guidelines of a highly structured and systematic approach for generating these forecasts and requires careful documentation for each step of the process. This structured process helps reduce the likelihood and effect of deliberate self-serving biases. Two detailed evaluation rounds of the company forecasts are implemented by a sub-committee,

one before the medicine is added to the PBS and one after it
is added. Finally comparisons of observed versus forecasts for
some selected new listings 12 months and also 24 months after
the listing are performed and the results are sent back to the
companies for comment.

Policy impact forecasts: In contrast to the highly structured
process used for new listings, there were no systematic proced-
ures for policy impact forecasts. On many occasions forecasts of
policy impacts were calculated by a small team, often heavily re-
liant on the work of one person. The forecasts were not usually
subject to a formal review process. There were no guidelines for
how to construct judgmental forecasts for policy impacts and
there was often a lack of adequate documentation about how
these forecasts were obtained, what assumptions underly them,
etc.

Consequently we recommended several changes:

- that guidelines for forecasting new policy impacts
  be developed to encourage a more systematic and
  structured forecasting approach;
- that the forecast methodology be documented in each
  case including all assumptions made in forming the
  forecasts;
- that new policy forecasts be made by at least two
  people from different areas of the organisation;
- that a review of forecasts be conducted one year after
  the implementation of each new policy by a review
  committee, especially for new policies that have a
  significant annual projected cost or saving. The review
  committee should include those involved in generating
  the forecasts but also others.

These recommendations reflect the principles outlined in
Section 3/3.

3/4   The Delphi method

The Delphi method was invented by Olaf Helmer and Norman
Dalkey of the Rand Corporation in the 1950s for the purpose of
addressing a specific military problem. The method relies on
the key assumption that forecasts from a group are generally
more accurate than those from individuals. The aim of the
Delphi method is to construct consensus forecasts from a group

of experts in a structured iterative manner. A facilitator is appointed in order to implement and manage the process. The Delphi method generally involves the following stages:

1. A panel of experts is assembled.
2. Forecasting tasks/challenges are set and distributed to the experts.
3. Experts return initial forecasts and justifications. These are compiled and summarised in order to provide feedback.
4. Feedback is provided to the experts who now review their forecasts in light of the feedback. This step may be iterated until a satisfactory level of consensus is reached.
5. Final forecasts are constructed by aggregating the experts' forecasts.

Each stage of the Delphi method comes with its own challenges. In what follows we provide some suggestions and discussion about each one of these.[4]

Experts and anonymity

The first challenge of the facilitator is to identify a group of experts that can contribute to the forecasting task. The usual suggestion is somewhere between 5 and 20 experts with diverse expertise. Experts submit forecasts and also provide detailed qualitative justifications for these.

A key feature of the Delphi method is that the participating experts remain anonymous at all times. This means that the experts cannot be influenced by political and social pressures in their forecasts. Furthermore, all experts are given an equal say and all are made accountable for their forecasts. This avoids the situation where a group meeting is held and some members do not contribute, while others dominate. It also prevents members exerting influence based on seniority or personality. There are suggestions that even something as simple as seating arrangements in a group setting can influence the group dynamics. Furthermore, there is ample evidence that a group meeting

[4] For further reading, refer to:
   G. Rowe (2007). A guide to Delphi. *Foresight: The International Journal of Applied Forecasting* (8), 11–16.
   G. Rowe and G. Wright (1999). The Delphi technique as a forecasting tool: issues and analysis. *International Journal of Forecasting* 15, 353–375.

setting promotes enthusiasm and influences individual judgement leading to optimism and overconfidence.[5]

A byproduct of anonymity is that the experts do not need to
meet as a group in a physical location. An important advantage
of this is that it increases the likelihood of gathering experts
with diverse skills and expertise from varying locations. Furthermore, it makes the process cost-effective by eliminating the
expense and inconvenience of travel, and it makes it flexible
as the experts only have to meet a common deadline for submitting forecasts rather than having to set a common meeting
time.

[5] R. Buehler, D. Messer-
vey and D. Griffin
(2005). Collaborative
planning and pre-
diction: Does group
discussion affect op-
timistic biases in time
estimation? *Organ-
izational Behavior
and Human Decision
Processes* **97**(1), 47–63.

Setting the forecasting task in a Delphi

In a Delphi setting, it may be useful to conduct a preliminary
round of information gathering from the experts before setting
the forecasting tasks. Alternatively, as experts submit their
initial forecasts and justifications, valuable information not
shared between all experts can be identified by the facilitator
when compiling the feedback.

Feedback

Feedback to the experts should include summary statistics of
forecasts and outlines of qualitative justifications. Numerical
data summaries and graphical representations can be used to
summarise experts' forecasts.

As the feedback is controlled by the facilitator, there may be
scope to direct attention and information from the experts to
areas where it is most required. For example the facilitator may
direct the experts' attention to responses that fall outside the
interquartile range, and the qualitative justification for such
forecasts.

Iteration

The process of the experts submitting forecasts, receiving
feedback, and re-viewing their forecasts in light of the feedback,
is repeated until a satisfactory level of consensus between
the experts is reached. Satisfactory consensus does not mean
complete convergence in the forecast value; it means that the
variability of the responses has decreased to a satisfactory level.

Usually two or three rounds are sufficient. Experts are more likely to drop out as the number of iterations increases, so too many rounds should be avoided.

Final forecasts

The final forecasts are usually constructed by giving equal weight to all experts' forecasts. The facilitator should keep in mind the possibility of extreme values which can distort the final forecast.

Limitations and variations

Applying the Delphi method can be time consuming. In a group meeting, final forecasts can possibly be reached in hours or even minutes — something almost impossible to do in a Delphi setting. If it is taking a long time to reach a consensus in a Delphi setting, the panel may lose interest and cohesiveness.

In a group setting, personal interactions can lead to quicker and better clarifications of qualitative justifications. A variation to the Delphi method often applied is the "estimate-talk-estimate method", where experts can interact between iterations. The forecast submissions can still remain anonymous. A disadvantage of this variation is the possibility of the loudest person exerting undue influence.

The facilitator

The role of the facilitator is of utmost importance. The facilitator is largely responsible for the design and administration of the Delphi process. The facilitator is also responsible for accommodating feedback to the experts and generating the final forecasts. In this role the facilitator needs to be experienced enough to recognise areas which may need more attention than others, and to direct the attention of the experts to these. Also, as there is no face-to-face interaction between the experts, the facilitator is responsible for disseminating important information. The efficiency and effectiveness of the facilitator can dramatically improve the probability of a successful Delphi method in a judgmental forecasting setting.

3/5   Forecasting by analogy

A useful judgmental approach often implemented in practice
is forecasting by analogy. A common everyday example is the
pricing of a house through an appraisal process. An appraiser
estimates the market value of a house by comparing it to similar
properties that have sold in the area. The degree of similarity
depends on the attributes considered. With house appraisals,
attributes such as land size, dwelling size, number of bedrooms,
number of bathrooms, and garage space are usually considered.

Even thinking and discussing analogous products or situations can generate useful (and sometimes crucial) information.
We illustrate this point with the following example.[6]

Example 3.2   Designing a high school curriculum

A small group of academics and teachers were assigned the
task of developing a curriculum for teaching judgement and
decision making under uncertainty for high schools in Israel.
Each group member was asked to forecast how long it would
take for the curriculum to be completed. Responses ranged
between 18 and 30 months. One of the group members who was
an expert in curriculum design was asked to consider analogous
curricula developments around the world. He concluded that
40% of analogous groups he considered never completed the
task. The rest took between 7 to 10 years. The Israel project was
completed in 8 years.

Obviously forecasting by analogy comes with challenges.
We should aspire to base forecasts on multiple analogies rather
than a single analogy, which may create biases. However these
may be challenging to identify. Similarly we should aspire to
consider multiple attributes. Identifying or even comparing
these may not always be straight forward. As always we suggest
performing these comparisons and the forecasting process
using a systematic approach. Developing a detailed scoring
mechanism to rank attributes and record the process of ranking
will always be useful.

[6] This example is
extracted from D.
Kahneman and D.
Lovallo (1993). Timid
choices and bold
forecasts: A cognitive
perspective on risk
taking. en. *Management
Science* **39**(1), 17–31.

A structured analogy

Alternatively a structured approach comprising a panel of experts can be implemented as proposed by Green and Armstrong[7]. The concept is similar to that of a Delphi; however, the forecasting task is completed by considering analogies. First of all a facilitator is appointed. Then the structured approach involves the following steps.

1. A panel of experts who are likely to have experience with analogous situations is assembled.
2. Tasks/challenges are set and distributed to the experts.
3. Experts identify and describe as many analogies as they can.
4. Experts list similarities and differences of each analogy to the target situation, then rate the similarity of each analogies to the target situation on a scale.
5. Forecasts are derived by facilitator by using a set rule. This can be a weighted average where the weights can be guided by the ranking scores of each analogy by the experts.

Similarly to the Delphi approach, anonymity of the experts could be an advantage in not suppressing creativity but could hinder collaboration. Green and Armstrong found no gain in collaboration between the experts in their results. A key finding was that experts with multiple analogies (more than two), and who had direct experience with the analogies, generated the most accurate forecasts.

[7] K. C. Green and J. S. Armstrong (2007). Structured analogies for forecasting. *International Journal of Forecasting* 23(3), 365–376.

3/6 Scenario Forecasting

A fundamentally different approach to judgmental forecasting is scenario-based forecasting. The aim of this approach is to generate forecasts based on plausible scenarios. In contrast to the two previous approaches (Delphi and forecasting by analogy) where the resulting forecast is intended to be a likely outcome, here each scenario-based forecast may have a low probability of occurrence. The scenarios are generated by considering all possible factors or drivers, their relative impacts, the interactions between them, and the targets to be forecasted.

Building forecasts based on scenarios allows for a wide range of possible forecasts to be generated and some extremes to be identified. For example is it usual for "best", "middle" and "worst" case scenarios to be presented, although many other scenarios will be generated. Thinking about and documenting these contrasting extremes can lead to early contingency planning.

With scenario forecasting, decision makers often participate directly in the generation of scenarios. While this may lead to some bias, it can ease the communication of the scenario-based forecasts, and lead to better understanding of the results.

3/7   New product forecasting

The definition of a new product can vary. It may be an entirely new product has been launched, a variation of an existing product ("new and improved"), a change in the pricing scheme of an existing product, or even an existing product entering a new market.

Judgmental forecasting is usually the only available method for new product forecasting as historical data are unavailable. The approaches we have already outlined (Delphi, forecasting by analogy and scenario forecasting) are all applicable when forecasting the demand of a new product.

Other methods more specific to the situation are also available. We briefly describe three such methods that are commonly applied in practice. These methods are less structured than those already discussed, and are likely to lead to more biased forecasts as a result.

Sales force composite

In this approach, forecasts for each outlet/branch/store of a company are generated by salespeople and are then aggregated. This usually involves sales managers forecasting demand for the outlet they manage. Salespeople are usually closest to the interaction between customers and products, and often develop an intuition about customer purchasing intentions. They bring to the forecast this valuable experience and expertise.

However having salespeople generate forecasts violates the key principle of segregating forecasters and users which can create biases in many directions. It is very common that the performance of a salesperson is evaluated against sales forecasts or expectations set beforehand. In this case the salesperson acting as a forecaster may introduce some self-serving bias by generating low forecasts. On the other hand we can think of the very enthusiastic salesperson full of optimism generating high forecasts.

Moreover a successful salesperson does not equate to a successful nor a well informed forecaster. A large proportion of salespeople will have no or very limited formal training in forecasting. Finally salespeople will feel customer displeasure at first hand if, for example, the product runs out or is not introduced in their store. Such interactions will cloud judgement.

Executive opinion

In contrast to the sales force composite, this approach involves staff at the top of the managerial structure generating aggregate forecasts. Forecasts are usually generated in a group meeting where executives contribute information from their own area of the company. Having executives from different functional areas of the company promotes great skill and knowledge diversity in the group.

This process carries all the advantages and disadvantages of a group meeting setting we have discussed earlier. It is important in this setting to justify and document the forecasting process. That is, executives need to be held accountable in order to reduce biases generated by the group meeting setting. There may also be scope to apply variations to a Delphi approach in this setting; for example, the estimate-talk-estimate process described earlier.

Customer intentions

Customer intentions can be used in forecasting demand for a new product or for a variation on an existing product. Questionnaires are filled by customers on their intentions to buy the product. A structured questionnaire is used, asking customers to rate the likelihood of purchasing a product on a scale; for example, highly likely, likely, possible, unlikely, highly unlikely.

Survey design challenges such as collecting a representative sample, applying a time- and cost-effective method, and dealing with non-responses, need to be addressed[8].

Furthermore, in this survey setting we must think about the relationship between purchase intention and purchase behaviour. Customers may not always do what they say they will. Many studies have found a positive correlation between purchase intentions and purchase behaviour; however the strength of these correlations varies substantially. Factors driving this variation include the timing between data collection and product launch, the definition of "new" for the product, and the type of industry. Behavioural theory tells us that intentions predict behaviour if the intentions are measured just before the behaviour.[9] The time between intention and behaviour will vary depending on whether it is a completely new product or a variation on an existing product. Also the correlation between intention and behaviour is found to be stronger for variations on existing and familiar products than for completely new products.

Whichever method of new product forecasting is used, it is important to thoroughly document the forecasts made, and the reasoning behind them, in order to evaluate them when data become available.

[8] R. M. Groves, F. J. Fowler, Jr., M. P. Couper, J. M. Lepkowski, E. Singer and R. Tourangeau (2009). *Survey Methodology*. 2nd ed. Wiley.

[9] D. M. Randall and J. A. Wolff (1994). The time interval in the intention-behaviour relationship: Meta-analysis. *British Journal of Social Psychology* 33, 405–418.

3/8   *Judgmental adjustments*

In this final section we consider the situation where historical data are available and used to generate statistical forecasts. It is common for practitioners to then apply judgmental adjustments to these forecasts. These adjustments can potentially provide all of the advantages of judgmental forecasting discussed earlier in the chapter. For example they provide an avenue for incorporating factors that may not be accounted for in the statistical model, such as promotions, large sporting events, holidays, or recent events that are not yet reflected in the data. However, these advantages come to fruition only when the right conditions are present. Judgmental adjustments, like judgmental forecasts, come with biases and limitations, and we must implement methodical strategies to minimise them.

Use adjustments sparingly

Practitioners adjust much more often than they should, and many times for the wrong reasons. By adjusting statistical forecasts, users of forecasts create a feeling of ownership and credibility. Users often do not understand or appreciate the mechanisms that generate the statistical forecasts (as they most likely will have no training in this area). By implementing judgmental adjustments, users feel that they have contributed and completed the forecasts, and they can now relate their own intuition and interpretations to these. The forecasts have become their own.

Judgmental adjustments should not aim to correct for a systematic pattern in the data that is thought to have been missed by the statistical model. This has proven to be ineffective as forecasters tend to read non-existent patterns in noisy series. Statistical models are much better at taking account of data patterns, and judgmental adjustments only hinder accuracy.

Judgmental adjustments are most effective when there is significant additional information at hand or strong evidence for the need of an adjustment. We should only adjust when we have important extra information not incorporated in the statistical model. Hence, adjustments seem to be most accurate when they are large in size. Small adjustments (especially in the positive direction promoting the illusion of optimism) are found to hinder accuracy and should be avoided.

Apply a structured approach

Using a structured and systematic approach will improve the accuracy of judgmental adjustments. Following the key principles outlined in Section 3/3 is vital. In particular, documenting and justifying adjustments will make it more challenging to override the statistical forecasts and will guard against adjusting unnecessarily.

It is common for adjustments to be implemented by a panel (see the example that follows). Using a Delphi setting carries great advantages. But if adjustments are implemented in a group meeting, it is wise to consider forecasts of key markets or products first as panel members will get tired during this process. Fewer adjustments tend to be made as the meeting goes on through the day.

Example 3.3   Tourism Forecasting Committee (TFC)

Tourism Australia publishes forecasts for all aspects of Australian tourism twice a year. The published forecasts are generated by the TFC, an independent body which comprises experts from various government and private industry sectors; for example, the Australian Commonwealth Treasury, airline companies, consulting firms, banking sector companies, and tourism bodies.

The forecasting methodology applied is an iterative process. First, model-based statistical forecasts are generated by the forecasting unit within Tourism Australia. Then judgmental adjustments are made to these in two rounds. In the first round, the TFC Technical Committee[10] (comprising senior researchers, economists and independent advisors) adjusts the model-based forecasts. In the second and final round, the TFC (comprising industry and government experts) makes final adjustments. Adjustments in both rounds are made by consensus.

[10] GA was an observor on this technical committee for a few years.

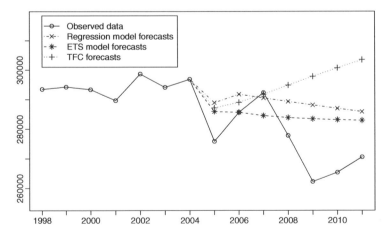

Figure 3.2: Long run annual forecasts for domestic visitor nights for Australia. We study regression models in Chapters 4 and 5, and ETS (ExponenTial Smoothing) models in Chapter 7.

In 2008 we[11] analysed forecasts for Australian domestic tourism. We concluded that the published TFC forecasts were optimistic, especially for the long-run, and we proposed alternative model-based forecasts. We now have observed data up to and including 2011. In Figure 3.2 we plot the published

[11] G. Athanasopoulos and R. J. Hyndman (2008). Modelling and forecasting Australian domestic tourism. *Tourism Management* **29**(1), 19–31.

forecasts against the actual data. We can see that the published TFC forecasts have continued to be optimistic.

What can we learn from this example? Although the TFC clearly states in its methodology that it produces 'forecasts' rather than 'targets', could this be a case were these have been confused? Are forecasters and users sufficiently well-segregated in this process? Could the iterative process itself be improved? Could the adjustment process in the meetings be improved? Could it be that the group meetings have promoted optimism? Could it be that domestic tourism should have been considered earlier in the day?

3/9   Further reading

Books

- Goodwin, P. and G. Wright (2009). *Decision analysis for management judgment*. 4th ed. Chichester: Wiley.
- Kahn, K. B. (2006). *New product forecasting: an applied approach*. M.E. Sharpe.
- Ord, J. K. and R. Fildes (2012). *Principles of business forecasting*. South-Western College Pub.

General papers

- Fildes, R. and P. Goodwin (2007a) Against your better judgment? How organizations can improve their use of management judgment in forecasting. *Interfaces* **37**(6), 570–576.
- Fildes, R. and P. Goodwin (2007b). Good and bad judgment in forecasting: lessons from four companies. *Foresight: The International Journal of Applied Forecasting* (8), 5–10.
- Harvey, N. (2001). "Improving judgment in forecasting". In: *Principles of Forecasting: a handbook for researchers and practitioners*. Ed. by J. S. Armstrong. Boston, MA: Kluwer Academic Publishers, pp.59–80.

Delphi

- Rowe, G. (2007). A guide to Delphi. *Foresight: The International Journal of Applied Forecasting* (8), 11–16.
- Rowe, G. and G. Wright (1999). The Delphi technique as a forecasting tool: issues and analysis. *International Journal of Forecasting* **15**, 353–375.

Adjustments

- Eroglu, C. and K. L. Croxton (2010). Biases in judgmental adjustments of statistical forecasts: The role of individual differences. *International Journal of Forecasting* **26**(1), 116–133.

- Franses, P. H. and R. Legerstee (2013). Do statistical forecasting models for SKU-level data benefit from including past expert knowledge? *International Journal of Forecasting* **29**(1), 80–87.

- Goodwin, P. (2000). Correct or combine? Mechanically integrating judgmental forecasts with statistical methods. *International Journal of Forecasting* **16**(2), 261–275.

- Sanders, N., P. Goodwin, D. Önkal, M. S. Gönül, N. Harvey, A. Lee and L. Kjolso (2005). When and how should statistical forecasts be judgmentally adjusted? *Foresight: The International Journal of Applied Forecasting* **1**(1), 5–23.

Analogy

- Green, K. C. and J. S. Armstrong (2007). Structured analogies for forecasting. *International Journal of Forecasting* **23**(3), 365–376.

Scenarios

- Önkal, D., K. Z. Sayım and M. S. Gönül (2012). Scenarios as channels of forecast advice. *Technological Forecasting and Social Change*.

Customer intentions

- Morwitz, V. G., J. H. Steckel and A. Gupta (2007). When do purchase intentions predict sales? *International Journal of Forecasting* **23**(3), 347–364.

4
Simple regression

In this chapter we introduce simple linear regression. The basic concept is that we forecast variable y assuming it has a linear relationship with variable x. The model is called "simple" regression as we only allow one predictor variable x. In Chapter 5 we will discuss forecasting with several predictor variables.

The forecast variable y is sometimes also called the regressand, dependent or explained variable. The predictor variable x is sometimes also called the regressor, independent or explanatory variable. In this book we will always refer to them as the "forecast variable" and "predictor variable".

4/1   *The simple linear model*

In this chapter, the forecast and predictor variables are assumed to be related by the simple linear model:

$$y = \beta_0 + \beta_1 x + \varepsilon.$$

An example of data from such a model is shown in Figure 4.1. The parameters β_0 and β_1 determine the intercept and the slope of the line respectively. The intercept β_0 represents the predicted value of y when $x = 0$. The slope β_1 represents the predicted increase in y resulting from a one unit increase in x.

Notice that the observations do not lie on the straight line but are scattered around it. We can think of each observation y_i consisting of the systematic or explained part of the model, $\beta_0 + \beta_1 x_i$, and the random "error", ε_i. The "error" term does not imply a mistake, but a deviation from the underlying straight line model. It captures anything that may affect y_i other than x_i.

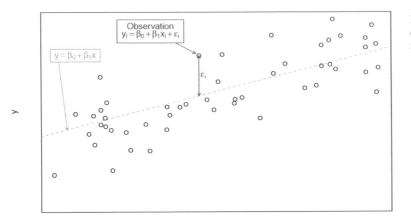

Figure 4.1: An example of data from a linear regression model.

We assume that these errors:

1. have mean zero; otherwise the forecasts will be systematically biased.
2. are not autocorrelated; otherwise the forecasts will be inefficient as there is more information to be exploited in the data.
3. are unrelated to the predictor variable; otherwise there would be more information that should be included in the systematic part of the model.

It is also useful to have the errors normally distributed with constant variance in order to produce prediction intervals and to perform statistical inference. While these additional conditions make the calculations simpler, they are not necessary for forecasting.

Another important assumption in the simple linear model is that x is not a random variable. If we were performing a controlled experiment in a laboratory, we could control the values of x (so they would not be random) and observe the resulting values of y. With observational data (including most data in business and economics) it is not possible to control the value of x, although they can still be non-random. For example, suppose we are studying the effect of interest rates on inflation. Then x is the interest rate and y is the rate of inflation. Interest rates are usually set by a committee and so they are not random.

4/2   Least squares estimation

In practice, of course, we have a collection of observations but we do not know the values of β_0 and β_1. These need to be estimated from the data. We call this "fitting a line through the data".

There are many possible choices for β_0 and β_1, each choice giving a different line. The least squares principle provides a way of choosing β_0 and β_1 effectively by minimizing the sum of the squared errors. That is, we choose the values of β_0 and β_1 that minimize

$$\sum_{i=1}^{N} \varepsilon_i^2 = \sum_{i=1}^{N} (y_i - \beta_0 - \beta_1 x_i)^2.$$

Using mathematical calculus, it can be shown that the resulting **least squares estimators** are

$$\hat{\beta}_1 = \frac{\sum\limits_{i=1}^{N} (y_i - \bar{y})(x_i - \bar{x})}{\sum\limits_{i=1}^{N} (x_i - \bar{x})^2}$$

and

$$\hat{\beta}_0 = \bar{y} - \hat{\beta}_1 \bar{x},$$

where $\bar{x}$ is the average of the x observations and $\bar{y}$ is the average of the y observations.

The *estimated* line is known as the "regression line" and is shown in Figure 4.2.

We imagine that there is a "true" line denoted by $y = \beta_0 + \beta_1 x$ (shown as the dashed green line in Figure 4.2, but we do not know β_0 and β_1 so we cannot use this line for forecasting. Therefore we obtain estimates $\hat{\beta}_0$ and $\hat{\beta}_1$ from the observed data to give the "regression line" (the solid purple line in Figure 4.2).

The regression line is used for forecasting. For each value of x, we can forecast a corresponding value of y using $\hat{y} = \hat{\beta}_0 + \hat{\beta}_1 x$.

Fitted values and residuals

The forecast values of y obtained from the observed x values are called "fitted values". We write these as $\hat{y}_i = \hat{\beta}_0 + \hat{\beta}_1 x_i$, for $i = 1,\ldots,N$. Each $\hat{y}_i$ is the point on the regression line corresponding to observation x_i.

The difference between the observed y values and the corresponding fitted $\hat{y}$ values are the "residuals":

$$e_i = y_i - \hat{y}_i = y_i - \hat{\beta}_0 - \hat{\beta}_1 x_i.$$

The residuals have some useful properties including the following two:

$$\sum_{i=1}^{N} e_i = 0 \quad \text{and} \quad \sum_{i=1}^{N} x_i e_i = 0.$$

As a result of these properties, it is clear that the average of the residuals is zero, and that the correlation between the residuals and the observations for predictor variable is also zero.

4/3   Regression and correlation

The correlation coefficient r was introduced in Section 2/2. Recall that r measures the strength and the direction (positive or negative) of the linear relationship between the two variables. The stronger the linear relationship, the closer the observed data points will cluster around a straight line.

The slope coefficient $\hat{\beta}_1$ can also be expressed as

$$\hat{\beta}_1 = r \frac{s_y}{s_x},$$

where s_y is the standard deviation of the y observations and s_x is the standard deviation of the x observations.

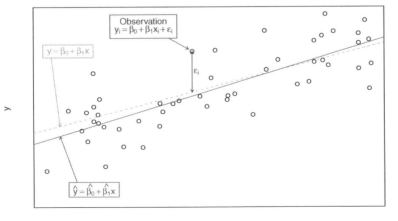

Figure 4.2: Estimated regression line for a random sample of size N.

So correlation and regression are strongly linked. The advantage of a regression model over correlation is that it asserts a predictive relationship between the two variables (x predicts y) and quantifies this in a way that is useful for forecasting.

Example 4.1   Car emissions

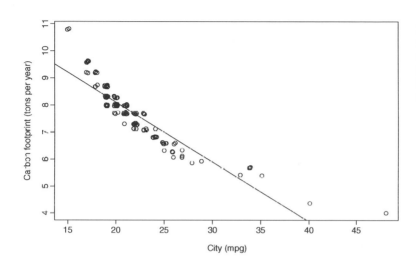

Figure 4.3: Fitted regression line from regressing the carbon footprint of cars versus their fuel economy in city driving conditions.

──────────────── R code ────────────────
```
plot(jitter(Carbon) ~ jitter(City), xlab="City (mpg)",
  ylab="Carbon footprint (tons per year)",data=fuel)
fit <- lm(Carbon ~ City, data=fuel)
abline(fit)
```

──────────────── R output ────────────────
```
> summary(fit)
Coefficients:
            Estimate Std. Error t value Pr(>|t|)
(Intercept) 12.525647   0.199232   62.87   <2e-16 ***
City        -0.220970   0.008878  -24.89   <2e-16 ***
---
Signif. codes:  0 *** 0.001 ** 0.01 * 0.05 . 0.1   1

Residual standard error: 0.4703 on 132 degrees of freedom
Multiple R-squared: 0.8244,        Adjusted R-squared: 0.823
F-statistic: 619.5 on 1 and 132 DF,  p-value: < 2.2e-16
```

Data on the carbon footprint and fuel economy for 2009 model cars were first introduced in Chapter 1. A scatter plot of

Carbon (carbon footprint in tonnes per year) versus City (fuel economy in city driving conditions in miles per gallon) for all 134 cars is presented in Figure 4.3. Also plotted is the estimated regression line

$$\hat{y} = 12.53 - 0.22x.$$

The regression estimation output from R is also shown. Notice the coefficient estimates in the column labelled "Estimate". The other features of the output will be explained later in this chapter.

Interpreting the intercept, $\hat{\beta}_0 = 12.53$. A car that has fuel economy of 0 mpg in city driving conditions can expect an average carbon footprint of 12.53 tonnes per year. As often happens with the intercept, this is a case where the interpretation is nonsense as it is impossible for a car to have fuel economy of 0 mpg.

The interpretation of the intercept requires that a value of $x = 0$ makes sense. When $x = 0$ makes sense, the intercept $\hat{\beta}_0$ is the predicted value of y corresponding to $x = 0$. Even when $x = 0$ does not make sense, the intercept is an important part of the model. Without it, the slope coefficient can be distorted unnecessarily.

Interpreting the slope, $\hat{\beta}_1 = -0.22$. For every extra mile per gallon, a car's carbon footprint will decrease on average by 0.22 tonnes per year. Alternatively, if we consider two cars whose fuel economies differ by 1 mpg in city driving conditions, their carbon footprints will differ, on average, by 0.22 tonnes per year (with the car travelling further per gallon of fuel having the smaller carbon footprint).

4/4 Evaluating the regression model

Residual plots

Recall that each residual is the unpredictable random component of each observation and is defined as

$$e_i = y_i - \hat{y}_i,$$

for $i = 1, \ldots, N$. We would expect the residuals to be randomly scattered without showing any systematic patterns. A simple and quick way for a first check is to examine a scatterplot of the residuals against the predictor variable.

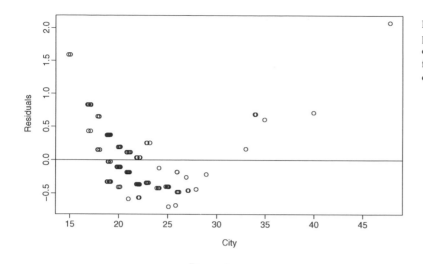

Figure 4.4: Residual plot from regressing carbon footprint versus fuel economy in city driving conditions.

────────────── R code ──────────────

```
res <- residuals(fit)
plot(jitter(res) ~ jitter(City), ylab="Residuals", xlab="City", data=fuel)
abline(0,0)
```

A non-random pattern may indicate that a non-linear relationship may be required, or some heteroscedasticity is present (i.e., the residuals show non-constant variance), or there is some left over serial correlation (only when the data are time series).

Figure 4.4 shows that the residuals from the Car data example display a pattern rather than being randomly scattered. Residuals corresponding to the lowest of the City values are mainly positive, for City values between 20 and 30 the residuals are mainly negative, and for larger City values (above 30 mpg) the residuals are positive again.

This suggests the simple linear model is not appropriate for these data. Instead, a non-linear model will be required.

Outliers and influential observations

Observations that take on extreme values compared to the majority of the data are called "outliers". Observations that have a large influence on the estimation results of a regression model are called "influential observations". Usually, influential observations are also outliers that are extreme in the x direction.

Example 4.2   Predicting weight from height

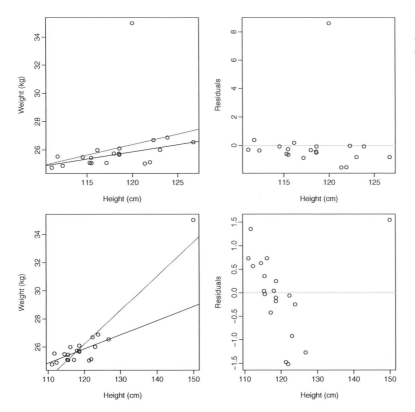

Figure 4.5: The effect of outliers and influential observations on regression.

In Figure 4.5 we consider simple linear models for predicting the weight of 7 year old children by regressing weight against height. The two samples considered are identical except for the one observation that is an outlier. In the first row of plots the outlier is a child who weighs 35kg and is 120cm tall. In the second row of plots the outlier is a child who also weighs 35kg but is much taller at 150cm (so more extreme in the *x* direction). The black lines are the estimated regression lines when the outlier in each case is not included in the sample. The red lines are the estimated regression lines when including the outliers. Both outliers have an effect on the regression line, but the second has a much bigger effect — so we call it an influential observation. The residual plots show that an influential observation does not always lead to a large residual.

There are formal methods for detecting outliers and influential observations that are beyond the scope of this textbook.

As we suggested at the beginning of Chapter 2, getting familiar with your data prior to performing any analysis is of vital importance. A scatter plot of y against x is always a useful starting point in regression analysis and often helps to identify unusual observations.

One source for an outlier occurring is an incorrect data entry. Simple descriptive statistics of your data can identify minima and maxima that are not sensible. If such an observation is identified, and it has been incorrectly recorded, it should be immediately removed from the sample.

Outliers also occur when some observations are simply different. In this case it may not be wise for these observations to be removed. If an observation has been identified as a likely outlier it is important to study it and analyze the possible reasons behind it. The decision of removing or retaining such an observation can be a challenging one (especially when outliers are influential observations). It is wise to report results both with and without the removal of such observations.

Goodness-of-fit

A common way to summarize how well a linear regression model fits the data is via the coefficient of determination or R^2. This can be calculated as **the square of the correlation between the observed y values and the predicted $\hat{y}$ values.** Alternatively, it can also be calculated as:

$$R^2 = \frac{\sum(\hat{y}_i - \bar{y})^2}{\sum(y_i - \bar{y})^2},$$

where the summations are over all observations. Thus, it is also **the proportion of variation in the forecast variable that is accounted for (or explained) by the regression model.**

If the predictions are close to the actual values, we would expect R^2 to be close to 1. On the other hand, if the predictions are unrelated to the actual values, then $R^2 = 0$. In all cases, R^2 lies between 0 and 1.

In simple linear regression, the value of R^2 is also equal to the square of the correlation between y and x. In the car data example $r = -0.91$, hence $R^2 = 0.82$. The coefficient of determination is presented as part of the R output obtained when estimation a linear regression and is labelled "Multiple R-squared: 0.8244" in Figure 4.3. Thus, 82% of the variation in the carbon footprint of cars is captured by the model. However, a "high" R^2 does not always indicate a good model for forecasting. Figure 4.4 shows that there are specific ranges of values of y for which the fitted y values are systematically under- or over-estimated.

The R^2 value is commonly used, often incorrectly, in forecasting. There are no set rules of what a good R^2 value is and typical values of R^2 depend on the type of data used. Validating a model's forecasting performance on the test data is much better than measuring the R^2 value on the training data

Standard error of the regression

Another measure of how well the model has fitted the data is the standard deviation of the residuals, which is often known as the "standard error of the regression" and is calculated by

$$s_e = \sqrt{\frac{1}{N-2} \sum_{i=1}^{N} e_i^2}. \tag{4.1}$$

Notice that this calculation is slightly different from the usual standard deviation where we divide by $N-1$ (see p.33). Here, we divide by $N-2$ because we have estimated two parameters (the intercept and slope) in computing the residuals. Normally, we only need to estimate the mean (i.e., one parameter) when computing a standard deviation. The divisor is always N minus the number of parameters estimated in the calculation.

The standard error is related to the size of the average error that the model produces. We can compare this error to the sample mean of y or with the standard deviation of y to gain some perspective on the accuracy of the model. In Figure 4.3, s_e is part of the R output labeled "Residual standard error" and takes the value 0.4703 tonnes per year.

We should warn here that the evaluation of the standard error can be highly subjective as it is scale dependent. The main reason we introduce it here is that it is required when generating forecast intervals, discussed in Section 4/5.

4/5   *Forecasting with regression*

Forecasts from a simple linear model are easily obtained using the equation

$$\hat{y} = \hat{\beta}_0 + \hat{\beta}_1 x$$

where x is the value of the predictor for which we require a forecast. That is, if we input a value of x in the equation we obtain a corresponding forecast $\hat{y}$.

When this calculation is done using an observed value of x from the data, we call the resulting value of $\hat{y}$ a "fitted value". This is not a genuine forecast as the actual value of y for that predictor value was used in estimating the model, and so the value of $\hat{y}$ is affected by the true value of y. When the values of x is a new value (i.e., not part of the data that were used to estimate the model), the resulting value of $\hat{y}$ is a genuine forecast.

Assuming that the regression errors are normally distributed, an approximate 95% **forecast interval** (also called a prediction interval) associated with this forecast is given by

$$\hat{y} \pm 1.96 s_e \sqrt{1 + \frac{1}{N} + \frac{(x - \bar{x})^2}{(N-1)s_x^2}}, \tag{4.2}$$

where N is the total number of observations, $\bar{x}$ is the mean of the observed x values, s_x is the standard deviation of the observed x values and s_e is given by equation (4.1). Similarly, an 80% forecast interval can be obtained by replacing 1.96 by 1.28 in equation (4.2). Other appropriate forecasting intervals can be obtained by replacing the 1.96 with the appropriate value given in Table 2.1. If R is used to obtain forecast intervals, more exact calculations are obtained (especially for small values of N) than what is given by equation (4.2).

Equation (4.2) shows that the forecast interval is wider when x is far from $\bar{x}$. That is, we are more certain about our forecasts when considering values of the predictor variable close to its sample mean.

The estimated regression line in the Car data example is

$$\hat{y} = 12.53 - 0.22x.$$

For the Chevrolet Aveo (the first car in the list) $x_1 = 25$ mpg and $y_1 = 6.6$ tons of CO_2 per year. The model returns a fitted value of $\hat{y}_1$=7.00, i.e., $e_1 = -0.4$. For a car with City driving fuel economy $x = 30$ mpg, the average footprint forecasted is $\hat{y} = 5.90$ tons of CO_2 per year. The corresponding 95% and 80% forecast intervals are [4.95, 6.84] and [5.28, 6.51] respectively (calculated using R).

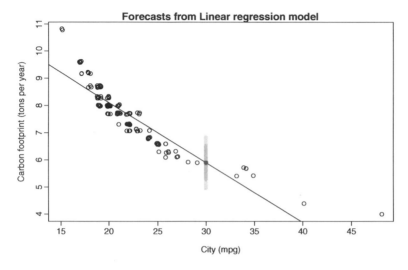

Figure 4.6: Forecast with 80% and 95% forecast intervals for a car with $x = 30$ mpg in city driving.

—————————————— R code ——————————————

```
fitted(fit)[1]
fcast <- forecast(fit, newdata=30)
plot(fcast, xlab="City (mpg)", ylab="Carbon footprint (tons per year)")
# The displayed graph uses jittering, while the code above does not.
```

4/6 Statistical inference

(This section is an optional digression.)

As well as being used for forecasting, simple linear regression models are also valuable in studying the historical effects of predictors. The analysis of the historical effect of a predictor uses statistical inference methods.

Hypothesis testing

If you are an analyst then you may also be interested in testing whether the predictor variable x has had an identifiable effect on y. That is, you may wish to explore whether there is enough evidence to show that x and y are related.

We use statistical hypothesis testing to formally examine this issue. If x and y are unrelated, then the slope parameter $\beta_1 = 0$. So we can construct a test to see if it is plausible that $\beta_1 = 0$ given the observed data.

The logic of hypothesis tests is to assume that the hypothesis you want to *disprove* is true, and then to look for evidence that the assumption is wrong. In this case, we assume that there is no relationship between x and y. This is called the "null hypothesis" and is stated as

$$H_0 : \beta_1 = 0.$$

Evidence against this hypothesis is provided by the value of $\hat{\beta}_1$, the slope estimated from the data. If $\hat{\beta}_1$ is very different from zero, we conclude that the null hypothesis is incorrect and that the evidence suggests there really is a relationship between x and y.

To determine how big the difference between $\hat{\beta}_1$ and β_1 must be before we would reject the null hypothesis, we calculate the probability of obtaining a value of $\hat{\beta}_1$ as large as we have calculated if the null hypothesis were true. This probability is known as the "p-value".

The details of the calculation need not concern us here, except to note that it involves assuming that the errors are normally distributed. R will provide the p-values if we need them.

In the car fuel example, R provides the following output.

———————————————— R output ————————————

```
Coefficients:
             Estimate Std. Error t value Pr(>|t|)
(Intercept) 12.525647   0.199232   62.87   <2e-16 ***
City        -0.220970   0.008878  -24.89   <2e-16 ***
---
Signif. codes:  0 *** 0.001 ** 0.01 * 0.05 . 0.1   1

Residual standard error: 0.4703 on 132 degrees of freedom
Multiple R-squared: 0.8244,       Adjusted R-squared: 0.823
F-statistic: 619.5 on 1 and 132 DF,  p-value: < 2.2e-16
```

The column headed $Pr > |t|$ provides the p-values. The p-value corresponding to the slope is in the row beginning City and takes value <2e-16. That is, it is so small, it is less than $2 \times 10^{-16} = 0.0000000000000002$. In other words, the observed data are extremely unlikely to have arisen if the null hypothesis were true. Therefore we reject H_0. It is much more likely that there is a relationship between city fuel consumption and the carbon footprint of a car. (Although, as we have seen, that relationship is more likely to be non-linear than linear.)

The asterisks to the right of the p-values give a visual indication of how small the p-values are. Three asterisks correspond to values less than 0.001, two asterisks indicate values less than 0.01, one asterisk means the value is less than 0.05, and so on. The legend is given in the line beginning Signif. codes.

There are two other p-values provided in the above output. The p-value corresponding to the intercept is also $< 2 \times 10^{-16}$; this p-value is usually not of great interest — it is a test on whether the intercept parameter is zero or not. The other p-value is on the last line and, in the case of simple linear regression, is identical to the p-value for the slope.

Confidence intervals

It is also sometimes useful to provide an interval estimate for β_1, usually referred to as a confidence interval (and not to be confused with a forecast or prediction interval). The interval estimate is a range of values that probably contain β_1.

In the car fuel example, R provides the following output.

──────────────────────── R output ────────────────────────
```
> confint(fit,level=0.95)
                 2.5 %      97.5 %
(Intercept) 12.1315464 12.9197478
City        -0.2385315 -0.2034092
```

So if the linear model is a correct specification of the relationship between x and y, then the interval $[-0.239, -0.203]$ contains the slope parameter, β_1, with probability 95%. Intervals for the intercept and for other probability values are obtained in the same way.

There is a direct relationship between p-values and confidence intervals. If the 95% confidence interval for β_1 does not contain 0, then the associated p-value must be less than 0.05. More generally, if the $100(1 - \alpha)$% confidence interval for a parameter does not contain 0, then the associated p-value must be less than α.

4/7   Non-linear functional forms

Although the linear relationship assumed at the beginning of this chapter is often adequate, there are cases for which a non-linear functional form is more suitable. The scatter plot of Carbon versus City in Figure 4.3 shows an example where a non-linear functional form is required.

Simply transforming variables y and/or x and then estimating a regression model using the transformed variables is the simplest way of obtaining a non-linear specification. The most commonly used transformation is the (natural) logarithmic (see Section 2/4). Recall that in order to perform a logarithmic transformation to a variable, all its observed values must be greater than zero.

A **log-log** functional form is specified as

$$\log y_i = \beta_0 + \beta_1 \log x_i + \varepsilon_i.$$

In this model, the slope β_1 can be interpreted as an elasticity: β_1 is the average percentage change in y resulting from a 1% change in x.

Figure 4.7 shows a scatter plot of Carbon versus City and the fitted log-log model in both the original scale and the logarithmic scale. The plot shows that in the original scale the slope of the fitted regression line using a log-log functional form is non-constant. The slope depends on x and can be calculated for each point (see Table 4.1). In the logarithmic scale the slope of the line which is now interpreted as an elasticity is constant. So estimating a log-log functional form produces a constant elasticity estimate in contrast to the linear model which produces a constant slope estimate.

Figure 4.8 shows a plot of the residuals from estimating the log-log model. They are now randomly scatted compared to the residuals from the linear model plotted in Figure 4.4. We can conclude that the log-log functional form clearly fits the data better.

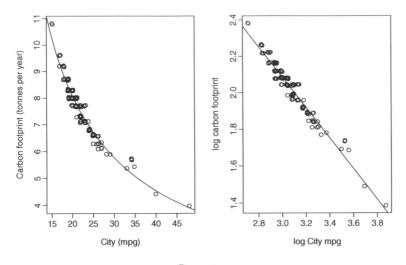

Figure 4.7: Fitting a log-log functional form to the Car data example. Plots show the estimated relationship both in the original and the logarithmic scales.

────────────── R code ──────────────

```
par(mfrow=c(1,2))
fit2 <- lm(log(Carbon) ~ log(City), data=fuel)
plot(jitter(Carbon) ~ jitter(City), xlab="City (mpg)",
  ylab="Carbon footprint (tonnes per year)", data=fuel)
lines(1:50, exp(fit2$coef[1]+fit2$coef[2]*log(1:50)))
plot(log(jitter(Carbon)) ~ log(jitter(City)),
  xlab="log City mpg", ylab="log carbon footprint", data=fuel)
abline(fit2)
```

Other useful forms are the log-linear form and the linear-log form. Table 4.1 summarises these.

Model	Functional form	Slope	Elasticity
linear	$y = \beta_0 + \beta_1 x$	β_1	$\beta_1 y/x$
log-log	$\log y = \beta_0 + \beta_1 \log x$	$\beta_1 y/x$	β_1
linear-log	$y = \beta_0 + \beta_1 \log x$	β_1/x	β_1/y
log-linear	$\log y = \beta_0 + \beta_1 x$	$\beta_1 y$	$\beta_1 x$

Table 4.1: Summary of selected functional forms. Elasticities that depend on the observed values of Y and X are commonly calculated for the sample means of these, $\bar{x}$ and $\bar{y}$.

4/8   Regression with time series data

When using regression for prediction, we are often considering time series data and we are aiming to forecast the future. There are a few issues that arise with time series data but not with cross-sectional data that we will consider in this section.

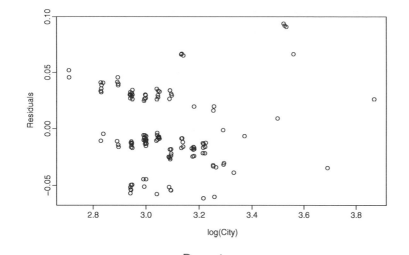

Figure 4.8: Residual plot from estimating a log-log functional form for the Car data example. The residuals now look much more randomly scattered compared to Figure 4.4.

─────────── R code ───────────

```
res <- residuals(fit2)
plot(jitter(res, amount= 005) ~ jitter(log(City)),
  ylab="Residuals", xlab="log(City)", data=fuel)
```

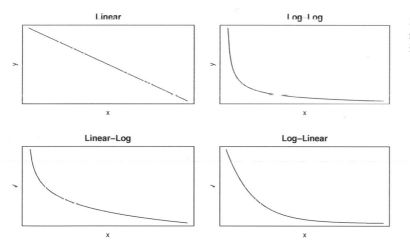

Figure 4.9: The four non-linear forms shown in Table 4.1, for $\beta_1 < 0$.

Example 4.3   US consumption expenditure

Figure 4.10 shows time series plots of quarterly percentage changes (growth rates) of real personal consumption expenditure (C) and real personal disposable income (I) for the US for the period March 1970 to Dec 2010. Also shown is a scatter plot

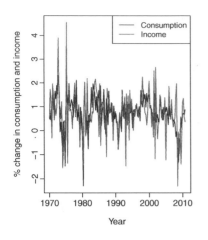 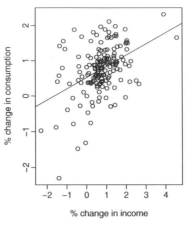

Figure 4.10: Percentage changes in personal consumption expenditure for the US.

─────────────── R code ───────────────
```
fit.ex3 <- lm(consumption ~ income, data=usconsumption)
plot(usconsumption, ylab="% change in consumption and income",
  plot.type="single", col=1:2, xlab="Year")
legend("topright", legend=c("Consumption","Income"),
  lty=1, col=c(1,2), cex=.9)
plot(consumption ~ income, data=usconsumption,
  ylab="% change in consumption", xlab="% change in income")
abline(fit.ex3)
summary(fit.ex3)
```

─────────────── R output ───────────────
```
Coefficients:
            Estimate Std. Error t value Pr(>|t|)
(Intercept)  0.52062    0.06231   8.356 2.79e-14 ***
income       0.31866    0.05226   6.098 7.61e-09 ***
```

including the estimated regression line

$$\hat{C} = 0.52 + 0.32I,$$

with the estimation results shown below the graphs. These show that a 1% increase in personal disposable income will result to an average increase of 0.84% in personal consumption expenditure. We are interested in forecasting consumption for the four quarters of 2011.

Using a regression model to forecast time series data poses a challenge in that future values of the predictor variable (income in this case) are needed to be input into the estimated model, but these are not known in advance. One solution to this problem is to use "scenario based forecasting".

Scenario based forecasting

In this setting the forecaster assumes possible scenarios for the predictor variable that are of interest. For example the US policy maker may want to forecast consumption if there is a 1% growth in income for each of the quarters in 2011. Alternatively a 1% decline in income for each of the quarters may be of interest. The resulting forecasts are calculated and shown in Figure 4.11.

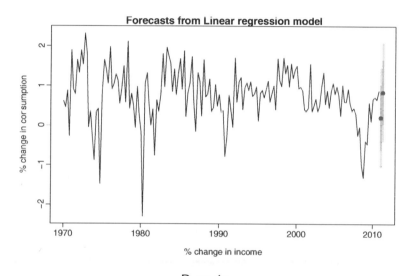

Figure 4.11: Forecasting percentage changes in personal consumption expenditure for the US.

─────────── R code ───────────
```
fcast <- forecast(fit.ex3, newdata=data.frame(income=c(-1,1)))
plot(fcast, ylab="% change in consumption", xlab="% change in income")
```

Forecast intervals for scenario based forecasts do not include the uncertainty associated with the future values of the predictor variables. They assume the value of the predictor is known in advance.

An alternative approach is to use genuine forecasts for the predictor variable. For example, a pure time series based approach can be used to generate forecasts for the predictor variable (more on this in Chapter 9) or forecasts published by some other source such as a government agency can be used.

Ex-ante versus ex-post forecasts

When using regression models with time series data, we need to distinguish between two different types of forecasts that can be produced, depending on what is assumed to be known when the forecasts are computed.

Ex ante forecasts are those that are made using only the information that is available in advance. For example, ex ante forecasts of consumption for the four quarters in 2011 should only use information that was available *before* 2011. These are the only genuine forecasts, made in advance using whatever information is available at the time.

Ex post forecasts are those that are made using later information on the predictors. For example, ex post forecasts of consumption for each of the 2011 quarters may use the actual observations of income for each of these quarters, once these have been observed. These are not genuine forecasts, but are useful for studying the behaviour of forecasting models.

The model from which ex-post forecasts are produced should not be estimated using data from the forecast period. That is, ex-post forecasts can assume knowledge of the predictor variable (the x variable), but should not assume knowledge of the data that are to be forecast (the y variable).

A comparative evaluation of ex ante forecasts and ex post forecasts can help to separate out the sources of forecast uncertainty. This will show whether forecast errors have arisen due to poor forecasts of the predictor or due to a poor forecasting model.

Example 4.4   Linear trend

A common feature of time series data is a trend. Using regression we can model and forecast the trend in time series data by including $t = 1, \ldots, T$, as a predictor variable:

$$y_t = \beta_0 + \beta_1 t + \varepsilon_t.$$

Figure 4.12 shows a time series plot of aggregate tourist arrivals to Australia over the period 1980 to 2010 with the fitted linear trend line $\hat{y}_t = 0.3375 + 0.1761t$. Also plotted are the point and forecast intervals for the years 2011 to 2015.

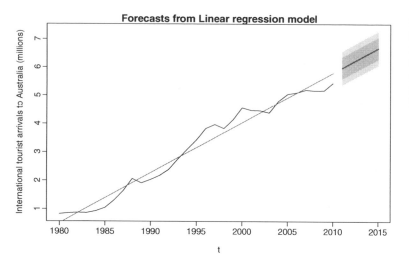

Figure 4.12: Forecasting international tourist arrivals to Australia for the period 2011-2015 using a linear trend. 80% and 95% forecast intervals are shown.

```
fit.ex4 <- tslm(austa ~ trend)
f < forecast(fit.ex4, h=5,level=c(80,95))
plot(f, ylab="International tourist arrivals to Australia (millions)",
  xlab="t")
lines(fitted(fit.ex4),col="blue")
summary(fit.ex4)
```

Coefficients:

	Estimate	Std. Error	t value	Pr(>|t|)	
(Intercept)	0.337535	0.100366	3.363	0.00218	**
trend	0.176075	0.005476	32.167	< 2e-16	***

Residual autocorrelation

With time series data it is highly likely that the value of a variable observed in the current time period will be influenced by its value in the previous period, or even the period before that, and so on. Therefore when fitting a regression model to time series data, it is very common to find autocorrelation in the residuals. In this case, the estimated model violates the assumption of no autocorrelation in the errors, and our forecasts may be inefficient — there is some information left over which should be utilized in order to obtain better forecasts. The forecasts from a model with autocorrelated errors are still unbiased, and so are not "wrong", but they will usually have larger prediction intervals than they need to.

Figure 4.13 plots the residuals from Examples 4.3 and 4.4, and the ACFs of the residuals (see Section 2/2 for an introduction to the ACF). The ACF of the consumption residuals shows a significant spike at lag 2 and 3 and the ACF of the tourism residuals shows significant spikes at lags 1 and 2. Usually plotting the ACFs of the residuals is adequate to reveal any potential autocorrelation in the residuals. More formal tests for autocorrelation are discussed in Section 5/4.

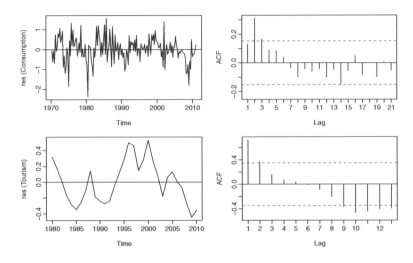

Figure 4.13: Residuals from the regression models for Consumption and Tourism. Because these involved time series data, it is important to look at the ACF of the residuals to see if there is any remaining information not accounted for by the model. In both these examples, there is some remaining autocorrelation in the residuals.

—————— R code ——————

```
par(mfrow=c(2,2))
res3 <- ts(resid(fit.ex3),s=1970.25,f=4)
plot.ts(res3,ylab="res (Consumption)")
abline(0,0)
Acf(res3)
res4 <- resid(fit.ex4)
plot(res4,ylab="res (Tourism)")
abline(0,0)
Acf(res4)
```

Spurious regression

More often than not, time series data are "non-stationary"; that is, the values of the time series do not fluctuate around a constant mean or with a constant variance. We will deal with time series stationarity in more detail in Chapter 8, but here we need to address the effect non-stationary data can have on regression models.

For example consider the two variables plotted in Figure 4.14, which appear to be related simply because they both trend upwards in the same manner. However, air passenger

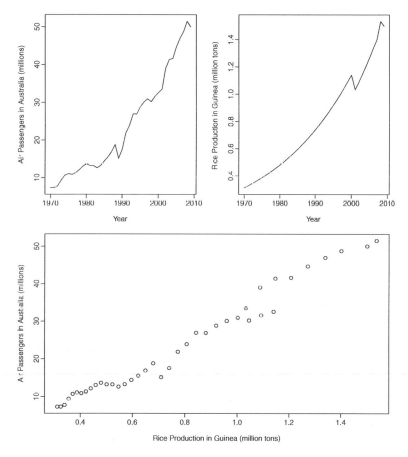

Figure 4.14: Trending time series data can appear to be related, as shown in this example in which air passengers in Australia are regressed against rice production in Guinea.

——————————— R output ———————————

```
Coefficients:
            Estimate Std. Error t value Pr(>|t|)
(Intercept)  -5.7297     0.9026  -6.348  1.9e-07 ***
guinearice   37.4101     1.0487  35.672  < 2e-16 ***

Multiple R-squared: 0.971.
  lag     Autocorrelation
   1           0.7496971
```

traffic in Australia has nothing to do with rice production in Guinea. Selected output obtained from regressing the number of air passengers transported in Australia versus rice production in Guinea (in metric tons) is also shown in Figure 4.14.

Regressing non-stationary time series can lead to spurious regressions. High R^2s and high residual autocorrelation can be signs of spurious regression. We discuss the issues surrounding non-stationary data and spurious regressions in detail in Chapter 9.

Cases of spurious regression might appear to give reasonable short-term forecasts, but they will generally not continue to work into the future.

4/9 *Summary of notation and terminology*

- x_i is observation i on variable x.
- $y_i = \beta_0 + \beta_1 x_i + \varepsilon_i$ is the **simple linear model** with intercept β_0 and slope β_1. The error is denoted by ε_i.
- $y_i = \hat{\beta}_0 + \hat{\beta}_1 x_i + e_i$ is the **estimated regression model** with intercept $\hat{\beta}_0$ and slope $\hat{\beta}_1$. The estimated error or **residual** is denoted by e_i.
- $\hat{y}_i = \hat{\beta}_0 + \hat{\beta}_1 x_i$ is the fitted or estimated **regression line**; $\hat{y}_i$ is the **fitted value** corresponding to observation y_i.

4/10   Exercises

4.1 Electricity consumption was recorded for a small town on 12 randomly chosen days. The following maximum temperatures (degrees Celsius) and consumption (megawatt-hours) were recorded for each day.

Day	1	2	3	4	5	6	7	8	9	10	11	12
Mwh	16.3	16.8	15.5	18.2	15.2	17.5	19.8	19.0	17.5	16.0	19.6	18.0
temp	29.3	21.7	23.7	10.4	29.7	11.9	9.0	23.4	17.8	30.0	8.6	11.8

(a) Plot the data and find the regression model for Mwh with temperature as an explanatory variable. Why is there a negative relationship?

(b) Produce a residual plot. Is the model adequate? Are there any outliers or influential observations?

(c) Use the model to predict the electricity consumption that you would expect for a day with maximum temperature 10° and a day with maximum temperature 35°. Do you believe these predictions?

(d) Give prediction intervals for your forecasts.

The following R code will get you started:

```
plot(Mwh ~ temp, data=econsumption)
fit <- lm(Mwh ~ temp, data=econsumption)
plot(residuals(fit) ~ temp, data=econsumption)
forecast(fit, newdata=data.frame(temp=c(10,35)))
```

4.2 The following table gives the winning times (in seconds) for the men's 400 meters final in each Olympic Games from 1896 to 2012 (data set olympic).

1896	54.2	1928	47.8	1964	45.1	1992	43.50
1900	49.4	1932	46.2	1968	43.8	1996	43.49
1904	49.2	1936	46.5	1972	44.66		
1908	50.0	1948	46.2	1976	44.27		
1912	48.2	1952	45.9	1980	44.60		
1920	49.6	1956	46.7	1984	44.27		
1924	47.6	1960	44.9	1988	43.87		

(a) Update the data set olympic to include the winning times from the last few Olympics.

(b) Plot the winning time against the year. Describe the main features of the scatterplot.

(c) Fit a regression line to the data. Obviously the winning times have been decreasing, but at what *average* rate per year?

(d) Plot the residuals against the year. What does this indicate about the suitability of the fitted line?

(e) Predict the winning time for the men's 400 meters final in the 2000, 2004, 2008 and 2012 Olympics. Give a prediction interval for each of your forecasts. What assumptions have you made in these calculations?

(f) Find out the actual winning times for these Olympics (see www.databaseolympics.com). How good were your forecasts and prediction intervals?

4.3 An elasticity coefficient is the ratio of the percentage change in the forecast variable (y) to the percentage change in the predictor variable (x). Mathematically, the elasticity is defined as $(dy/dx) \times (x/y)$. Consider the log-log model,

$$\log y = \beta_0 + \beta_1 \log x + \varepsilon.$$

Express y as a function of x and show that the coefficient β_1 is the elasticity coefficient.

4/11   *Further reading*

- Chatterjee, S. and A. S. Hadi (2012). *Regression analysis by example*. 5th ed. New York: John Wiley & Sons.

- Fox, J. and H. S. Weisberg (2010). *An R Companion to Applied Regression*. SAGE Publications, Inc.

- Pardoe, I. (2006). *Applied regression modeling: a business approach*. Hoboken, NJ: John Wiley & Sons.

5
Multiple regression

In multiple regression there is one variable to be forecast and several predictor variables. Throughout this chapter we will use two examples of multiple regression, one based on cross-sectional data and the other on time series data.

Example: credit scores

Banks score loan customers based on a lot of personal inform ation. A sample of 500 customers from an Australian bank provided the following information.

Score	Savings ($'000)	Income ($'000)	Time current address (Months)	Time current job (Months)
39.40	0.01	111.17	27	8
51.79	0.65	56.40	29	33
32.82	0.75	36.74	2	16
57.31	0.62	55.99	14	7
37.17	4.13	62.04	2	14
33.69	0.00	43.75	7	7
25.56	0.94	79.01	4	11
32.04	0.00	45.41	3	3
41.34	4.26	55.22	16	18
⋮	⋮	⋮	⋮	⋮

The credit score in the left hand column is used to determine if a customer will be given a loan or not. For these data, the score is on a scale between 0 and 100. It would save a lot of time if the credit score could be predicted from the other variables listed above. Then there would be no need to collect all the other information that banks require. Even if the credit score can only be roughly forecast using these four predictors, it might provide a way of filtering out customers that are unlikely to receive a high enough score to obtain a loan.

This is an example of cross-sectional data where we want to predict the value of the credit score variable using the values of the other variables.

Example: Australian quarterly beer production

Recall the Australian quarterly beer production data shown below.

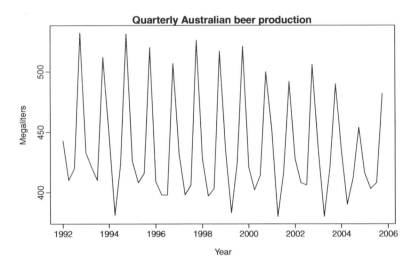

Figure 5.1: Australian quarterly beer production

These are time series data and we want to forecast the value of future beer production. There are no other variables available for predictors. Instead, with time series data, we use the number of quarters since the start of the series as a predictor variable. We may also use the quarter of the year corresponding to each observation as a predictor variable. Then, knowing the number of quarters since the start of the series and the specific quarter of interest, we can forecast the value of beer production in that quarter.

5/1 Introduction to multiple linear regression

The general form of a multiple regression is

$$y_i = \beta_0 + \beta_1 x_{1,i} + \beta_2 x_{2,i} + \cdots + \beta_k x_{k,i} + \varepsilon_i,$$

where y_i is the variable to be forecast and $x_{1,i}, \ldots, x_{k,i}$ are the k predictor variables. Each of the predictor variables must be numerical. The coefficients $\beta_1, \ldots, \beta_k$ measure the effect of each predictor after taking account of the effect of all other predictors in the model. Thus, the coefficients measure the *marginal effects* of the predictor variables.

As for simple linear regression, when forecasting we require the following assumptions for the errors $(\varepsilon_1, \ldots, \varepsilon_N)$:

1. the errors have mean zero;
2. the errors are uncorrelated with each other;
3. the errors are uncorrelated with each predictor $x_{j,i}$.

It is also useful to have the errors normally distributed with constant variance in order to produce prediction intervals, but this is not necessary for forecasting.

Example: credit scores

All 500 observations of the credit score data are shown in Figure 5.2. The top row shows the relationship between each predictor and credit score. While there appear to be some relationships here, particularly between credit score and income, the predictors are all highly skewed and the few outlying obser-vations are making it hard to see what is going on in the bulk of the data.

A way around this problem is to take transformations of the predictors. However, we cannot take logarithms of the predictors because they contain some zeros. Instead, we use the transformation $\log(x + 1)$ where x is the predictor value. That is, we add one to the value of the predictor and then take logarithms. This has a similar effect to taking logarithms but avoids the problem of zeros. It also has the neat side-effect of zeros on the original scale remaining zeros on the transformed scale. The scatterplot matrix showing the transformed data is shown in Figure 5.3.

Now the relationships between the variables are clearer, although there is a great deal of random variation present. We shall try fitting the following model:

$$y = \beta_0 + \beta_1 x_1 + \beta_2 x_2 + \beta_3 x_3 + \beta_4 x_4 + \varepsilon,$$

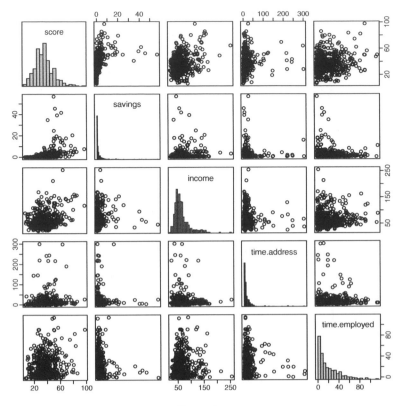

Figure 5.2: Scatterplot matrix of the credit scores and the four predictors.

———————— R code ————————
```
pairs(credit[,-(4:5)],diag.panel=panel.hist)
#The panel.hist function is defined in help(pairs).
```

where

y = credit score,

x_1 = log savings,

x_2 = log income,

x_3 = log time at current address,

x_4 = log time in current job,

ε = error.

Here "log" means the transformation $\log(x + 1)$.

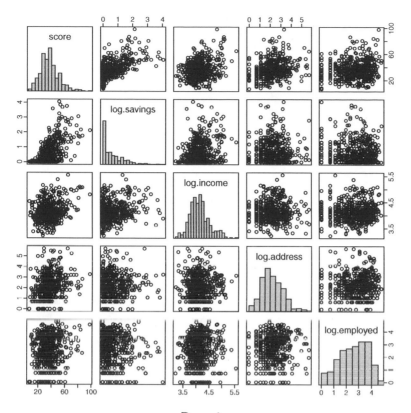

Figure 5.3: Scatterplot matrix of the credit scores and the four predictors, after transforming the four predictors using logarithms.

―――――――――― R code ――――――――――
```
creditlog <- data.frame(score=credit$score,
  log.savings=log(credit$savings+1),
  log.income=log(credit$income+1),
  log.address=log(credit$time.address+1),
  log.employed=log(credit$time.employed+1),
  fte=credit$fte, single=credit$single)
pairs(creditlog[,1:5],diag.panel=panel.hist)
```

Estimation of the model

The values of the coefficients $\beta_0, \ldots, \beta_k$ are obtained by finding the minimum sum of squares of the errors. That is, we find the values of $\beta_0, \ldots, \beta_k$ which minimize

$$\sum_{i=1}^{N} \varepsilon_i^2 = \sum_{i=1}^{N} (y_i - \beta_0 - \beta_1 x_{1,i} - \cdots - \beta_k x_{k,i})^2.$$

This is called "least squares" estimation because it gives the least value for the sum of squared errors. In practice, the calculation is always done using a computer package. Finding the best estimates of the coefficients is often called "fitting" the model to the data.

When we refer to the *estimated* coefficients, we will use the notation $\hat{\beta}_0, \ldots, \hat{\beta}_k$. The equations for these will be given in Section 5/5.

Example: credit scores (continued)

The following computer output is obtained after fitting the regression model described earlier.

——————————— R code ———————————

```
fit <- lm(score ~ log.savings + log.income + log.address
  + log.employed + single, data=creditlog)
summary(fit)
```

——————————— R output ———————————

Coefficients:

	Estimate	Std. Error	t value	P value
(Intercept)	-0.219	5.231	-0.04	0.9667
log.savings	10.353	0.612	16.90	< 2e-16
log.income	5.052	1.258	4.02	6.8e-05
log.address	2.667	0.434	6.14	1.7e-09
log.employed	1.314	0.409	3.21	0.0014

Residual standard error: 10.16 on 495 degrees of freedom
Multiple R-squared: 0.4701,   Adjusted R-squared: 0.4658
F-statistic: 109.8 on 4 and 495 DF, p-value: < 2.2e-16

The first column gives the estimates of each β coefficient and the second column gives its "standard error" (i.e., the standard deviation which would be obtained from repeatedly estimating the β coefficients on similar data sets). The standard error gives a measure of the uncertainty in the estimated β coefficient.

For forecasting purposes, the final two columns are of limited interest. The "t value" is the ratio of a β coefficient to its standard error and the last column gives the p-value: the probability of the estimated β coefficient being as large as it is if there was no real relationship between the credit score and the predictor. This is useful when studying the effect of each predictor, but is not particularly useful when forecasting.

Fitted values, forecast values and residuals

Predictions of y can be calculated by ignoring the error in the regression equation. That is

$$\hat{y} = \hat{\beta}_0 + \hat{\beta}_1 x_1 + \hat{\beta}_2 x_2 + \cdots + \hat{\beta}_k x_k.$$

Plugging in values of $x_1, \ldots, x_k$ into the right hand side of this equation gives a prediction of y for that combination of predictors.

When this calculation is done using values of the predictors from the data that were used to estimate the model, we call the resulting values of $\hat{y}$ the "fitted values". These are "predictions" of the data used in estimating the model. They are not genuine forecasts as the actual value of y for that set of predictors was used in estimating the model, and so the value of $\hat{y}$ is affected by the true value of y.

When the values of $x_1, \ldots, x_k$ are new values (i.e., not part of the data that were used to estimate the model), the resulting value of $\hat{y}$ is a genuine forecast.

The difference between the y observations and the fitted values are the "residuals":

$$e_i = y_i - \hat{y}_i = y_i - \hat{\beta}_0 - \hat{\beta}_1 x_{1,i} - \hat{\beta}_2 x_{2,i} - \cdots - \hat{\beta}_k x_{k,i}.$$

As with simple regression (see Section 4/2), the residuals have zero mean and are uncorrelated with any of the predictors.

R^2: the coefficient of determination

The R^2 value was introduced in Section 4/4. It is the square of the correlation between the actual values and the predicted values. The following graph shows the actual values plotted against the fitted values for the credit score data.

Recall that the value of R^2 can also be calculated as the proportion of variation in the forecast variable that is explained by the regression model:

$$R^2 = \frac{\sum (\hat{y}_i - \bar{y})^2}{\sum (y_i - \bar{y})^2}$$

In this case, $R^2 = 0.47$, so about half of the variation in the scores can be predicted using the model.

Thus, the model is not really sufficient to replace a more detailed approach to credit scoring, but it might be helpful in

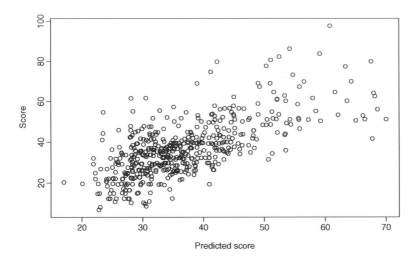

Figure 5.4: Actual credit scores plotted against fitted credit scores using the multiple regression model. The correlation is 0.6856, so the squared correlation is $(0.6856)^2 = 0.4701$.

————————————— R code —————————————

```
plot(fitted(fit), creditlog$score,
 ylab="Score", xlab="Predicted score")
```

filtering out customers who will get a very low score. In the above graph it is evident that anyone with a predicted score below 35 has a true score not much more than 60. Consequently, if the bank wanted to identify high scoring customers quickly, using this model will provide a first filter, and more detailed information need only be collected on a subset of the customers.

5/2   Some useful predictors

Dummy variables

So far, we have assumed that each predictor takes numerical values. But what about when a predictor is a categorical variable taking only two values (e.g., "yes" and "no"). Such a variable might arise, for example, when forecasting credit scores and you want to take account of whether the customer is in full-type employment. So the predictor takes value "yes" when the customer is in full-time employment, and "no" otherwise.

This situation can still be handled within the framework of multiple regression models by creating a "dummy variable" taking value 1 corresponding to "yes" and 0 corresponding to "no". A dummy variable is also known as an "indicator variable".

If there are more than two categories, then the variable can be coded using several dummy variables (one fewer than the total number of categories).

Seasonal dummy variables   For example, suppose we are fore-casting daily electricity demand and we want to account for the day of the week as a predictor. Then the following dummy variables can be created.

Day	D1	D2	D3	D4	D5	D6
Monday	1	0	0	0	0	0
Tuesday	0	1	0	0	0	0
Wednesday	0	0	1	0	0	0
Thursday	0	0	0	1	0	0
Friday	0	0	0	0	1	0
Saturday	0	0	0	0	0	1
Sunday	0	0	0	0	0	0
Monday	1	0	0	0	0	0
Tuesday	0	1	0	0	0	0
Wednesday	0	0	1	0	0	0
Thursday	0	0	0	1	0	0
$\vdots$	$\vdots$	$\vdots$	$\vdots$	$\vdots$	$\vdots$	$\vdots$

Notice that only six dummy variables are needed to code seven categories. That is because the seventh category (in this case Sunday) is specified when the dummy variables are all set to zero.

Many beginners will try to add a seventh dummy variable for the seventh category. This is known as the "dummy variable trap" because it will cause the regression to fail. There will be too many parameters to estimate. The general rule is to use one fewer dummy variables than categories. So for quarterly data, use three dummy variables; for monthly data, use 11 dummy variables; and for daily data, use six dummy variables.

The interpretation of each of the coefficients associated with the dummy variables is that it is *a measure of the effect of that category relative to the omitted category*. In the above example, the coefficient associated with Monday will measure the effect of Monday compared to Sunday on the forecast variable.

Outliers   If there is an outlier in the data, rather than omit it, you can use a dummy variable to remove its effect. In this case, the dummy variable takes value one for that observation and zero everywhere else.

Public holidays   For daily data, the effect of public holidays can be accounted for by including a dummy variable predictor taking value one on public holidays and zero elsewhere.

Easter   Easter is different from most holidays because it is not held on the same date each year and the effect can last for several days. In this case, a dummy variable can be used with value one where any part of the holiday falls in the particular time period and zero otherwise.

For example, with monthly data, when Easter falls in March then the dummy variable takes value 1 in March, when it falls in April, the dummy variable takes value 1 in April, and when it starts in March and finishes in April, the dummy variable takes value 1 for both months.

Trend

A linear trend is easily accounted for by including the predictor $x_{1,t} = t$. A quadratic or higher order trend is obtained by specifying

$$x_{1,t} = t, \quad x_{2,t} = t^2, \quad \ldots$$

However, it is not recommended that quadratic or higher order trends are used in forecasting. When they are extrapolated, the resulting forecasts are often very unrealistic.

A better approach is to use a piecewise linear trend which bends at some time. If the trend bends at time τ, then it can be specified by including the following predictors in the model.

$$x_{1,t} = t$$

$$x_{2,t} = \begin{cases} 0 & t < \tau \\ (t - \tau) & t \geq \tau \end{cases}$$

If the associated coefficients of $x_{1,t}$ and $x_{2,t}$ are β_1 and β_2, then β_1 gives the slope of the trend before time τ, while the slope of the line after time τ is given by $\beta_1 + \beta_2$.

An extension of this idea is to use a spline (see Section 5/6).

Ex post and ex ante forecasting

As discussed in Section 4/8, ex ante forecasts are those that are made using only the information that is available in advance, while ex post forecasts are those that are made using later information on the predictors.

Normally, we cannot use future values of the predictor variables when producing ex ante forecasts because their values will not be known in advance. However, the special predictors introduced in this section are all known in advance, as they are based on calendar variables (e.g., seasonal dummy variables or public holiday indicators) or deterministic functions of time. In such cases, there is no difference betweeen ex ante and ex post forecasts.

Example: Australian quarterly beer production

We can model the Australian beer production data using a regression model with a linear trend and quarterly dummy variables:

$$y_t = \beta_0 + \beta_1 t + \beta_2 d_{2,t} + \beta_3 d_{3,t} + \beta_4 d_{4,t} + \varepsilon_t,$$

where $d_{i,t} = 1$ if t is in quarter i and 0 otherwise. The first quarter variable has been omitted, so the coefficients associated with the other quarters are measures of the difference between those quarters and the first quarter.

Computer output from this model is given below.

──────────────────────────── R code ────────────────────────────
```
beer2 <- window(ausbeer,start=1992,end=2006-.1)
fit <- tslm(beer2 ~ trend + season)
summary(fit)
```

──────────────────────────── R output ──────────────────────────
```
Coefficients:
            Estimate Std. Error t value Pr(>|t|)
(Intercept) 441.8141     4.5338  97.449  < 2e-16
trend        -0.3820     0.1078  -3.544 0.000854
season2     -34.0466     4.9174  -6.924 7.18e-09
season3     -18.0931     4.9209  -3.677 0.000568
season4      76.0746     4.9268  15.441  < 2e-16

Residual standard error: 13.01 on 51 degrees of freedom
Multiple R-squared: 0.921,       Adjusted R-squared: 0.9149
```

So there is a strong downward trend of 0.382 megalitres per quarter. On average, the second quarter has production of 34.0 megalitres lower than the first quarter, the third quarter has production of 18.1 megalitres lower than the first quarter, and the fourth quarter has production 76.1 megalitres higher than the first quarter. The model explains 92.1% of the variation in the beer production data.

The following plots show the actual values compared to the predicted (i.e., fitted) values.

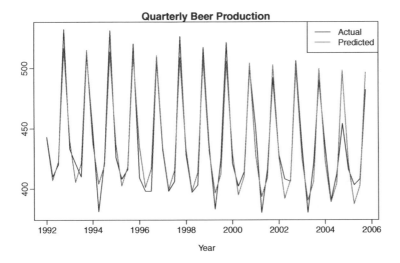

Figure 5.5: Time plot of beer production and predicted beer production.

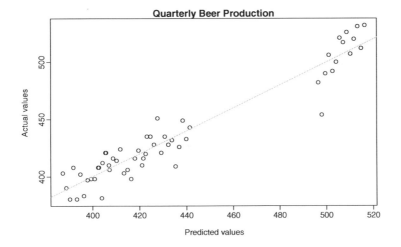

Figure 5.6: Actual beer production plotted against predicted beer production.

Forecasts obtained from the model are shown in Figure 5.7.

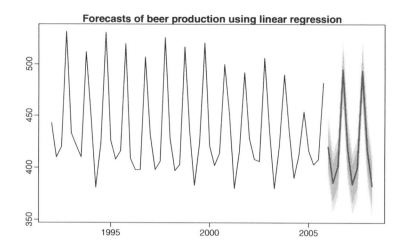

Figure 5.7: Forecasts from the regression model for beer production. The dark shaded region shows 80% prediction intervals and the light shaded region shows 95% prediction intervals.

Intervention variables

It is often necessary to model interventions that may have affected the variable to be forecast. For example, competitor activity, advertising expenditure, industrial action, and so on, can all have an effect.

When the effect lasts only for one period, we use a spike variable. This is a dummy variable taking value one in the period of the intervention and zero elsewhere. A spike variable is equivalent to a dummy variable for handling an outlier.

Other interventions have an immediate and permanent effect. If an intervention causes a level shift (i.e., the value of the series changes suddenly and permanently from the time of intervention), then we use a step variable. A step variable takes value zero before the intervention and one from the time of intervention onwards.

Another form of permanent effect is a change of slope. Here the intervention is handled using a piecewise linear trend as discussed earlier (where τ is the time of intervention).

Trading days

The number of trading days in a month can vary considerably and can have a substantial effect on sales data. To allow for this, the number of trading days in each month can be included as a predictor. An alternative that allows for the effects of different days of the week has the following predictors:

$$x_1 = \text{\# Mondays in month;}$$
$$x_2 = \text{\# Tuesdays in month;}$$
$$\vdots$$
$$x_7 = \text{\# Sundays in month.}$$

Distributed lags

It is often useful to include advertising expenditure as a predictor. However, since the effect of advertising can last beyond the actual campaign, we need to include lagged values of advertising expenditure. So the following predictors may be used.

$$x_1 = \text{advertising for previous month;}$$
$$x_2 = \text{advertising for two months previously;}$$
$$\vdots$$
$$x_m = \text{advertising for } m \text{ months previously.}$$

It is common to require the coefficients to decrease as the lag increases. In Chapter 9 we discuss methods to allow this constraint to be implemented.

5/3   Selecting predictors

When there are many possible predictors, we need some strategy to select the best predictors to use in a regression model.

A common approach that is *not recommended* is to plot the forecast variable against a particular predictor and if it shows no noticeable relationship, drop it. This is invalid because it is not always possible to see the relationship from a scatterplot, especially when the effect of other predictors has not been accounted for.

Another common approach which is also invalid is to do a multiple linear regression on all the predictors and disregard all variables whose p-values are greater than 0.05. To start with, statistical significance does not always indicate predictive value. Even if forecasting is not the goal, this is not a good strategy because the p-values can be misleading when two or more predictors are correlated with each other (see Section 5/7).

Instead, we will use a measure of predictive accuracy. Five such measures are introduced in this section.

Adjusted R^2

Computer output for regression will always give the R^2 value, discussed in Section 5/1. However, it is not a good measure of the predictive ability of a model. Imagine a model which produces forecasts that are exactly 20% of the actual values. In that case, the R^2 value would be 1 (indicating perfect correlation), but the forecasts are not very close to the actual values.

In addition, R^2 does not allow for "degrees of freedom". Adding *any* variable tends to increase the value of R^2, even if that variable is irrelevant. For these reasons, forecasters should not use R^2 to determine whether a model will give good predictions.

An equivalent idea is to select the model which gives the minimum sum of squared errors (SSE), given by

$$\text{SSE} = \sum_{i=1}^{N} e_i^2.$$

Minimizing the SSE is equivalent to maximizing R^2 and will always choose the model with the most variables, and so is not a valid way of selecting predictors.

An alternative, designed to overcome these problems, is the adjusted R^2 (also called "R-bar-squared"):

$$\bar{R}^2 = 1 - (1 - R^2)\frac{N-1}{N-k-1},$$

where N is the number of observations and k is the number of predictors. This is an improvement on R^2 as it will no longer increase with each added predictor. Using this measure, the best model will be the one with the largest value of $\bar{R}^2$.

Maximizing $\bar{R}^2$ is equivalent to minimizing the following estimate of the variance of the forecast errors:

$$\hat{\sigma}^2 = \frac{\text{SSE}}{N-k-1}.$$

Maximizing $\bar{R}^2$ works quite well as a method of selecting predictors, although it does tend to err on the side of selecting too many predictors.

Cross-validation

As discussed in Section 2/5, cross-validation is a very useful way of determining the predictive ability of a model. In general, leave-one-out cross-validation for regression can be carried out using the following steps.

1. Remove observation i from the data set, and fit the model using the remaining data. Then compute the error ($e_i^* = y_i - \hat{y}_i$) for the omitted observation. (This is not the same as the residual because the ith observation was not used in estimating the value of $\hat{y}_i$.)
2. Repeat step 1 for $i = 1, \ldots, N$.
3. Compute the MSE from $e_1^*, \ldots, e_N^*$. We shall call this the CV.

For many forecasting models, this is a time-consuming procedure, but for regression there are very fast methods of calculating CV so it takes no longer than fitting one model to the full data set. The equation for computing CV is given in Section 5/5.

Under this criterion, the best model is the one with the smallest value of CV.

Akaike's Information Criterion

A closely-related method is Akaike's Information Criterion, which we define as

$$\text{AIC} = N \log\left(\frac{\text{SSE}}{N}\right) + 2(k + 2),$$

where N is the number of observations used for estimation and k is the number of predictors in the model. Different computer packages use slightly different definitions for the AIC, although they should all lead to the same model being selected. The $k + 2$ part of the equation occurs because there are $k + 2$ parameters in the model — the k coefficients for the predictors, the intercept and the variance of the residuals. The idea here is to penalize the fit of the model (SSE) with the number of parameters that need to be estimated.

The model with the minimum value of the AIC is often the best model for forecasting. For large values of N, minimizing the AIC is equivalent to minimizing the CV value.

Corrected Akaike's Information Criterion

For small values of N, the AIC tends to select too many predictors, and so a bias-corrected version of the AIC has been developed.

$$\text{AIC}_c = \text{AIC} + \frac{2(k+2)(k+3)}{N-k-3}.$$

As with the AIC, the AIC_c should be minimized.

Schwarz Bayesian Information Criterion

A related measure is Schwarz's Bayesian Information Criterion (known as SBIC, BIC or SC):

$$\text{BIC} = N \log\left(\frac{\text{SSE}}{N}\right) + (k+2)\log(N).$$

As with the AIC, minimizing the BIC is intended to give the best model. The model chosen by BIC is either the same as that chosen by AIC, or one with fewer terms. This is because BIC penalizes the SSE more heavily than the AIC. For large values of N, minimizing BIC is similar to leave-v-out cross-validation when $v = N[1 - 1/(\log(N) - 1)]$.

Many statisticians like to use BIC because it has the feature that if there is a true underlying model, then with enough data the BIC will select that model. However, in reality there is rarely if ever a true underlying model, and even if there was a true underlying model, selecting that model will not necessarily give the best forecasts (because the parameter estimates may not be accurate).

——————————————— R code ———————————————
```
# To obtain all these measures in R, use
CV(fit)
```

Example: credit scores (continued)

In the credit scores regression model we used four predictors. Now we can check if all four predictors are actually useful, or whether we can drop one or more of them. With four predictors, there are $2^4 = 16$ possible models. All 16 models were fitted, and the results are summarized in the table below.

Savings	Income	Address	Employ.	CV	AIC	AIC_c	BIC	Adj R^2
X	X	X	X	104.7	2325.8	2325.9	2351.1	0.4658
X	X	X		106.5	2334.1	2334.2	2355.1	0.4558
X		X	X	107.7	2339.8	2339.9	2360.9	0.4495
X		X		109.7	2349.3	2349.3	2366.1	0.4379
X	X		X	112.2	2360.4	2360.6	2381.5	0.4263
X			X	115.1	2373.4	2373.5	2390.3	0.4101
X	X			116.1	2377.7	2377.8	2394.6	0.4050
X				119.5	2392.1	2392.2	2404.8	0.3864
	X	X	X	164.2	2551.6	2551.7	2572.7	0.1592
	X	X		164.9	2553.8	2553.9	2570.7	0.1538
	X		X	176.1	2586.7	2586.8	2603.6	0.0963
		X	X	177.5	2591.4	2591.5	2608.3	0.0877
		X		178.6	2594.6	2594.6	2607.2	0.0801
	X			179.1	2595.3	2595.3	2607.9	0.0788
			X	190.0	2625.3	2625.4	2638.0	0.0217
				193.8	2635.3	2635.3	2643.7	0.0000

An X indicates that the variable was included in the model. The best models are given at the top of the table, and the worst models are at the bottom of the table.

The model with all four predictors has the lowest CV, AIC, AIC_c and BIC values and the highest $\bar{R}^2$ value. So in this case, all the measures of predictive accuracy indicate the same "best" model which is the one that includes all four predictors. The different measures do not always lead to the same model being selected.

Best subset regression

Where possible, all potential regression models can be fitted (as was done in the above example) and the best one selected based on one of the measures discussed here. This is known as "best subsets" regression or "all possible subsets" regression.

It is recommended that one of CV, AIC or AIC_c be used for this purpose. If the value of N is large enough, they will all lead to the same model. Most software packages will at least produce AIC, although CV and AIC_c will be more accurate for smaller values of N.

While $\bar{R}^2$ is very widely used, and has been around longer than the other measures, its tendency to select too many predictor variables makes it less suitable for forecasting than either CV, AIC or AIC_c. Also, the tendency of BIC to select too few variables makes it less suitable for forecasting than either CV, AIC or AIC_c.

Stepwise regression

If there are a large number of predictors, it is not possible to fit all possible models. For example, 40 predictors leads to $2^{40} > 1$ trillion possible models! Consequently, a strategy is required to limit the number of models to be explored.

An approach that works quite well is *backwards stepwise regression*:

- Start with the model containing all potential predictors.
- Try subtracting one predictor at a time. Keep the model if it improves the measure of predictive accuracy.
- Iterate until no further improvement.

It is important to realise that a stepwise approach is not guaranteed to lead to the best possible model. But it almost always leads to a good model.

If the number of potential predictors is too large, then this backwards stepwise regression will not work and the starting model will need to use only a subset of potential predictors. In this case, an extra step needs to be inserted in which predictors are also added one at a time, with the model being retained if it improves the measure of predictive accuracy.

5/4   Residual diagnostics

The residuals from a regression model are calculated as the difference between the actual values and the fitted values: $e_i = y_i - \hat{y}_i$. Each residual is the unpredictable component of the associated observation.

After selecting the regression variables and fitting a regression model, it is necessary to plot the residuals to check that the assumptions of the model have been satisfied. There are a series of plots that should be produced in order to check different aspects of the fitted model and the underlying assumptions.

Scatterplots of residuals against predictors

Do a scatterplot of the residuals against each predictor in the model. If these scatterplots show a pattern, then the relationship may be nonlinear and the model will need to be modified accordingly. See Section 5/6 for a discussion of nonlinear regression.

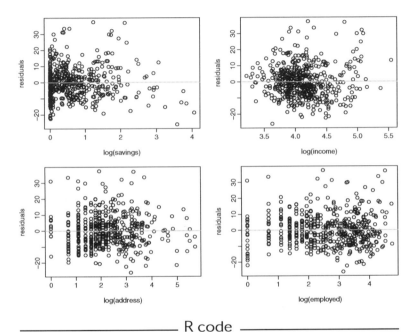

Figure 5.8: The residuals from the regression model for credit scores plotted against each of the predictors in the model.

———— R code ————

```
fit <- lm(score ~ log.savings + log.income +
  log.address + log.employed, data=creditlog)
par(mfrow=c(2,2))
plot(creditlog$log.savings,residuals(fit),xlab="log(savings)")
plot(creditlog$log.income,residuals(fit),xlab="log(income)")
plot(creditlog$log.address,residuals(fit),xlab="log(address)")
plot(creditlog$log.employed,residuals(fit),xlab="log(employed)")
```

It is also necessary to plot the residuals against any predictions *not* in the model. If these show a pattern, then the predictor may need to be added to the model (possibly in a nonlinear form).

Figure 5.8 shows the residuals from the model fitted to credit scores. In this case, the scatterplots show no obvious patterns, although the residuals tend to be negative for large values of the savings predictor. This suggests that the credit scores tend to be over-estimated for people with large amounts of savings. To correct this bias, we would need to use a non-linear model (see Section 5/6).

Scatterplot of residuals against fitted values

A plot of the residuals against the fitted values should show no pattern. If a pattern is observed, there may be "heteroscedasticity" in the errors. That is, the variance of the residuals may not be constant. To overcome this problem, a transformation of the forecast variable (such as a logarithm or square root) may be required.

Figure 5.9 shows a plot of the residuals against the fitted values for the credit score model.

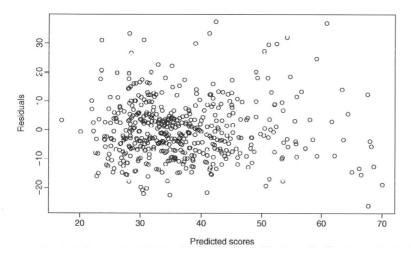

Figure 5.9: The residuals from the credit score model plotted against the fitted values obtained from the model.

——————— R code ———————
```
plot(fitted(fit), residuals(fit),
  xlab="Predicted scores", ylab="Residuals")
```

Again, the plot shows no systematic patterns and the variation in the residuals does not seem to change with the size of the fitted value.

Autocorrelation in the residuals

When the data are a time series, you should look at an ACF plot of the residuals. This will reveal if there is any autocorrelation in the residuals (suggesting that there is information that has not been accounted for in the model).

Figure 5.10 shows a time plot and ACF of the residuals from the model fitted to the beer production data discussed in Section 5/2.

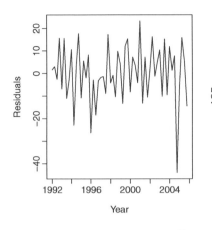
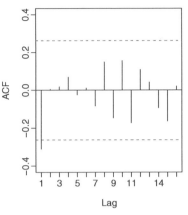

Figure 5.10: Residuals from the regression model for beer production.

```
──────────── R code ────────────
fit <- tslm(beer2 ~ trend + season)
res <- residuals(fit)
par(mfrow=c(1,2))
plot(res, ylab="Residuals",xlab="Year")
Acf(res, main="ACF of residuals")
```

There is an outlier in the residuals (2004:Q4) which suggests there was something unusual happening in that quarter. It would be worth investigating that outlier to see if there were any unusual circumstances or events that may have reduced beer production for the quarter.

The remaining residuals show that the model has captured the patterns in the data quite well, although there is a small amount of autocorrelation left in the residuals (seen in the significant spike in the ACF plot). This suggests that the model can be slightly improved, although it is unlikely to make much difference to the resulting forecasts.

Another test of autocorrelation that is designed to take account of the regression model is the **Durbin-Watson** test. It is used to test the hypothesis that there is no lag one autocorrelation in the residuals. If there is no autocorrelation, the

Durbin-Watson distribution is symmetric around 2. Most computer packages will report the DW statistic automatically, and should also provide a p-value. A small p-value indicates there is significant autocorrelation remaining in the residuals. For the beer model, the Durbin-Watson test reveals some significant lag one autocorrelation.

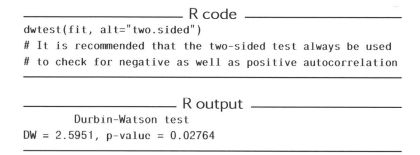

───────────────── R code ─────────────────
```
dwtest(fit, alt="two.sided")
# It is recommended that the two-sided test always be used
# to check for negative as well as positive autocorrelation
```

───────────────── R output ─────────────────
```
          Durbin-Watson test
DW = 2.5951, p-value = 0.02764
```

Both the ACF plot and the Durbin-Watson test show that there is some autocorrelation remaining in the residuals. This means there is some information remaining in the residuals that can be exploited to obtain better forecasts. The forecasts from the current model are still unbiased, but will have larger prediction intervals than they need to. A better model in this case will be a dynamic-regression model which will be covered in Chapter 9.

A third possible test is the **Breusch-Godfrey** test designed to look for significant higher-lag autocorrelations.

───────────────── R code ─────────────────
```
# Test for autocorrelations up to lag 5.
bgtest(fit,5)
```

Histogram of residuals

Finally, it is a good idea to check if the residuals are normally distributed. As explained earlier, this is not essential for forecasting, but it does make the calculation of prediction intervals much easier.

In this case, the residuals seem to be slightly negatively skewed, although that is probably due to the outlier.

Figure 5.11: Histogram of residuals from regression model for beer production.

──────── R code ────────
```
hist(res, breaks="FD", xlab="Residuals",
 main="Histogram of residuals", ylim=c(0,22))
x <- -50:50
lines(x, 560*dnorm(x,0,sd(res)),col=2)
```

5/5   Matrix formulation

Warning: this is a more advanced optional section and assumes knowledge of matrix algebra.

The multiple regression model can be written as

$$y_i = \beta_0 + \beta_1 x_{1,i} + \beta_2 x_{2,i} + \cdots + \beta_k x_{k,i} + \varepsilon_i.$$

This expresses the relationship between a single value of the forecast variable and the predictors. It can be convenient to write this in matrix form where all the values of the forecast variable are given in a single equation. Let $y = (y_1,\ldots,y_N)'$, $\varepsilon = (\varepsilon_1,\ldots,\varepsilon_N)'$, $\beta = (\beta_0,\ldots,\beta_k)'$ and

$$X = \begin{bmatrix} 1 & x_{1,1} & x_{2,1} & \cdots & x_{k,1} \\ 1 & x_{1,2} & x_{2,2} & \cdots & x_{k,2} \\ \vdots & \vdots & \vdots & & \vdots \\ 1 & x_{1,N} & x_{2,N} & \cdots & x_{k,N} \end{bmatrix}.$$

Then

$$y = X\beta + \varepsilon.$$

Least squares estimation

Least squares estimation is obtained by minimizing the expression $\varepsilon'\varepsilon = (Y - X\beta)'(Y - X\beta)$. It can be shown that this is minimized when β takes the value

$$\hat{\beta} = (X'X)^{-1}X'Y$$

This is sometimes known as the "normal equation". The estimated coefficients require the inversion of the matrix $X'X$. If this matrix is singular, then the model cannot be estimated. This will occur, for example, if you fall for the "dummy variable trap" (having the same number of dummy variables as there are categories of a categorical predictor).

The residual variance is estimated using

$$\hat{\sigma}^2 = \frac{1}{N - k}(Y - X\hat{\beta})'(Y - X\hat{\beta}).$$

Fitted values and cross-validation

The normal equation shows that the fitted values can be calculated using

$$\hat{Y} = X\hat{\beta} = X(X'X)^{-1}X'Y = HY,$$

where $H = X(X'X)^{-1}X'$ is known as the "hat-matrix" because it is used to compute $\hat{Y}$ ("Y-hat").

If the diagonal values of H are denoted by $h_1, \ldots, h_N$, then the cross-validation statistic can be computed using

$$CV = \frac{1}{N}\sum_{i=1}^{N}[e_i/(1 - h_i)]^2,$$

where e_i is the residual obtained from fitting the model to all N observations. Thus, it is not necessary to actually fit N separate models when computing the CV statistic.

Forecasts

Let X^* be a row vector containing the values of the predictors for the forecasts (in the same format as X). Then the forecast is given by

$$\hat{y} = X^*\hat{\beta} = X^*(X'X)^{-1}X'Y$$

and its variance by

$$\sigma^2\left[1 + X^*(X'X)^{-1}(X^*)'\right].$$

Then a 95% prediction interval can be calculated (assuming normally distributed errors) as

$$\hat{y} \pm 1.96\hat{\sigma}\sqrt{1 + X^*(X'X)^{-1}(X^*)'}.$$

This takes account of the uncertainty due to the error term ε and the uncertainty in the coefficient estimates. However, it ignores any errors in X^*. So if the future values of the predictors are uncertain, then the prediction interval calculated using this expression will be too narrow.

5/6 Non-linear regression

Sometimes the relationship between the forecast variable and a predictor is not linear, and then the usual multiple regression equation needs modifying. In Section 4/7, we discussed using log transformations to deal with a variety of non-linear forms, and in Section 5/2 we showed how to include a piecewise-linear trend in a model; that is a nonlinear trend constructed out of linear pieces. Allowing other variables to enter in a nonlinear manner can be handled in exactly the same way.

To keep things simple, suppose we have only one predictor x. Then the model we use is

$$y = f(x) + e,$$

where f is a possibly nonlinear function. In standard (linear) regression, $f(x) = \beta_0 + \beta_1 x$, but in nonlinear regression, we allow f to be a nonlinear function of x.

One of the simplest ways to do nonlinear regression is to make f piecewise linear. That is, we introduce points where the slope of f can change. These points are called "knots".

Example 5.1 Car emissions continued

In Chapter 4, we considered an example of forecasting the carbon footprint of a car from its city-based fuel economy. Our previous analysis (Section 4/7) showed that this relationship was nonlinear. Close inspection of Figure 4.3 suggests that a change in slope occurs at about 25mpg. This can be achieved using the following variables: x (the City mpg) and

$$z = (x - 25)_+ = \begin{cases} 0 & \text{if } x < 25 \\ x - 25 & \text{if } x \geq 25. \end{cases}$$

The resulting fitted values are shown as the red line below.

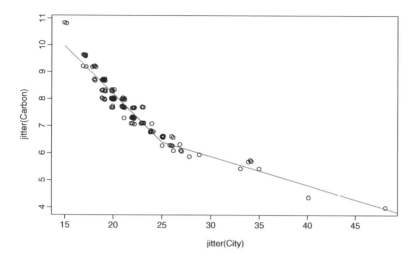

Figure 5.12: Piecewise linear trend to fuel economy data.

R code

```
Cityp <- pmax(fuel$City-25,0)
fit2 <- lm(Carbon ~ City + Cityp, data=fuel)
x <- 15:50; z <- pmax(x-25,0)
fcast2 <- forecast(fit2, newdata=data.frame(City=x,Cityp=z))
plot(jitter(Carbon) ~ jitter(City), data=fuel)
lines(x, fcast2$mean,col="red")
```

Additional bends can be included in the relationship by adding further variables of the form $(x - c)_+$ where c is the "knot" or point at which the line should bend. As above, the notation $(x - c)_+$ means the value $x - c$ if it is positive and 0 otherwise.

Regression splines

Piecewise linear relationships constructed in this way are a special case of *regression splines*. In general, a linear regression spline is obtained using

$$x_1 = x \quad x_2 = (x - c_1)_+ \quad \ldots \quad x_k = (x - c_{k-1})_+,$$

where $c_1, \ldots, c_{k-1}$ are the knots (the points at which the line can bend). Selecting the number of knots $(k - 1)$ and where they should be positioned can be difficult and somewhat arbitrary. Automatic knot selection algorithms are available in some software, but are not yet widely used.

A smoother result is obtained using piecewise cubics rather than piecewise lines. These are constrained so they are continuous (they join up) and they are smooth (so there are no sudden changes of direction as we see with piecewise linear splines). In general, a cubic regression spline is written as

$$x_1 = x \quad x_2 = x^2 \quad x_3 = x^3 \quad x_4 = (x - c_1)_+^3 \quad \ldots \quad x_k = (x - c_{k-3})_+^3.$$

An example of a cubic regression spline fitted to the fuel economy data is shown below with a single knot at $c_1 = 25$.

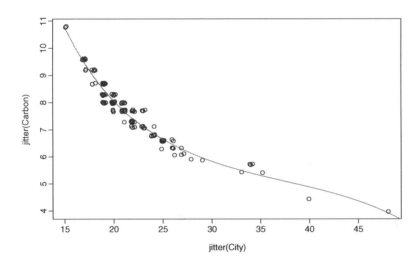

Figure 5.13: Cubic regression spline fitted to the fuel economy data.

———————————— R code ————————————
```
fit3 <- lm(Carbon ~ City + I(City^2) + I(City^3) + I(Cityp^3), data=fuel)
fcast3 <- forecast(fit3,newdata=data.frame(City=x,Cityp=z))
plot(jitter(Carbon) ~ jitter(City), data=fuel)
lines(x, fcast3$mean,col="red")
```

This usually gives a better fit to the data, although forecasting values of Carbon when City is outside the range of the historical data becomes very unreliable.

5/7   Correlation, causation and forecasting

Correlation is not causation

It is important not to confuse correlation with causation, or causation with forecasting. A variable x may be useful for predicting a variable y, but that does not mean x is causing y. It is possible that *x* *is* causing *y*, but it may be that the relationship between them is more complicated than simple causality.

For example, it is possible to model the number of drownings at a beach resort each month with the number of ice-creams sold in the same period. The model can give reasonable forecasts, not because ice-creams cause drownings, but because people eat more ice-creams on hot days when they are also more likely to go swimming. So the two variables (ice-cream sales and drownings) are correlated, but one is not causing the other. It is important to understand that **correlations are useful for forecasting, even when there is no causal relationship between the two variables**.

However, often a better model is possible if a causal mechanism can be determined. In this example, both ice-cream sales and drownings will be affected by the temperature and by the numbers of people visiting the beach resort. Again, high temperatures do not actually *cause* people to drown, but they are more directly related to why people are swimming. So a better model for drownings will probably include temperatures and visitor numbers and exclude ice-cream sales.

Confounded predictors

A related issue involves confounding variables. Suppose we are forecasting monthly sales of a company for 2012, using data from 2000–2011. In January 2008 a new competitor came into the market and started taking some market share. At the same time, the economy began to decline. In your forecasting model, you include both competitor activity (measured using advertising time on a local television station) and the health of the economy (measured using GDP). It will not be possible to separate the effects of these two predictors because they are correlated. We say two variables are **confounded** when their effects on the forecast variable cannot be separated. Any pair of correlated predictors will have some level of confounding, but we would not normally describe them as confounded unless there was a relatively high level of correlation between them.

Confounding is not really a problem for forecasting, as we can still compute forecasts without needing to separate out the effects of the predictors. However, it becomes a problem with scenario forecasting as the scenarios should take account of the relationships between predictors. It is also a problem if some historical analysis of the contributions of various predictors is required.

Multicollinearity and forecasting

A closely related issue is **multicollinearity** which occurs when similar information is provided by two or more of the predictor variables in a multiple regression. It can occur in a number of ways.

- Two predictors are highly correlated with each other (that is, they have a correlation coefficient close to +1 or -1). In this case, knowing the value of one of the variables tells you a lot about the value of the other variable. Hence, they are providing similar information.
- A linear combination of predictors is highly correlated with another linear combination of predictors. In this case, knowing the value of the first group of predictors tells you a lot about the value of the second group of predictors. Hence, they are providing similar information.

The dummy variable trap is a special case of multicollinearity. Suppose you have quarterly data and use four dummy variables, D_1, D_2, D_3 and D_4. Then $D_4 = 1 - D_1 - D_2 - D_3$; so there is perfect correlation between D_4 and $D_1 + D_2 + D_3$.

When multicollinearity occurs in a multiple regression model, there are several consequences that you need to be aware of.

1. If there is perfect correlation (i.e., a correlation of +1 or -1, such as in the dummy variable trap), it is not possible to estimate the regression model.
2. If there is high correlation (close to but not equal to +1 or -1), then the estimation of the regression coefficients is computationally difficult. In fact, some software (notably Microsoft Excel) may give highly inaccurate estimates of the coefficients. Most reputable statistical software will use algorithms to limit the effect of multicollinearity on the coefficient estimates, but you do need to be careful. The major software packages

such as R, SPSS, SAS and Stata all use estimation algorithms to avoid the problem as much as possible.

3. The uncertainty associated with individual regression coefficients will be large. This is because they are difficult to estimate. Consequently, statistical tests (e.g., t-tests) on regression coefficients are unreliable. (In forecasting we are rarely interested in such tests.) Also, it will not be possible to make accurate statements about the contribution of each separate predictor to the forecast.

4. Forecasts will be unreliable if the values of the future predictors are outside the range of the historical values of the predictors. For example, suppose you have fitted a regression model with predictors X and Z which are highly correlated with each other, and suppose that the values of X in the fitting data ranged between 0 and 100. Then forecasts based on $X > 100$ or $X < 0$ will be unreliable. It is always a little dangerous when future values of the predictors lie much outside the historical range, but it is especially problematic when multicollinearity is present.

Note that if you are using good statistical software, if you are not interested in the specific contributions of each predictor, and if the future values of your predictor variables are within their historical ranges, there is nothing to worry about — multicollinearity is not a problem.

5/8 Exercises

5.1 The data below (data set fancy) concern the monthly
sales figures of a shop which opened in January 1987
and sells gifts, souvenirs, and novelties. The shop is situ-
ated on the wharf at a beach resort town in Queensland,
Australia. The sales volume varies with the seasonal
population of tourists. There is a large influx of visitors
to the town at Christmas and for the local surfing festival, held every March since 1988. Over time, the shop
has expanded its premises, range of products, and staff.

	1987	1988	1989	1990	1991	1992	1993
Jan	1664.81	2499.81	4717.02	5921.10	4826.64	7615.03	10243.24
Feb	2397.53	5198.24	5702.63	5814.58	6470.23	9849.69	11266.88
Mar	2840.71	7225.14	9957.58	12421.25	9638.77	14558.40	21826.84
Apr	3547.29	4806.03	5304.78	6369.77	8821.17	11587.33	17357.33
May	3752.96	5900.88	6492.43	7609.12	8722.37	9332.56	15997.79
Jun	3714.74	4951.34	6630.80	7224.75	10209.48	13082.09	18601.53
Jul	4349.61	6179.12	7349.62	8121.22	11276.55	16732.78	26155.15
Aug	3566.34	4752.15	8176.62	7979.25	12552.22	19888.61	28586.52
Sep	5021.82	5496.43	8573.17	8093.06	11637.39	23933.38	30505.41
Oct	6423.48	5835.10	9690.50	8476.70	13606.89	25391.35	30821.33
Nov	7600.60	12600.08	15151.84	17914.66	21822.11	36024.80	46634.38
Dec	19756.21	28541.72	34061.01	30114.41	45060.69	80721.71	104660.67

(a) Produce a time plot of the data and describe
the patterns in the graph. Identify any unusual
or unexpected fluctuations in the time series.

(b) Explain why it is necessary to take logarithms
of these data before fitting a model.

(c) Use R to fit a regression model to the logarithms of these sales data with a linear trend,
seasonal dummies and a "surfing festival"
dummy variable.

(d) Plot the residuals against time and against
the fitted values. Do these plots reveal any
problems with the model?

(e) Do boxplots of the residuals for each month.
Does this reveal any problems with the model?

(f) What do the values of the coefficients tell you
about each variable?

(g) What does the Durbin-Watson statistic tell you about your model?

(h) Regardless of your answers to the above questions, use your regression model to predict the monthly sales for 1994, 1995, and 1996. Produce prediction intervals for each of your forecasts.

(i) Transform your predictions and intervals to obtain predictions and intervals for the raw data.

(j) How could you improve these predictions by modifying the model?

5.2 The data below (data set texasgas) shows the demand for natural gas and the price of natural gas for 20 towns in Texas in 1969.

City	Average price P (cents per thousand cubic feet)	Consumption per customer C (thousand cubic feet)
Amarillo	30	134
Borger	31	112
Dalhart	37	136
Shamrock	42	109
Royalty	43	105
Texarkana	45	87
Corpus Christi	50	56
Palestine	54	43
Marshall	54	77
Iowa Park	57	35
Palo Pinto	58	65
Millsap	58	56
Memphis	60	58
Granger	73	55
Llano	88	49
Brownsville	89	39
Mercedes	92	36
Karnes City	97	46
Mathis	100	40
La Pryor	102	42

(a) Do a scatterplot of consumption against price. The data are clearly not linear. Three possible nonlinear models for the data are given below

$$C_i = \exp(a + bP_i + e_i)$$

$$C_i = \begin{cases} a_1 + b_1 P_i + e_i & \text{when } P_i \le 60 \\ a_2 + b_2 P_i + e_i & \text{when } P_i > 60; \end{cases}$$

$$C_i = a + b_1 P + b_2 P^2.$$

The second model divides the data into two sections, depending on whether the price is above or below 60 cents per 1,000 cubic feet.

(b) Can you explain why the slope of the fitted line should change with P?

(c) Fit the three models and find the coefficients, and residual variance in each case.

For the second model, the parameters a_1, a_2, b_1, b_2 can be estimated by simply fitting a regression with four regressors but no constant: (i) a dummy taking value 1 when $P \le 60$ and 0 otherwise; (ii) $P1 = P$ when $P \le 60$ and 0 otherwise; (iii) a dummy taking value 0 when $P \le 60$ and 1 otherwise; (iv) $P2 = P$ when $P > 60$ and 0 otherwise.

(d) For each model, find the value of R^2 and AIC, and produce a residual plot. Comment on the adequacy of the three models.

(e) For prices 40, 60, 80, 100, and 120 cents per 1,000 cubic feet, compute the forecasted per capita demand using the best model of the three above.

(f) Compute 95% prediction intervals. Make a graph of these prediction intervals and discuss their interpretation.

(g) What is the correlation between P and P^2? Does this suggest any general problem to be considered in dealing with polynomial regressions—especially of higher orders?

5/9   Further reading

Regression with cross-sectional data

- Chatterjee, S. and A. S. Hadi (2012). *Regression analysis by example*. 5th ed. New York: John Wiley & Sons.
- Fox, J. and H. S. Weisberg (2010). *An R Companion to Applied Regression*. SAGE Publications, Inc.
- Harrell, Jr, F. E. (2001). *Regression modelling strategies: with applications to linear models, logistic regression, and survival analysis*. New York: Springer.
- Pardoe, I. (2006). *Applied regression modeling: a business approach*. Hoboken, NJ: John Wiley & Sons.
- Sheather, S. J. (2009). *A modern approach to regression with R*. New York: Springer.

Regression with time series data

- Shumway, R. H. and D. S. Stoffer (2011). *Time series analysis and its applications: with R examples*. 3rd ed. New York: Springer.

6
Time series decomposition

Time series data can exhibit a huge variety of patterns and it is helpful to categorize some of the patterns and behaviours that can be seen in time series. It is also sometimes useful to try to split a time series into several components, each representing one of the underlying categories of patterns.

In this chapter, we consider some common patterns and methods to extract the associated components from a time series. Often this is done to help understand the time series better, but it can also be used to improve forecasts.

6/1 Time series components

Time series patterns

In this chapter, we will refer to three types of time series patterns.

Trend A trend exists when there is a long-term increase or decrease in the data. It does not have to be linear. Sometimes we will refer to a trend "changing direction" when it might go from an increasing trend to a decreasing trend.

Seasonal A seasonal pattern exists when a series is influenced by seasonal factors (e.g., the quarter of the year, the month, or day of the week). Seasonality is always of a fixed and known period.

Cyclic A cyclic pattern exists when data exhibit rises and falls that are *not of fixed period*. The duration of these fluctuations is usually of at least 2 years.

Many people confuse cyclic behaviour with seasonal behaviour, but they are really quite different. If the fluctuations are not of fixed period then they are cyclic; if the period is unchanging and associated with some aspect of the calendar, then the pattern is seasonal. In general, the average length of cycles is longer than the length of a seasonal pattern, and the magnitude of cycles tends to be more variable than the magnitude of seasonal patterns.

The following four examples shows different combinations of the above components.

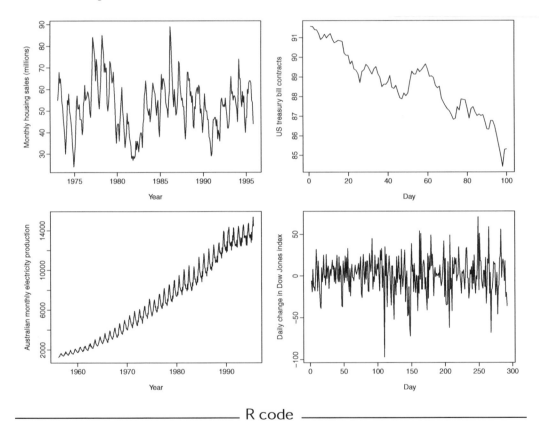

```
                        ─── R code ───
par(mfrow=c(2,2))
plot(hsales,xlab="Year",ylab="Monthly housing sales (millions)")
plot(ustreas,xlab="Day",ylab="US treasury bill contracts")
plot(elec,xlab="Year",ylab="Australian monthly electricity production")
plot(diff(dj),xlab="Day",ylab="Daily change in Dow Jones index")
```

Figure 6.1: Four time series exhibiting different types of time series patterns.

1. The monthly housing sales (top left) show strong seasonality within each year, as well as some strong cyclic behaviour with period about 6–10 years. There is no apparent trend in the data over this period.

2. The US treasury bill contracts (top right) show results from the Chicago market for 100 consecutive trading days in 1981. Here there is no seasonality, but an obvious downward trend. Possibly, if we had a much longer series, we would see that this downward trend is actually part of a long cycle, but when viewed over only 100 days it appears to be a trend.

3. The Australian monthly electricity production (bottom left) shows a strong increasing trend, with strong seasonality. There is no evidence of any cyclic behaviour here.

4. The daily change in the Dow Jones index (bottom right) has no trend, seasonality or cyclic behaviour. There are random fluctuations which do not appear to be very predictable, and no strong patterns that would help with developing a forecasting model.

Time series decomposition

We shall think of the time series y_t as comprising three components: a seasonal component, a trend-cycle component (containing both trend and cycle), and a remainder component (containing anything else in the time series). For example, if we assume an additive model, then we can write

$$y_t = S_t + T_t + E_t,$$

where y_t is the data at period t, S_t is the seasonal component at period t, T_t is the trend-cycle component at period t and E_t is the remainder (or irregular or error) component at period t. Alternatively, a multiplicative model would be written as

$$y_t = S_t \times T_t \times E_t.$$

The additive model is most appropriate if the magnitude of the seasonal fluctuations or the variation around the trend-cycle does not vary with the level of the time series. When the variation in the seasonal pattern, or the variation around the trend-cycle, appears to be proportional to the level of the time series, then a multiplicative model is more appropriate. With economic time series, multiplicative models are common.

An alternative to using a multiplicative model, is to first transform the data until the variation in the series appears to be stable over time, and then use an additive model. When a log transformation has been used, this is equivalent to using a multiplicative decomposition because

$$y_t = S_t \times T_t \times E_t \quad \text{is equivalent to} \quad \log y_t = \log S_t + \log T_t + \log E_t.$$

Sometimes, the trend-cycle component is simply called the "trend" component, even though it may contain cyclic behaviour as well.

Example 6.1 *Electrical equipment manufacturing*

We will look at several methods for obtaining the components S_t, T_t and E_t later in this chapter. But first, it is helpful to see an example. We will decompose the new orders index for electrical equipment shown in Figure 6.2. These data show the number of new orders for electrical equipment (computer, electronic and optical products) in the Euro area (16 countries). The data have been adjusted by working days and normalized so a value of 100 corresponds to 2005.

Figure 6.2 shows the trend-cycle component, T_t, in red and the original data, y_t, in grey. The trend-cycle shows the overall movement in the series, ignoring the seasonality and any small random fluctuations.

Figure 6.3 shows an additive decomposition of these data. The method used for extracting components in this example is STL which is discussed in Section 6/5.

All three components are shown in the bottom three panels of Figure 6.3. These three components can be added together to reconstruct the data shown in the top panel. Notice that the seasonal component changes very slowly over time, so any two consecutive years have very similar pattern, but years far apart may have different seasonal patterns. The remainder component shown in the bottom panel is what is left over when the seasonal and trend-cycle components have been subtracted from the data.

The grey bars to the right of each panel show the relative scales of the components. Each grey bar represents the same

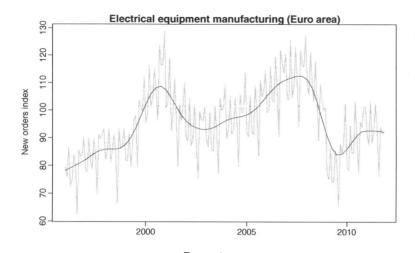

Figure 6.2: Electrical equipment orders: the trend-cycle component (red) and raw data (grey).

─────── R code ───────

```
fit <- stl(elecequip, s.window=5)
plot(elecequip, col="gray",
 main="Electrical equipment manufacturing",
 ylab="New orders index", xlab="")
lines(fit$time.series[,2],col="red",ylab="Trend")
```

length but because the plots are on different scales, the bars vary in size. The large grey bar in the bottom panel shows that the variation in the remainder component is small compared to the variation in the data which has a bar about one quarter the size. In other words, if we shrunk the bottom three panels until their bars became the same size as that in the data panel, then all the panels would be on the same scale.

It can be useful to use seasonal plots and seasonal sub-series plots of the seasonal component. These help us to visualize the variation in the seasonal component over time. Figure 6.4 shows a seasonal sub-series plot of the seasonal component from Figure 6.3. In this case, there are only very small changes over time.

Seasonally adjusted data

If the seasonal component is removed from the original data, the resulting values are called the "seasonally adjusted" data. For an additive model, the seasonally adjusted data are given by $y_t - S_t$, and for multiplicative data, the seasonally adjusted

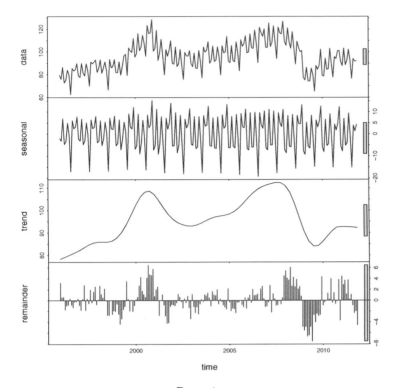

Figure 6.3: The electrical equipment orders (top) and its three additive components.

────────── R code ──────────

```
plot(fit)
```

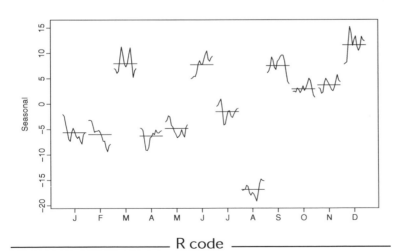

Figure 6.4: Seasonal sub-series plot of the seasonal component from the STL decomposition shown in Figure 6.3.

────────── R code ──────────

```
monthplot(fit$time.series[,"seasonal"], main="", ylab="Seasonal")
```

values are obtained using y_t/S_t. Figure 6.5 shows the seasonally adjusted electrical equipment orders.

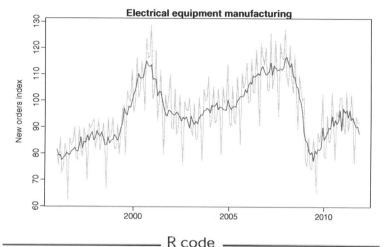

Figure 6.5: Seasonally adjusted electrical equipment orders (red) and the original data (grey).

──────────── R code ────────────

```
plot(elecequip, col="grey",
 main="Electrical equipment manufacturing",
  xlab="", ylab="New orders index")
lines(seasadj(fit),col="red",ylab="Seasonally adjusted")
```

If the variation due to seasonality is not of primary interest, the seasonally adjusted series can be useful. For example, monthly unemployment data are usually seasonally adjusted to highlight variation due to the underlying state of the economy than the seasonal variation. An increase in unemployment due to school leavers seeking work is seasonal variation while an increase in unemployment due to large employers laying off workers is non-seasonal. Most people who study unemployment data are more interested in the non-seasonal variation. Consequently, employment data (and many other economic series) are usually seasonally adjusted.

Seasonally adjusted series contain the remainder component as well as the trend-cycle. Therefore they are not "smooth" and "downturns" or "upturns" can be misleading. If the purpose is to look for turning points in the series, and interpret any changes in the series, then it is better to use the trend-cycle component rather than the seasonally adjusted data.

6/2   Moving averages

The classical method of time series decomposition originated in the 1920s and was widely used until the 1950s. It still forms the basis of later time series methods, and so it is important to understand how it works. The first step in a classical decomposition is to use a moving average method to estimate the trend-cycle, so we begin by discussing moving averages.

Moving average smoothing

A moving average of order m can be written as

$$\hat{T}_t = \frac{1}{m} \sum_{j=-k}^{k} y_{t+j},$$

where $m = 2k + 1$. That is, the estimate of the trend-cycle at time t is obtained by averaging values of the time series within k periods of t. Observations that are nearby in time are also likely to be close in value, and the average eliminates some of the randomness in the data, leaving a smooth trend-cycle component. We call this an "m-MA" meaning a moving average of order m.

For example, consider Figure 6.6 showing the volume of electricity sold to residential customers in South Australia each

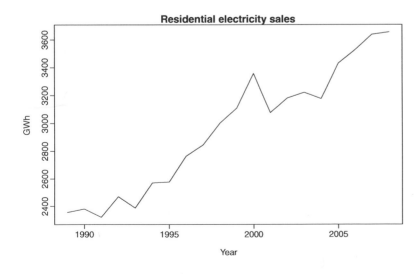

Figure 6.6: Residential electricity sales (excluding hot water) for South Australia: 1989–2008.

year from 1989 to 2008 (hot water sales have been excluded). The data are also shown in Table 6.1.

Year	Sales (GWh)	5-MA
1989	2354.34	
1990	2379.71	
1991	2318.52	2381.53
1992	2468.99	2424.56
1993	2386.09	2463.76
1994	2569.47	2552.60
1995	2575.72	2627.70
1996	2762.72	2750.62
1997	2844.50	2858.35
1998	3000.70	3014.70
1999	3108.10	3077.30
2000	3357.50	3144.52
2001	3075.70	3188.70
2002	3180.60	3202.32
2003	3221.60	3216.94
2004	3176.20	3307.30
2005	3430.60	3398.75
2006	3527.48	3485.43
2007	3637.89	
2008	3655.00	

Table 6.1: Annual electricity sales to residential customers in South Australia, 1989–2008.

——————————— R code ———————————

```
ma(elecsales, order=5)
```

In the second column of this table, a moving average of order 5 is shown, providing an estimate of the trend-cycle. The first value in this column is the average of the first five observations (1989–1993); the second value in the 5-MA column is the average of the values 1990–1994; and so on. Each value in the 5-MA column is the average of the observations in the five year period centered on the corresponding year. There are no values for the first two years or last two years because we don't have two observations on either side. In the formula above, column 5-MA contains the values of $\hat{T}_t$ with $k = 2$. To see what the trend-cycle estimate looks like, we plot it along with the original data in Figure 6.7.

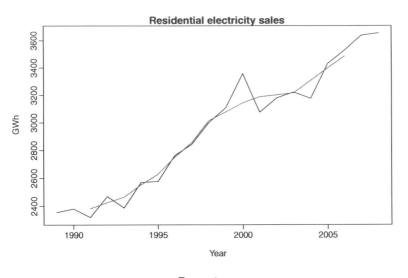

Figure 6.7: Residential electricity sales (black) along with the 5-MA estimate of the trend-cycle (red).

─────────── R code ───────────

```
plot(elecsales, main="Residential electricity sales",
  ylab="GWh", xlab="Year")
lines(ma(elecsales,5),col="red")
```

Notice how the trend (in red) is smoother than the original data and captures the main movement of the time series without all the minor fluctuations. The moving average method does not allow estimates of T_t where t is close to the ends of the series; hence the red line does not extend to the edges of the graph on either side. Later we will use more sophisticated methods of trend-cycle estimation which do allow estimates near the endpoints.

The order of the moving average determines the smoothness of the trend-cycle estimate. In general, a larger order means a smoother curve. Figure 6.8 shows the effect of changing the order of the moving average for the residential electricity sales data.

Simple moving averages such as these are usually of odd order (e.g., 3, 5, 7, etc.) This is so they are symmetric: in a moving average of order $m = 2k + 1$, there are k earlier observations, k later observations and the middle observation that are averaged. But if m was even, it would no longer be symmetric.

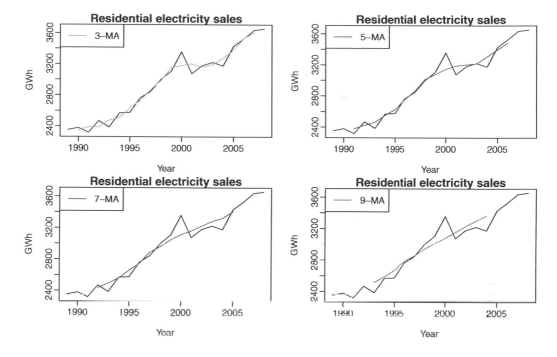

Figure 6.8: Different moving averages applied to the residential electricity sales data.

Moving averages of moving averages

It is possible to apply a moving average to a moving average. One reason for doing this is to make an even-order moving average symmetric.

For example, we might take a moving average of order 4, and then apply another moving average of order 2 to the results. In the following table, this has been done for the first few years of the Australian quarterly beer production data.

The notation "2 × 4-MA" in the last column means a 4-MA followed by a 2-MA. The values in the last column are obtained by taking a moving average of order 2 of the values in the previous column. For example, the first two values in the 4-MA column are 451.2=(443+410+420+532)/4 and 448.8=(410+420+532+433)/4. The first value in the 2 × 4-MA column is the average of these two: 450.0=(451.2+448.8)/2.

When a 2-MA follows a moving average of even order (such as 4), it is called a "centered moving average of order 4". This is because the results are now symmetric. To see that this is the

Year	Data	4-MA	2 × 4-MA
1992 Q1	443.00		
1992 Q2	410.00	451.25	
1992 Q3	420.00	448.75	450.00
1992 Q4	532.00	451.50	450.12
1993 Q1	433.00	449.00	450.25
1993 Q2	421.00	444.00	446.50
1993 Q3	410.00	448.00	446.00
1993 Q4	512.00	438.00	443.00
1994 Q1	449.00	441.25	439.62
1994 Q2	381.00	446.00	443.62
1994 Q3	423.00	440.25	443.12
1994 Q4	531.00	447.00	443.62
1995 Q1	426.00	445.25	446.12
1995 Q2	408.00	442.50	443.88
1995 Q3	416.00	438.25	440.38
1995 Q4	520.00	435.75	437.00
1996 Q1	409.00	431.25	433.50
1996 Q2	398.00	428.00	429.62
1996 Q3	398.00	433.75	430.88

Table 6.2: A moving average of order 4 applied to the quarterly beer data, followed by a moving average of order 2.

―――――――――― R code ――――――――――

```
beer2 <- window(ausbeer,start=1992)
ma4 <- ma(beer2, order=4, centre=FALSE)
ma2x4 <- ma(beer2, order=4, centre=TRUE)
```

case, we can write the 2 × 4-MA as follows:

$$\hat{T}_t = \frac{1}{2}\left[\frac{1}{4}(y_{t-2} + y_{t-1} + y_t + y_{t+1}) + \frac{1}{4}(y_{t-1} + y_t + y_{t+1} + y_{t+2})\right]$$
$$= \frac{1}{8}y_{t-2} + \frac{1}{4}y_{t-1} + \frac{1}{4}y_t + \frac{1}{4}y_{t+1} + \frac{1}{8}y_{t+2}.$$

It is now a weighted average of observations, but it is symmetric.

Other combinations of moving averages are also possible. For example a 3 × 3-MA is often used, and consists of a moving average of order 3 followed by another moving average of order 3. In general, an even order MA should be followed by an even order MA to make it symmetric. Similarly, an odd order MA should be followed by an odd order MA.

Estimating the trend-cycle with seasonal data

The most common use of centered moving averages is in estimating the trend-cycle from seasonal data. Consider the 2×4-MA:

$$\hat{T}_t = \frac{1}{8}y_{t-2} + \frac{1}{4}y_{t-1} + \frac{1}{4}y_t + \frac{1}{4}y_{t+1} + \frac{1}{8}y_{t+2}.$$

When applied to quarterly data, each quarter of the year is given equal weight as the first and last terms apply to the same quarter in consecutive years. Consequently, the seasonal variation will be averaged out and the resulting values of $\hat{T}_t$ will have little or no seasonal variation remaining. A similar effect would be obtained using a 2×8-MA or a 2×12-MA.

In general, a $2 \times m$-MA is equivalent to a weighted moving average of order $m + 1$ with all observations taking weight $1/m$ except for the first and last terms which take weights $1/(2m)$. So if the seasonal period is even and of order m, use a $2 \times m$-MA to estimate the trend-cycle. If the seasonal period is odd and of order m, use a m-MA to estimate the trend cycle. In particular, a 2×12-MA can be used to estimate the trend-cycle of monthly data and a 7-MA can be used to estimate the trend-cycle of daily data.

Other choices for the order of the MA will usually result in trend cycle estimates being contaminated by the seasonality in the data.

Example 6.2   Electrical equipment manufacturing

Figure 6.9 shows a 2×12-MA applied to the electrical equipment orders index. Notice that the smooth line shows no seasonality; it is almost the same as the trend-cycle shown in Figure 6.2 which was estimated using a much more sophisticated method than moving averages. Any other choice for the order of the moving average (except for 24, 36, etc.) would have resulted in a smooth line that shows some seasonal fluctuations.

Weighted moving averages

Combinations of moving averages result in weighted moving averages. For example, the 2×4-MA discussed above is equivalent to a weighted 5-MA with weights given by $[\frac{1}{8}, \frac{1}{4}, \frac{1}{4}, \frac{1}{4}, \frac{1}{8}]$. In

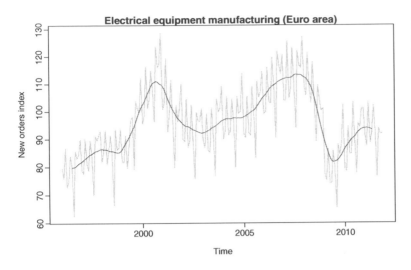

Figure 6.9: A 2×12-MA applied to the electrical equipment orders index.

──────── R code ────────

```
plot(elecequip, ylab="New orders index", col="gray",
 main="Electrical equipment manufacturing (Euro area)")
lines(ma(elecequip, order=12), col="red")
```

general, a weighted m-MA can be written as

$$\hat{T}_t = \sum_{j=-k}^{k} a_j y_{t+j},$$

where $k = (m - 1)/2$ and the weights are given by $[a_{-k}, \dots, a_k]$. It is important that the weights all sum to one and that they are symmetric so that $a_j = a_{-j}$. The simple m-MA is a special case where all the weights are equal to $1/m$.

A major advantage of weighted moving averages is that they yield a smoother estimate of the trend-cycle. Instead of observations entering and leaving the calculation at full weight, their weights are slowly increased and then slowly decreased resulting in a smoother curve.

Some specific sets of weights are widely used. Some of these are given in Table 6.3.

Name	a_0	a_1	a_2	a_3	a_4	a_5	a_6	a_7	a_8	a_9	a_{10}	a_{11}
3-MA	.333	.333										
5 MA	.200	.200	.200									
2×12-MA	.083	.083	.083	.083	.083	.083	.042					
3×3-MA	.333	.222	.111									
3×5-MA	.200	.200	.133	.067								
S15-MA	.231	.209	.144	.066	.009	−.016	−.019	−.009				
S21-MA	.171	.163	.134	.037	.051	.017	−.006	−.014	−.014	−.009	−.003	
H5-MA	.558	.294	−.073									
H9-MA	.330	.267	.119	−.010	−.041							
H13-MA	.240	.214	.147	.066	.000	−.028	−.019					
H23-MA	.148	.138	.122	.097	.068	.039	.013	−.005	−.015	−.016	−.011	−.004

S = Spencer's weighted moving average
H = Henderson's weighted moving average

Table 6.3: Commonly used weights in weighted moving averages.

6/3   Classical decomposition

The classical decomposition method originated in the 1920s. It is a relatively simple procedure and forms the basis for most other methods of time series decomposition. There are two forms of classical decomposition: an additive decomposition and a multiplicative decomposition. These are described below for a time series with seasonal period m (e.g., $m = 4$ for quarterly data, $m = 12$ for monthly data, $m = 7$ for daily data with a weekly pattern).

In classical decomposition, we assume the seasonal component is constant from year to year. These m values are sometimes called the "seasonal indices".

Additive decomposition

Step 1 If m is an even number, compute the trend-cycle component using a $2 \times m$-MA to obtain $\hat{T}_t$. If m is an odd number, compute the trend-cycle component using an m-MA to obtain $\hat{T}_t$.

Step 2 Calculate the detrended series: $y_t - \hat{T}_t$.

Step 3 To estimate the seasonal component for each month, simply average the detrended values for that month. For example, the seasonal index for March is the average of all the detrended March values in the data. These seasonal indexes are then adjusted to ensure that they add to zero. The seasonal component is obtained by stringing together all the seasonal indices for each year of data. This gives $\hat{S}_t$.

Step 4 The remainder component is calculated by subtracting the estimated seasonal and trend-cycle components: $\hat{E}_t = y_t - \hat{T}_t - \hat{S}_t$.

Multiplicative decomposition

A classical multiplicative decomposition is very similar except the subtractions are replaced by divisions.

Step 1 If m is an even number, compute the trend-cycle component using a $2 \times m$-MA to obtain $\hat{T}_t$. If m is an odd number, compute the trend-cycle component using an m-MA to obtain $\hat{T}_t$.

Step 2 Calculate the detrended series: $y_t/\hat{T}_t$.

Step 3 To estimate the seasonal component for each month, simply average the detrended values for that month. For example, the seasonal index for March is the average of all the detrended March values in the data. These seasonal indexes are then adjusted to ensure that they add to m. The seasonal component is obtained by stringing together all the seasonal indices for each year of data. This gives $\hat{S}_t$.

Step 4 The remainder component is calculated by dividing out the estimated seasonal and trend-cycle components: $\hat{E}_t = y_t/(\hat{T}_t \hat{S}_t)$.

————————————— R code —————————————

```
# x is the time series
fit <- decompose(x, type="multiplicative")
plot(fit)
```

Comments on classical decomposition

While classical decomposition is still widely used, it is not recommended. There are now several much better methods. Some of the problems with classical decomposition are summarised below.

- The estimate of the trend is unavailable for the first few and last few observations. For example, if $m = 12$, there is no trend estimate for the first six and last six observations. Consequently, there is also no estimate of the remainder component for the same time periods.

- Classical decomposition methods assume that the seasonal component repeats from year to year. For many series, this is a reasonable assumption, but for some longer series it is not. For example, electricity demand patterns have changed over time as air conditioning has become more widespread. So in many locations, the seasonal usage pattern from several decades ago had maximum demand in winter (due to heating), while the current seasonal pattern has maximum demand in summer (due to air conditioning). The classical decomposition methods are unable to capture these seasonal changes over time.

- Occasionally, the value of the time series in a small number of periods may be particularly unusual. For example, monthly air passenger traffic may be affected by an industrial dispute making the traffic during the dispute very different from usual. The classical method is not robust to these kinds of unusual values.

6/4   X-12-ARIMA decomposition

One of the most popular methods for decomposing quarterly and monthly data is X-12-ARIMA, which has its origins in methods developed by the US Bureau of the Census. It is now widely used by the Bureau and government agencies around the world. Earlier versions of the method included X-11 and X-11-ARIMA. An X-13-ARIMA method is currently under development at the US Bureau of the Census.

The X-12-ARIMA method is based on classical decomposition, but with many extra steps and features to overcome the drawbacks of classical decomposition that were discussed in the previous section. In particular, the trend estimate is available for all observations including the end points, and the seasonal component is allowed to vary slowly over time. It is also relatively robust to occasional unusual observations. X-12-ARIMA handles both additive and multiplicative decomposition, but only allows for quarterly and monthly data.

The "ARIMA" part of X-12-ARIMA refers to the use of an ARIMA model (see Chapter 7) that provides forecasts of the series forward in time, as well as backwards in time. Then, when a moving average is applied to obtain an estimate of the trend-cycle, there is no loss of observations at the start and end of the series.

The algorithm begins in a similar way to classical decomposition, and then the components are refined through several iterations. The following outline of the method describes a multiplicative decomposition applied to monthly data. Similar algorithms are used for additive decompositions and quarterly data.

1. Compute a 2×12 moving average applied to the original data to obtain a rough estimate of the trend-cycle $\hat{T}_t$ for all periods.

2. Calculate ratios of the data to trend (called "centered ratios"): $y_t/\hat{T}_t$.

3. Apply separate 3×3 MAs to each month of the centered ratios to form a rough estimate of $\hat{S}_t$.

4. Divide the centered ratios by $\hat{S}_t$ to get an estimate of the remainder, $\hat{E}_t$.

5. Reduce extreme values of E_t to get modified $\hat{E}_t$.

6. Multiply modified $\hat{E}_t$ by $\hat{S}_t$ to get modified centered ratios.

7. Repeat Step 3 to obtain revised $\hat{S}_t$.

8. Divide original data by the new estimate of $\hat{S}_t$ to give the preliminary seasonally adjusted series, $y_t/\hat{S}_t$.

9. The trend-cycle $\hat{T}_t$ is estimated by applying a weighted Henderson MA to the preliminary seasonally adjusted values. (The greater the randomness, the longer the length of the moving average used.) For monthly series: either a 9-, 13-, or 23-term Henderson moving average is used.

10. Repeat Step 2. New ratios are obtained by dividing the original data by the new estimate of $\hat{T}_t$.

11. Repeat Steps 3–6 using the new ratios and applying a 3×5 MA instead of a 3×3 MA.

12. Repeat Step 7 but using a 3×5 MA instead of a 3×3 MA.
13. Repeat Step 8.
14. The remainder component is obtained by dividing the seasonally adjusted data from Step 13 by the trend-cycle obtained in Step 9.
15. Extreme values of the remainder component are replaced as in Step 5.
16. A series of modified data is obtained by multiplying the trend-cycle, seasonal component, and adjusted remainder component together.

The whole process is repeated two more times using the data obtained in the Step 16 each time. On the final iteration, the 3×5 MA of Steps 11 and 12 is replaced by either a 3×3, 3×5, or 3×9 moving average, depending on the variability in the data.

X-12-ARIMA also has some sophisticated methods to handle trading day variation, holiday effects and the effects of known predictors, which are not covered here.

A complete discussion of the method is available in[1] Ladiray and Quenneville (2001).

There is currently no R package for X-12-ARIMA decomposition. However, free software that implements the method is available from the US Census Bureau and an R interface to that software is provided by the x12 package.

[1] Ladiray, D., & Quenneville, B. (2001) *Seasonal Adjustment with the X-11 Method*, Lecture Notes in Statistics 158, Springer Verlag: New York.

6/5   STL decomposition

STL is a very versatile and robust method for decomposing time series. STL is an acronym for "Seasonal and Trend decomposition using Loess", while Loess is a method for estimating nonlinear relationships. The STL method was developed by[2] Cleveland et al. (1990)

STL has several advantages over the classical decomposition method and X-12-ARIMA:

- Unlike X-12-ARIMA, STL will handle any type of seasonality, not only monthly and quarterly data.
- The seasonal component is allowed to change over time, and the rate of change can be controlled by the user.
- The smoothness of the trend-cycle can also be controlled by the user.

[2] Cleveland, R.B. and Cleveland, W.S. and McRae, J.E. and Terpenning, I. (1990) "STL: A seasonal-trend decomposition procedure based on loess", *Journal of Official Statistics*, **6**(1), 3–73.

- It can be robust to outliers (i.e., the user can specify a robust decomposition). So occasional unusual observations will not affect the estimates of the trend-cycle and seasonal components. They will, however, affect the remainder component.

On the other hand, STL has some disadvantages. In particular, it does not automatically handle trading day or calendar variation, and it only provides facilities for additive decompositions.

It is possible to obtain a multiplicative decomposition by first taking logs of the data, and then back-transforming the components. Decompositions some way between additive and multiplicative can be obtained using a Box-Cox transformation of the data with $0 < \lambda < 1$. A value of $\lambda = 0$ corresponds to the multiplicative decomposition while $\lambda = 1$ is equivalent to an additive decomposition.

The best way to begin learning how to use STL is to see some examples and experiment with the settings. Figure 6.3 showed an example of STL applied to the electrical equipment orders data. Figure 6.10 shows an alternative STL decomposition where the trend is more flexible, the seasonal component does not change over time, and the robust option has been used. Here it is more obvious that there has been a down-turn at the end of the series, and that the orders in 2009 were unusually low (corresponding to some large negative values in the remainder component).

The two main parameters to be chosen when using STL are the trend window (t.window) and seasonal window (s.window). These control how rapidly the trend and seasonal components can change. Small values allow more rapid change. Setting the seasonal window to be infinite is equivalent to forcing the seasonal component to be periodic (i.e., identical across years).

6/6 *Forecasting with decomposition*

While decomposition is primarily useful for studying time series data, and exploring the historical changes over time, it can also be used in forecasting.

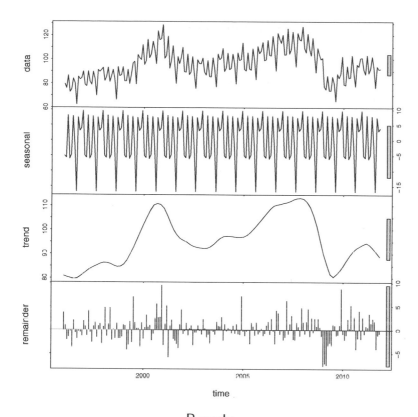

Figure 6.10: The electrical equipment orders (top) and its three additive components obtained from a robust STL decomposition with flexible trend and fixed seasonality.

———————— R code ————————

```
fit <- stl(elecequip, t.window=15, s.window="periodic", robust=TRUE)
plot(fit)
```

Assuming an additive decomposition, the decomposed time series can be written as

$$y_t = \hat{S}_t + \hat{A}_t$$

where $\hat{A}_t = \hat{T}_t + \hat{E}_t$ is the seasonally adjusted component. Or if a multiplicative decomposition has been used, we can write

$$y_t = \hat{S}_t \hat{A}_t,$$

where $\hat{A}_t = \hat{T}_t \hat{E}_t$.

To forecast a decomposed time series, we separately forecast the seasonal component, $\hat{S}_t$, and the seasonally adjusted component $\hat{A}_t$. It is usually assumed that the seasonal component is unchanging, or changing extremely slowly, and so it is forecast by simply taking the last year of the estimated component. In other words, a seasonal naïve method is used for the seasonal component.

To forecast the seasonally adjusted component, any non-seasonal forecasting method may be used. For example, a random walk with drift model, or Holt's method (discussed in the next chapter), or a non-seasonal ARIMA model (discussed in Chapter 8), may be used.

Example 6.3   Electrical equipment manufacturing

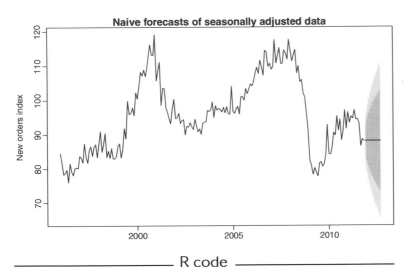

Figure 6.11: Naïve forecasts of the seasonally adjusted data obtained from an STL decomposition of the electrical equipment orders data.

```
———————————————— R code ————————————————
fit <- stl(elecequip, t.window=15, s.window="periodic",
  robust=TRUE)
eeadj <- seasadj(fit)
plot(naive(eeadj), ylab="New orders index",
  main="Naive forecasts of seasonally adjusted data")
```

Figure 6.11 shows naïve forecasts of the seasonally adjusted electrical equipment orders data. These are then "reseasonalized" by adding in the seasonal naïve forecasts of the seasonal component. The resulting forecasts of the original data are shown in Figure 6.12. The prediction intervals shown in this graph are constructed in the same way as the point forecasts. That is, the upper and lower limits of the prediction intervals on the seasonally adjusted data are "reseasonalized" by adding in the forecasts of the seasonal component. In this calculation, the uncertainty in the forecasts of the seasonal component has

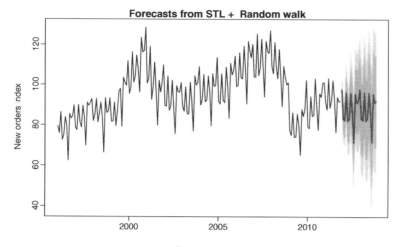

Figure 6.12: Forecasts of the electrical equipment orders data based on a naïve forecast of the seasonally adjusted data and a seasonal naïve forecast of the seasonal component, after an an STL decomposition of the data.

———————— R code ————————

```
fcast <- forecast(fit, method="naive")
plot(fcast, ylab="New orders index")
```

been ignored. The rationale for this choice is that the uncertainty in the seasonal component is much smaller than that for the seasonally adjusted data, and so it is a reasonable approximation to ignore it.

6/7   Exercises

6.1 Show that a 3×5 MA is equivalent to a 7-term weighted moving average with weights of 0.067, 0.133, 0.200, 0.200, 0.200, 0.133, and 0.067.

6.2 The data below represent the monthly sales (in thousands) of product A for a plastics manufacturer for years 1 through 5 (data set plastics).

	1	2	3	4	5
Jan	742	741	896	951	1030
Feb	697	700	793	861	1032
Mar	776	774	885	938	1126
Apr	898	932	1055	1109	1285
May	1030	1099	1204	1274	1468
Jun	1107	1223	1326	1422	1637
Jul	1165	1290	1303	1486	1611
Aug	1216	1349	1436	1555	1608
Sep	1208	1341	1473	1604	1528
Oct	1131	1296	1453	1600	1420
Nov	971	1066	1170	1403	1119
Dec	783	901	1023	1209	1013

(a) Plot the time series of sales of product A. Can you identify seasonal fluctuations and/or a trend?

(b) Use a classical multiplicative decomposition to calculate the trend-cycle and seasonal indices.

(c) Do the results support the graphical interpretation from part (a)?

(d) Compute and plot the seasonally adjusted data.

(e) Change one observation to be an outlier (e.g., add 500 to one observation), and recompute the seasonally adjusted data. What is the effect of the outlier?

(f) Does it make any difference if the outlier is near the end rather than in the middle of the time series?

(g) Use a random walk with drift to produce forecasts of the seasonally adjusted data.

(h) Reseasonalize the results to give forecasts on the original scale.

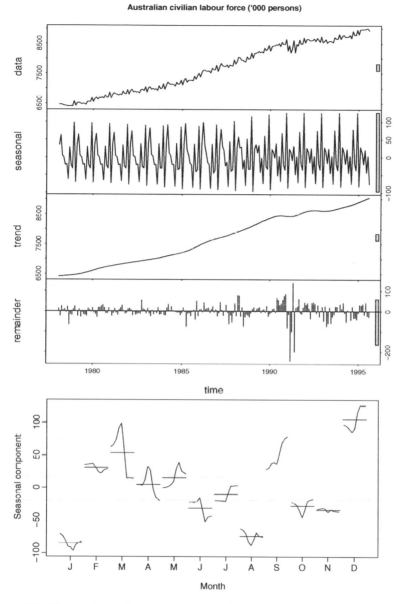

Figure 6.13: Decomposition of the number of persons in the civilian labor force in Australia each month from February 1978 to August 1995.

6.3 Figure 6.13 shows the result of decomposing the number of persons in the civilian labor force in Australia each month from February 1978 to August 1995.

(a) Write about 3–5 sentences describing the results of the seasonal adjustment. Pay particular attention to the scales of the graphs in making your interpretation.

(b) Is the recession of 1991/1992 visible in the estimated components?

6/8 *Further reading*

- Cleveland, R. B., W. S. Cleveland, J. E. McRae and I. J. Terpenning (1990). STL : A seasonal-trend decomposition procedure based on loess. *Journal of Official Statistics* **6**(1), 3–73.

- Gómez, V. and A. Maravall (2001). "Seasonal adjustment and signal extraction in economic time series". In: *A course in time series analysis*. Ed. by D. Peña, G. C. Tiao and R. S. Tsay. New York: John Wiley & Sons. Chap. 8, pp.202–246.

- Ladiray, D. and B. Quenneville (2001). *Seasonal adjustment with the X-11 method*. Lecture notes in statistics. Springer-Verlag.

- Miller, D. M. and D. Williams (2003). Shrinkage estimators of time series seasonal factors and their effect on forecasting accuracy. *International Journal of Forecasting* **19**(4), 669–684.

- Theodosiou, M. (2011). Forecasting monthly and quarterly time series using STL decomposition. *International Journal of Forecasting* **27**(4), 1178–1195.

7

Exponential smoothing

Exponential smoothing was proposed in the late 1950s (Brown 1959, Holt 1957 and Winters 1960 are key pioneering works) and has motivated some of the most successful forecasting methods. Forecasts produced using exponential smoothing methods are weighted averages of past observations, with the weights decaying exponentially as the observations get older. In other words, the more recent the observation the higher the associated weight. This framework generates reliable forecasts quickly and for a wide range of time series which is a great advantage and of major importance to applications in industry.

This chapter is divided into two parts. In the first part we present in detail the mechanics of all exponential smoothing methods and their application in forecasting time series with various characteristics. This is key in understanding the intuition behind these methods. In this setting, selecting and using a forecasting method may appear to be somewhat ad-hoc. The selection of the method is generally based on recognising key components of the time series (trend and seasonal) and how these enter the smoothing method (in an additive or multiplicative manner).

In the second part of the chapter we present statistical models that underlie exponential smoothing methods. These models generate identical point forecasts to the methods discussed in the first part of the chapter, but also generate prediction intervals. Furthermore, this statistical framework allows for genuine model selection between competing models.

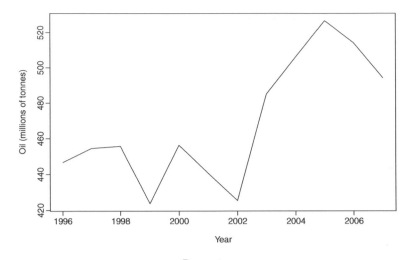

Figure 7.1: Oil production in Saudi Arabia from 1996 to 2007.

─────────────── R code ───────────────

```
oildata <- window(oil,start=1996,end=2007)
plot(oildata, ylab="Oil (millions of tonnes)",xlab="Year")
```

7/1   Simple exponential smoothing

The simplest of the exponentially smoothing methods is naturally called "simple exponential smoothing" (SES)[1]. This method is suitable for forecasting data with no trend or seasonal pattern. For example, the data in Figure 7.1 do not display any clear trending behaviour or any seasonality, although the mean of the data may be changing slowly over time. We have already considered the naïve and the average as possible methods for forecasting such data (Section 2/3).

[1] In some books, it is called "single exponential smoothing".

Using the naïve method, all forecasts for the future are equal to the last observed value of the series,

$$\hat{y}_{T+h|T} = y_T,$$

for $h = 1, 2, \dots$. Hence, the naïve method assumes that the most current observation is the only important one and all previous observations provide no information for the future. This can be thought of as a weighted average where all the weight is given to the last observation.

Using the average method, all future forecasts are equal to a simple average of the observed data,

$$\hat{y}_{T+h|T} = \frac{1}{T} \sum_{t=1}^{T} y_t,$$

for $h = 1, 2, \ldots$. Hence, the average method assumes that all observations are of equal importance and they are given equal weight when generating forecasts.

We often want something between these two extremes. For example it may be sensible to attach larger weights to more recent observations than to observations from the distant past. This is exactly the concept behind simple exponential smoothing. Forecasts are calculated using weighted averages where the weights decrease exponentially as observations come from further in the past — the smallest weights are associated with the oldest observations:

$$\hat{y}_{T+1|T} = \alpha y_T + \alpha(1-\alpha)y_{T-1} + \alpha(1-\alpha)^2 y_{T-2} + \alpha(1-\alpha)^3 y_{T-3} + \cdots,$$
(7.1)

where $0 \leq \alpha \leq 1$ is the smoothing parameter. The one-step-ahead forecast for time $T + 1$ is a weighted average of all the observations in the series $y_1, \ldots, y_T$. The rate at which the weights decrease is controlled by the parameter α.

Table 7.1 shows the weights attached to observations for four different values of α when forecasting using simple exponential smoothing. Note that the sum of the weights even for a small α will be approximately one for any reasonable sample size.

	Weights assigned to observations for:			
Observation	$\alpha = 0.2$	$\alpha = 0.4$	$\alpha = 0.6$	$\alpha = 0.8$
y_T	0.2	0.4	0.6	0.8
y_{T-1}	0.16	0.24	0.24	0.16
y_{T-2}	0.128	0.144	0.096	0.032
y_{T-3}	0.1024	0.0864	0.0384	0.0064
y_{T-4}	$(0.2)(0.8)^4$	$(0.4)(0.6)^4$	$(0.6)(0.4)^4$	$(0.8)(0.2)^4$
y_{T-5}	$(0.2)(0.8)^5$	$(0.4)(0.6)^5$	$(0.6)(0.4)^5$	$(0.8)(0.2)^5$

Table 7.1: Exponentially decaying weights attached to observations of the time series when generating forecasts using simple exponential smoothing.

For any α between 0 and 1, the weights attached to the observations decrease exponentially as we go back in time, hence the name "exponential smoothing". If α is small (i.e., close to 0), more weight is given to observations from the more distant past. If α is large (i.e., close to 1), more weight is given to the more recent observations. At the extreme case where $\alpha = 1$, $\hat{y}_{T+1|T} = y_T$ and forecasts are equal to the naïve forecasts.

We present three equivalent forms of simple exponential smoothing, each of which leads to the forecast equation (7.1).

Weighted average form

The forecast at time $t + 1$ is equal to a weighted average between the most recent observation y_t and the most recent forecast $\hat{y}_{t|t-1}$,

$$\hat{y}_{t+1|t} = \alpha y_t + (1 - \alpha)\hat{y}_{t|t-1}$$

for $t = 1, \ldots, T$, where $0 \le \alpha \le 1$ is the smoothing parameter.

The process has to start somewhere, so we let the first forecast of y_1 be denoted by ℓ_0. Then

$$\hat{y}_{2|1} = \alpha y_1 + (1 - \alpha)\ell_0$$
$$\hat{y}_{3|2} = \alpha y_2 + (1 - \alpha)\hat{y}_{2|1}$$
$$\hat{y}_{4|3} = \alpha y_3 + (1 - \alpha)\hat{y}_{3|2}$$
$$\vdots$$
$$\hat{y}_{T+1|T} = \alpha y_T + (1 - \alpha)\hat{y}_{T|T-1}$$

Then substituting each equation into the following equation, we obtain

$$\hat{y}_{3|2} = \alpha y_2 + (1 - \alpha)[\alpha y_1 + (1 - \alpha)\ell_0]$$
$$= \alpha y_2 + \alpha(1 - \alpha)y_1 + (1 - \alpha)^2\ell_0$$
$$\hat{y}_{4|3} = \alpha y_3 + (1 - \alpha)[\alpha y_2 + \alpha(1 - \alpha)y_1 + (1 - \alpha)^2\ell_0]$$
$$= \alpha y_3 + \alpha(1 - \alpha)y_2 + \alpha(1 - \alpha)^2 y_1 + (1 - \alpha)^3\ell_0$$
$$\vdots$$
$$\hat{y}_{T+1|T} = \sum_{j=0}^{T-1} \alpha(1 - \alpha)^j y_{T-j} + (1 - \alpha)^T\ell_0. \tag{7.2}$$

So the weighted average form leads to the same forecast equation (7.1).

Component form

An alternative representation is the component form. For simple exponential smoothing the only component included is the level, ℓ_t. (Other methods considered later in this chapter may also include a trend b_t and seasonal component s_t.) Component form representations of exponential smoothing methods comprise a forecast equation and a smoothing equation for each of the components included in the method. The component form of simple exponential smoothing is given by:

Forecast equation $\hat{y}_{t+1|t} = \ell_t$

Smoothing equation $\ell_t = \alpha y_t + (1-\alpha)\ell_{t-1},$

where ℓ_t is the level (or the smoothed value) of the series at time t. The forecast equation shows that the forecasted value at time $t+1$ is the estimated level at time t. The smoothing equation for the level (usually referred to as the level equation) gives the estimated level of the series at each period t.

Applying the forecast equation for time T gives, $\hat{y}_{T+1|T} = \ell_T$, the most recent estimated level.

If we replace ℓ_t by $\hat{y}_{t+1|t}$ and ℓ_{t-1} by $\hat{y}_{t|t-1}$ in the smoothing equation, we will recover the weighted average form of simple exponential smoothing.

Error correction form

The third form of simple exponential smoothing is obtained by re-arranging the level equation in the component form to get what we refer to as the error correction form

$$\ell_t = \ell_{t-1} + \alpha(y_t - \ell_{t-1})$$
$$= \ell_{t-1} + \alpha e_t$$

where $e_t = y_t - \ell_{t-1} = y_t - \hat{y}_{t|t-1}$ for $t = 1, \ldots, T$. That is, e_t is the one-step error at time t computed on the training data. The training data errors lead to the adjustment/correction of the estimated level throughout the smoothing process for $t = 1, \ldots, T$.

For example, if the error at time t is negative, then $\hat{y}_{t|t-1} > y_t$ and so the level at time $t-1$ has been over-estimated. The new level ℓ_t is then the previous level ℓ_{t-1} adjusted downwards. The closer α is to one the "rougher" the estimate of the level (large adjustments take place). The smaller the α the "smoother" the level (small adjustments take place).

Multi-horizon Forecasts

So far we have given forecast equations for only one step ahead. Simple exponential smoothing has a "flat" forecast function, and therefore for longer forecast horizons,

$$\hat{y}_{T+h|T} = \hat{y}_{T+1|T} = \ell_T, \qquad h = 2, 3, \ldots.$$

Remember these forecasts will only be suitable if the time series has no trend or seasonal component.

Initialisation

The application of every exponential smoothing method requires the initialisation of the smoothing process. For simple exponential smoothing we need to specify an initial value for the level, ℓ_0, which appears in the last term of equation (7.2). Hence ℓ_0 plays a role in all forecasts generated by the process. In general, the weight attached to ℓ_0 is small. However, in the case that α is small and/or the time series is relatively short, the weight may be large enough to have a noticeable effect on the resulting forecasts. Therefore, selecting suitable initial values can be quite important. A common approach is to set $\ell_0 = y_1$ (recall that $\ell_0 = \hat{y}_{1|0}$).

Other exponential smoothing methods that also involve a trend and/or a seasonal component require initial values for these components also. We tabulate common strategies for selecting initial values in Table 7.9.

An alternative approach (see below) is to use optimization to estimate the value of ℓ_0 rather than set it to some value. Even if optimization is used, selecting appropriate initial values can assist the speed and precision of the optimization process.

Optimization

For every exponential smoothing method we also need to choose the value for the smoothing parameters. For simple exponential smoothing, there is only one smoothing parameter (α), but for the methods that follow there is usually more than one smoothing parameter.

There are cases where the smoothing parameters may be chosen in a subjective manner — the forecaster specifies the value of the smoothing parameters based on previous experience. However, a more robust and objective way to obtain values for the unknown parameters included in any exponential smoothing method is to estimate them from the observed data.

In Section 4/2 we estimated the coefficients of a regression model by minimizing the sum of the squared errors (SSE). Similarly, the unknown parameters and the initial values for any exponential smoothing method can be estimated by minimizing the SSE. The errors are specified as $e_t = y_t - \hat{y}_{t|t-1}$ for $t = 1,\ldots,T$ (the one-step-ahead training errors). Hence we find the values of the unknown parameters and the initial values that minimize

$$\text{SSE} = \sum_{t=1}^{T}(y_t - \hat{y}_{t|t-1})^2 = \sum_{t=1}^{T} e_t^2. \tag{7.3}$$

Unlike the regression case (where we have formulae that return the values of the regression coefficients which minimize the SSE) this involves a non-linear minimization problem and we need to use an optimization tool to perform this.

Example 7.1   Oil production

In this example, simple exponential smoothing is applied to forecast oil production in Saudi Arabia. The black line in Figure 7.2 is a plot of the data over the period 1996–2007, which shows a changing level over time but no obvious trending behaviour.

In Table 7.2 we demonstrate the application of simple exponential smoothing. The last three columns show the estimated level for times $t = 0$ to $t = 12$, then the forecasts for $h = 1,2,3$, for three different values of α. For the first two columns the smoothing parameter α is set to 0.2 and 0.6 respectively and the initial level ℓ_0 is set to y_1 in both cases. In the third column both the smoothing parameter and the initial level are estimated. Using an optimization tool, we find the values of α and ℓ_0 that minimize the SSE, subject to the restriction that $0 \leq \alpha \leq 1$. Note that the SSE values presented in the last row of the table is smaller for this estimated α and ℓ_0 than for the other values of α and ℓ_0.

The three different sets of forecasts for the period 2008–2010 are plotted in Figure 7.2. Also plotted are one-step-ahead training forecasts alongside the data over the period 1996–2007.

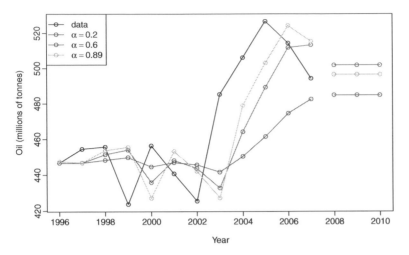

Figure 7.2: Simple exponential smoothing applied to oil production in Saudi Arabia (1996–2007).

R code

```
fit1 <- ses(oildata, alpha=0.2, initial="simple", h=3)
fit2 <- ses(oildata, alpha=0.6, initial="simple", h=3)
fit3 <- ses(oildata, h=3)
plot(fit1, plot.conf=FALSE, ylab="Oil (millions of tonnes)",
  xlab="Year", main="", fcol="white", type="o")
lines(fitted(fit1), col="blue", type="o")
lines(fitted(fit2), col="red", type="o")
lines(fitted(fit3), col="green", type="o")
lines(fit1$mean, col="blue", type="o")
lines(fit2$mean, col="red", type="o")
lines(fit3$mean, col="green", type="o")
legend("topleft",lty=1, col=c(1,"blue","red","green"),
  c("data", expression(alpha == 0.2), expression(alpha == 0.6),
  expression(alpha == 0.89)),pch=1)
```

The influence of α on the smoothing process is clearly visible. The larger the α the greater the adjustment that takes place in the next forecast in the direction of the previous data point; smaller α leads to less adjustment and so the series of one-step training forecasts is smoother.

Year	Time period t	Observed values y_t	$\alpha = 0.2$	$\alpha = 0.6$ Level ℓ_t	$\alpha = 0.89^*$
1995	0	–	446.7	446.7	447.5*
1996	1	446.7	446.7	446.7	446.7
1997	2	454.5	448.2	451.3	453.6
1998	3	455.7	449.7	453.9	455.4
1999	4	423.6	444.5	435.8	427.1
2000	5	456.3	446.8	448.1	453.1
2001	6	440.6	445.6	443.6	441.9
2002	7	425.3	441.5	432.6	427.1
2003	8	485.1	450.3	464.1	478.9
2004	9	506.0	461.4	489.3	503.1
2005	10	526.8	474.5	511.8	524.2
2006	11	514.3	482.5	513.3	515.3
2007	12	494.2	484.8	501.8	496.5
	h		Forecasts $\hat{y}_{T+h|T}$		
2008	13		484.8	501.8	496.5
2009	14		484.8	501.8	496.5
2010	15		484.8	501.8	496.5

Table 7.2: Forecasting total oil production in millions of tonnes for Saudi Arabia using simple exponential smoothing with three different values for the smoothing parameter α

Analysis of one-step-ahead training errors over period 1–12			
MAE	24.7	20.2	20.1
RMSE	32.1	26.0	25.1
MAPE	5.1	4.2	4.3
SSE	12391.7	8098.6	7573.4

*$\alpha = 0.89$ and $\ell_0 = 447.5$ are obtained by minimizing SSE over periods $t = 1, 2, \ldots, 12$.

7/2   Holt's linear trend method

Holt (1957) extended simple exponential smoothing to allow forecasting of data with a trend. This method involves a forecast equation and two smoothing equations (one for the level and one for the trend):

Forecast equation $\qquad \hat{y}_{t+h|t} = \ell_t + hb_t$

Level equation $\qquad \ell_t = \alpha y_t + (1 - \alpha)(\ell_{t-1} + b_{t-1})$

Trend equation $\qquad b_t = \beta^*(\ell_t - \ell_{t-1}) + (1 - \beta^*)b_{t-1}$

where ℓ_t denotes an estimate of the level of the series at time t, b_t denotes an estimate of the trend (slope) of the series at time t, α is the smoothing parameter for the level, $0 \leq \alpha \leq 1$ and β^* is the smoothing parameter for the trend, $0 \leq \beta^* \leq 1$ (we denote this as β^* instead of β for reasons that will be explained in Section 7/7).

As with simple exponential smoothing, the level equation here shows that ℓ_t is a weighted average of observation y_t and the one-step-ahead training forecast for time t, here given by $\ell_{t-1}+b_{t-1}$. The trend equation shows that b_t is a weighted average of the estimated trend at time t based on $\ell_t - \ell_{t-1}$ and b_{t-1}, the previous estimate of the trend.

The forecast function is no longer flat but trending. The h-step-ahead forecast is equal to the last estimated level plus h times the last estimated trend value. Hence the forecasts are a linear function of h.

The error correction form of the level and the trend equations show the adjustments in terms of the one-step training errors:

$$\ell_t = \ell_{t-1} + b_{t-1} + \alpha e_t$$
$$b_t = b_{t-1} + \alpha \beta^* e_t$$

where $e_t = y_t - (\ell_{t-1} + b_{t-1}) = y_t - \hat{y}_{t|t-1}$.

Example 7.2   Air Passengers

In Table 7.3 we demonstrate the application of Holt's linear method to air transportation data for all passengers with an Australian airline. To initialise the method we set $\ell_0 = y_1$ and $b_0 = y_2 - y_1$ as suggested in Table 7.9. Alternatively we could fit a linear trend to the first few observations (see Section 4/8) and use the estimates of the intercept and the slope as the initial values for the level and the trend respectively.

For demonstration purposes the smoothing parameters are set to $\alpha = 0.8$ and $\beta^* = 0.2$. Otherwise, the smoothing parameters together with the initial values could be estimated by minimizing the SSE for the one-step training errors as in Section 7/1.

Year	t	y_t	Holt's linear method			Exponential trend method		
			ℓ_t	b_t	$\hat{y}_t$	ℓ_t	b_t	$\hat{y}_t$
1989	0	–	17.55	4.31	–	17.55	1.25	–
1990	1	17.55	18.41	3.62	21.86	18.41	1.21	21.86
1991	2	21.86	21.89	3.59	22.03	21.93	1.20	22.21
1992	3	23.89	24.21	3.33	25.48	24.39	1.18	26.38
1993	4	26.93	27.05	3.24	27.54	27.32	1.17	28.89
1994	5	26.89	27.57	2.69	30.29	27.91	1.14	32.02
1995	6	28.83	29.12	2.46	30.26	29.44	1.12	31.88
1996	7	30.08	30.38	2.22	31.58	30.68	1.11	33.10
1997	8	30.95	31.28	1.96	32.60	31.56	1.09	33.99
1998	9	30.19	30.80	1.47	33.24	31.04	1.07	34.47
1999	10	31.58	31.72	1.36	32.27	31.91	1.06	33.23
2000	11	32.58	32.68	1.28	33.08	32.84	1.06	33.89
2001	12	33.48	33.57	1.20	33.96	33.71	1.05	34.66
2002	13	39.02	38.17	1.88	34.78	38.29	1.07	35.39
2003	14	41.39	41.12	2.10	40.06	41.28	1.07	40.86
2004	15	41.60	41.92	1.84	43.22	42.10	1.06	44.13
	h				$\hat{y}_{T+h|T}$			$\hat{y}_{T+h|T}$
2005	1				43.76			44.60
2006	2				45.59			47.24
2007	3				47.43			50.04
2008	4				49.27			53.01
2009	5				51.10			56.15

Table 7.3: Applying Holt's linear method and the Exponential trend method with $\alpha = 0.8$ and $\beta^* = 0.2$ to Australian Air Passenger data, (thousands of passengers)

——————————— R code ———————————
```
air <- window(ausair,start=1990,end=2004)
fit1 <- holt(air, alpha=0.8, beta=0.2, initial="simple", h=5)
fit2 <- holt(air, alpha=0.8, beta=0.2, initial="simple", exponential=TRUE, h=5)
# Results for first model:
fit1$model$state
fitted(fit1)
fit1$mean
```

7/3   Exponential trend method

A variation from Holt's linear trend method is achieved by allowing the level and the slope to be multiplied rather than added:

$$\hat{y}_{t+h|t} = \ell_t b_t^h$$
$$\ell_t = \alpha y_t + (1 - \alpha)(\ell_{t-1} b_{t-1})$$
$$b_t = \beta^* \frac{\ell_t}{\ell_{t-1}} + (1 - \beta^*)b_{t-1}$$

where b_t now represents an estimated growth rate (in relative terms rather than absolute) which is multiplied rather than added to the estimated level. The trend in the forecast function is now exponential rather than linear, so that the forecasts project a constant growth rate rather than a constant slope. The

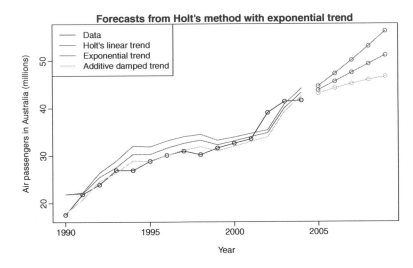

Figure 7.3: Forecasting Air Passengers in Australia (thousands of passengers). For all methods $\alpha = 0.8$ and $\beta^* = 0.2$, and for the additive damped trend method $\phi = 0.85$.

——————— R code ———————

```
fit3 <- holt(air, alpha=0.8, beta=0.2, damped=TRUE, initial="simple", h=5)
plot(fit2, type="o", ylab="Air passengers in Australia (millions)", xlab="Year",
    fcol="white", plot.conf=FALSE)
lines(fitted(fit1), col="blue")
lines(fitted(fit2), col="red")
lines(fitted(fit3), col="green")
lines(fit1$mean, col="blue", type="o")
lines(fit2$mean, col="red", type="o")
lines(fit3$mean, col="green", type="o")
legend("topleft", lty=1, col=c("black","blue","red","green"),
    c("Data","Holt's linear trend","Exponential trend","Additive damped trend"))
```

error correction form is

$$\ell_t = \ell_{t-1} b_{t-1} + \alpha e_t$$
$$b_t = b_{t-1} + \alpha \beta^* \frac{e_t}{\ell_{t-1}}$$

where $e_t = y_t - (\ell_{t-1} b_{t-1}) = y_t - \hat{y}_{t|t-1}$.

Example 7.2   Air Passengers (continued)

In Table 7.3 we also demonstrate the application of the exponential trend method. As for Holt's linear method we set, $\alpha = 0.8$, $\beta^* = 0.2$ and $\ell_0 = y_1$, however $b_0 = y_2/y_1$ as suggested in Table 7.9.

Notice the difference between the trend and the growth rate in the two methods in the columns labelled b_t. In Holt's linear method, b_t is added to the corresponding level term in the calculations; in the exponential trend method, b_t is multiplied with the corresponding level term in the calculations.

7/4   Damped trend methods

The forecasts generated by Holt's linear method display a constant trend (increasing or decreasing) indefinitely into the future. Even more extreme are the forecasts generated by the exponential trend method which include exponential growth or decline.

Empirical evidence indicates that these methods tend to over-forecast, especially for longer forecast horizons. Motivated by this observation, Gardner and McKenzie (1985) introduced a parameter that "dampens" the trend to a flat line some time in the future. Methods that include a damped trend have proven to be very successful and are arguably the most popular individual methods when forecasts are required automatically for many series.

Additive damped trend

In conjunction with the smoothing parameters α and β^* (with values between 0 and 1 as in Holt's method), this method also includes a damping parameter $0 < \phi < 1$:

$$\hat{y}_{t+h|t} = \ell_t + (\phi + \phi^2 + \cdots + \phi^h)b_t$$
$$\ell_t = \alpha y_t + (1 - \alpha)(\ell_{t-1} + \phi b_{t-1})$$
$$b_t = \beta^*(\ell_t - \ell_{t-1}) + (1 - \beta^*)\phi b_{t-1}.$$

If $\phi = 1$ the method is identical to Holt's linear method. For values between 0 and 1, ϕ dampens the trend so that it approaches a constant some time in the future. In fact the forecasts converge to $\ell_T + \phi b_T/(1 - \phi)$ as $h \to \infty$ for any value $0 < \phi < 1$. The effect of this is that short-run forecasts are trended while long-run forecasts are constant.

The error correction form of the smoothing equations is

$$\ell_t = \ell_{t-1} + \phi b_{t-1} + \alpha e_t$$
$$b_t = \phi b_{t-1} + \alpha \beta^* e_t.$$

Example 7.2   Air Passengers (continued)

Figure 7.3 shows the one-step training forecasts, and the forecasts for years 2005–2010 generated from Holt's linear trend method, exponential trend and additive damped trend. The most optimistic forecasts come from the exponential trend method while the least optimistic come from the damped trend method, with the forecasts generated by Holt's linear trend method somewhere between the two.

Multiplicative damped trend

Motivated by the improvements in forecasting performance seen in the additive damped trend case, Taylor (2003) introduced a damping parameter to the exponential trend method resulting to a multiplicative damped trend method:

$$\hat{y}_{t+h|t} = \ell_t b_t^{(\phi + \phi^2 + \cdots + \phi^h)}$$
$$\ell_t = \alpha y_t + (1 - \alpha)\ell_{t-1} b_{t-1}^{\phi}$$
$$b_t = \beta^* \frac{\ell_t}{\ell_{t-1}} + (1 - \beta^*)b_{t-1}^{\phi}.$$

This method will produce even more conservative forecasts than the additive damped trend method when compared to

Holt's linear method. The error correction form of the smoothing equations is

$$\ell_t = \ell_{t-1} b_{t-1}^{\phi} + \alpha e_t$$
$$b_t = b_{t-1}^{\phi} + \alpha \beta^* \frac{e_t}{\ell_{t-1}}.$$

Example 7.3   Sheep in Asia

In this example we compare the forecasting performance of all the non-seasonal methods we have considered so far in forecasting the sheep livestock population in Asia. The data spans the period 1970–2007. We withhold the period 2001–2007 as a test set, and use the data up to and including year 2000 for the training set (see Section 2.5 for a definition of training and test sets). Figure 7.5 shows that data and the forecasts from all methods.

The parameters and initial values of the methods are estimated for all methods by minimizing SSE (as specified in Equation (7.3)) over the training set. In Table 7.4 we present the estimation results and error measures over the training and the test sets.

─────────────── R code ───────────────
```
livestock2 <- window(livestock,start=1970,end=2000)
fit1 <- ses(livestock2)
fit2 <- holt(livestock2)
fit3 <- holt(livestock2,exponential=TRUE)
fit4 <- holt(livestock2,damped=TRUE)
fit5 <- holt(livestock2,exponential=TRUE,damped=TRUE)
# Results for first model:
fit1$model
accuracy(fit1) # training set
accuracy(fit1,livestock) # test set
```

For the simple exponential smoothing method, the estimated smoothing parameter is $\alpha = 1$. This is expected as the series is clearly trending over time and simple exponential smoothing requires the largest possible adjustment in each step to capture this trend.

For the other methods, there is also a trend component. With the exception of the multiplicative damped trend method, the smoothing parameter for the slope parameter is estimated to

	SES	Holt's linear	Exponential trend	Additive damped	Multiplicative damped
Parameter estimates and initial values					
α	1.00	0.98	0.98	0.99	0.98
β^*	–	0	0	0	0
ϕ	–	–	–	0.98[†]	0.98[†]
ℓ_0	263.92	257.78	255.52	254.58	254.69
b_0	–	5.01	1.01	5.39	1.02
training errors over the training set 1970–2000					
RMSE	14.77	13.92	14.06	14.00	14.03
SSE	6761.47	6006.06	6128.46	6080.26	6100.11
Forecast errors over the test set 2001–2007					
MAE	20.38	10.69	9.64	14.18	11.77
RMSE	25.46	11.88	12.50	15.78	12.62
MAPE	4.60	2.54	2.33	3.26	2.76
MASE	2.26	1.19	1.07	1.57	1.31

Table 7.4: Estimation results for Example 7.3.

[†] the parameter is restricted to $\phi \leq 0.98$. See text for more details.

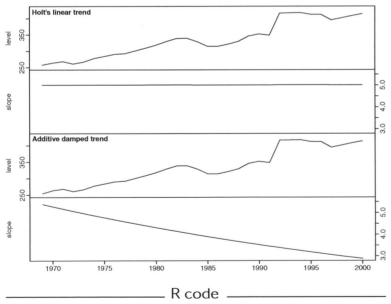

Figure 7.4: Level and slope components for Holt's linear trend method and the additive damped trend method.

──────── R code ────────

```
plot(fit2$model$state)
plot(fit4$model$state)
```

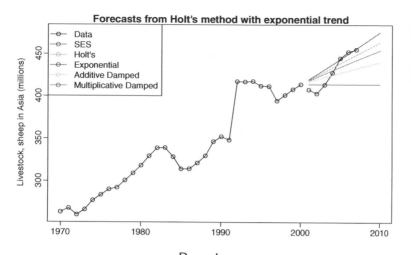

Figure 7.5: Forecasting livestock, sheep in Asia: comparing forecasting performance of non-seasonal methods.

```
──────────────── R code ────────────────
plot(fit3, type="o", ylab="Livestock, sheep in Asia (millions)",
   flwd=1, plot.conf=FALSE)
lines(window(livestock,start=2001),type="o")
lines(fit1$mean,col=2)
lines(fit2$mean,col=3)
lines(fit4$mean,col=5)
lines(fit5$mean,col=6)
legend("topleft", lty=1, pch=1, col=1:6,
   c("Data","SES","Holt's","Exponential",
      "Additive Damped","Multiplicative Damped"))
```

be zero, indicating that the trend is not changing over time. Of course, the trend estimated using the damped trend methods will change in the future due to the damping.

In Figure 7.4, we plot the level and trend components for Holt's method and for the additive damped trend method. The slope of the trend component for Holt's method is constant, showing that the trend is linear. In contrast, the slope of the trend component for the damped trend method is decreasing, showing that the trend is levelling off.

For the additive damped trend method, the damping parameter ϕ is restricted to a maximum of 0.98 (the estimation returned an optimal value of $\phi = 1$). This restriction is imposed to ensure that the additive damped trend method generates noticeably different forecasts from Holt's linear method, otherwise we get identical forecasts.

The SSE measures calculated over the training set show that Holt's linear trend method provides the best fit to the data followed by the additive damped trend method. Simple exponential smoothing generates the largest one-step training errors. In Figure 7.5 we can examine the forecasts generated by the methods. Pretending that we have not seen the data over the test-set we would conclude that all forecasts are quite plausible especially from the methods that account for the trend in the data.

Comparing the forecasting performance of the methods over the test set in Table 7.4, all measures show that the two damped methods forecast more accurately overall. The additive damped trend is the most accurate method according to the MAE and the MASE but the multiplicative damped trend method is most accurate according to RMSE and MAPE. Conflicting results like this are very common when performing forecasting competitions between methods. As forecasting tasks can vary by many dimensions (length of forecast horizon, size of test set, forecast error measures, frequency of data, etc.), it is unlikely that one method will be better than all others for all forecasting scenarios. What we require from a forecasting method are consistently sensible forecasts, and these should be frequently evaluated against the task at hand.

7/5   Holt-Winters seasonal method

Holt (1957) and Winters (1960) extended Holt's method to capture seasonality. The Holt-Winters seasonal method comprises the forecast equation and three smoothing equations — one for the level ℓ_t, one for trend b_t, and one for the seasonal component denoted by s_t, with smoothing parameters α, β^* and γ. We use m to denote the period of the seasonality, i.e., the number of seasons in a year. For example, for quarterly data $m = 4$, and for monthly data $m = 12$.

There are two variations to this method that differ in the nature of the seasonal component. The additive method is preferred when the seasonal variations are roughly constant through the series, while the multiplicative method is preferred when the seasonal variations are changing proportional to the level of the series. With the additive method, the seasonal component is expressed in absolute terms in the scale of the observed series, and in the level equation the series is seasonally adjusted by subtracting the seasonal component. Within each year the seasonal component will add up to approximately zero. With the multiplicative method, the seasonal component is expressed in relative terms (percentages) and the series is seasonally adjusted by dividing through by the seasonal component. Within each year, the seasonal component will sum up to approximately m.

Holt-Winters additive method

The component form for the additive method is:

$$\hat{y}_{t+h|t} = \ell_t + hb_t + s_{t-m+h_m^+}$$
$$\ell_t = \alpha(y_t - s_{t-m}) + (1-\alpha)(\ell_{t-1} + b_{t-1})$$
$$b_t = \beta^*(\ell_t - \ell_{t-1}) + (1-\beta^*)b_{t-1}$$
$$s_t = \gamma(y_t - \ell_{t-1} - h_{t-1}) + (1-\gamma)s_{t-m},$$

where $h_m^+ = \lfloor(h-1) \mod m\rfloor + 1$, which ensures that the estimates of the seasonal indices used for forecasting come from the final year of the sample. The level equation shows a weighted average between the seasonally adjusted observation $(y_t - s_{t-m})$ and the non-seasonal forecast $(\ell_{t-1} + b_{t-1})$ for time t. The trend equation is identical to Holt's linear method. The seasonal equation shows a weighted average between the current seasonal index, $(y_t - \ell_{t-1} - b_{t-1})$, and the seasonal index of the same season last year (i.e., m time periods ago).

The notation $\lfloor u \rfloor$ means the largest integer not greater than u.

The equation for the seasonal component is often expressed as

$$s_t = \gamma^*(y_t - \ell_t) + (1 - \gamma^*)s_{t-m}.$$

If we substitute ℓ_t from the smoothing equation for the level of the component form above, we get

$$s_t = \gamma^*(1-\alpha)(y_t - \ell_{t-1} - b_{t-1}) + [1 - \gamma^*(1-\alpha)]s_{t-m}$$

which is identical to the smoothing equation for the seasonal component we specify here with $\gamma = \gamma^*(1 - \alpha)$. The usual parameter restriction is $0 \le \gamma^* \le 1$, which translates to $0 \le \gamma \le 1 - \alpha$.

The error correction form of the smoothing equations is:

$$\ell_t = \ell_{t-1} + b_{t-1} + \alpha e_t$$
$$b_t = b_{t-1} + \alpha \beta^* e_t$$
$$s_t = s_{t-m} + \gamma e_t.$$

where $e_t = y_t - (\ell_{t-1} + b_{t-1} + s_{t-m}) = y_t - \hat{y}_{t|t-1}$ are the one-step training forecast errors.

Holt-Winters multiplicative method

The component form for the multiplicative method is:

$$\hat{y}_{t+h|t} = (\ell_t + hb_t)s_{t-m+h_m^+}.$$
$$\ell_t = \alpha \frac{y_t}{s_{t-m}} + (1 - \alpha)(\ell_{t-1} + b_{t-1})$$
$$b_t = \beta^*(\ell_t - \ell_{t-1}) + (1 - \beta^*)b_{t-1}$$
$$s_t = \gamma \frac{y_t}{(\ell_{t-1} + b_{t-1})} + (1 - \gamma)s_{t-m}$$

and the error correction representation is:

$$\ell_t = \ell_{t-1} + b_{t-1} + \alpha \frac{e_t}{s_{t-m}}$$
$$b_t = b_{t-1} + \alpha \beta^* \frac{e_t}{s_{t-m}}$$
$$s_t = s_t + \gamma \frac{e_t}{(\ell_{t-1} + b_{t-1})}$$

where $e_t = y_t - (\ell_{t-1} + b_{t-1})s_{t-m}.$

Example 7.4   International tourist visitor nights in Australia

In this example we employ the Holt-Winters method with both additive and multiplicative seasonality to forecast tourists visitor nights in Australia by international arrivals. Figure 7.6 shows the data alongside the one-step-ahead training forecasts over the sample period 2005Q1–2010Q4 and the forecasts for the period 2011Q1–2012Q4. The data show an obvious seasonal pattern with peaks observed in the March quarter of each year as this corresponds to the Australian summer.

The application of the method with additive and multiplicative seasonality are presented in Tables 7.5 and 7.6 respectively. The results show that the method with the multiplicative seasonality fits the data best. This was expected as the time plot shows the seasonal variation in the data increases as the level of the series increases. This is also reflected in the two sets of forecasts; the forecasts generated by the method with the multiplicative seasonality portray larger and increasing seasonal variation as the level of the forecasts increases compared to the forecasts generated by the method with additive seasonality.

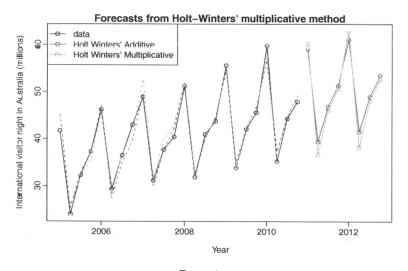

Figure 7.6: Forecasting international visitor nights in Australia using Holt-Winters method with both additive and multiplicative seasonality.

```
────────────── R code ──────────────
aust <- window(austourists,start=2005)
fit1 <- hw(aust,seasonal="additive")
fit2 <- hw(aust,seasonal="multiplicative")

plot(fit2,ylab="International visitor night in Australia (millions)",
    plot.conf=FALSE, type="o", fcol="white", xlab="Year")
lines(fitted(fit1), col="red", lty=2)
lines(fitted(fit2), col="green", lty=2)
lines(fit1$mean, type="o", col="red")
lines(fit2$mean, type="o", col="green")
legend("topleft",lty=1, pch=1, col=1:3,
  c("data","Holt Winters' Additive","Holt Winters' Multiplicative"))
```

Qtr-Year	t	y_t	ℓ_t	b_t	s_t	$\hat{y}_t$
2004 Q1	−3	−	−	−	10.7	−
2004 Q2	−2	−	−	−	−9.5	−
2004 Q3	−1	−	−	−	−2.6	−
2004 Q4	0		33.8	0.65	1.4	
2005 Q1	1	41.7	34.4	0.57	10.7	45.1
2005 Q2	2	24.0	34.9	0.53	−9.5	25.5
2005 Q3	3	32.3	35.4	0.52	−2.6	32.9
2005 Q4	4	37.3	35.9	0.52	1.4	37.3
2006 Q1	5	46.2	36.4	0.50	10.7	47.1
2006 Q2	6	29.3	37.0	0.54	−9.5	27.5
2006 Q3	7	36.5	37.6	0.58	−2.6	35.0
2006 Q4	8	43.0	38.2	0.66	1.4	39.5
2007 Q1	9	48.9	38.9	0.64	10.7	49.6
2007 Q2	10	31.2	39.6	0.67	−9.5	30.0
2007 Q3	11	37.7	40.2	0.67	−2.6	37.7
2007 Q4	12	40.4	40.9	0.63	1.4	42.3
2008 Q1	13	51.2	41.5	0.61	10.7	52.1
2008 Q2	14	31.9	42.0	0.59	−9.5	32.6
2008 Q3	15	41.0	42.7	0.61	−2.6	40.1
2008 Q4	16	43.8	43.2	0.59	1.4	44.7
2009 Q1	17	55.6	43.9	0.62	10.7	54.5
2009 Q2	18	33.9	44.4	0.59	−9.5	35.0
2009 Q3	19	42.1	45.0	0.58	−2.6	42.5
2009 Q4	20	45.6	45.6	0.55	1.4	47.0
2010 Q1	21	59.8	46.2	0.62	10.7	56.8
2010 Q2	22	35.2	46.8	0.57	−9.5	37.3
2010 Q3	23	44.3	47.3	0.56	−2.6	44.8
2010 Q4	24	47.9	47.8	0.53	1.4	49.3
	h					$y_{T+h|T}$
2011 Q1	1					59.0
2011 Q2	2					39.4
2011 Q3	3					46.9
2011 Q4	4					51.3
2012 Q1	5					61.1
2012 Q2	6					41.5
2012 Q3	7					49.0
2012 Q4	8					53.4

Table 7.5: Applying Holt-Winters method with additive seasonality for forecasting international visitor nights in Australia. Notice the additive seasonal component summing to approximately zero.

The smoothing parameters and initial estimates for the components have been estimated by minimizing SSE ($\alpha = 0.025$, $\beta^* = 0.023$, $\gamma = 0$ and SSE= 60.27, RMSE= 1.585).

Qtr-Year	t	y_t	ℓ_t	b_t	s_t	$\hat{y}_t$
2004 Q1	−3	−	−	−	1.3	−
2004 Q2	−2	−	−	−	0.8	−
2004 Q3	−1	−	−	−	0.9	−
2004 Q4	0		32.2	0.93	1.0	
2005 Q1	1	41.7	33.1	0.93	1.3	41.8
2005 Q2	2	24.0	32.9	0.78	0.8	25.9
2005 Q3	3	32.3	33.9	0.81	0.9	31.9
2005 Q4	4	37.3	35.4	0.91	1.0	35.7
2006 Q1	5	46.2	36.4	0.92	1.3	45.9
2006 Q2	6	29.3	37.9	1.00	0.8	28.4
2006 Q3	7	36.5	38.7	0.98	0.9	36.8
2006 Q4	8	43.0	40.6	1.11	1.0	40.8
2007 Q1	9	48.9	40.4	0.92	1.3	52.7
2007 Q2	10	31.2	41.2	0.90	0.8	31.5
2007 Q3	11	37.7	41.1	0.76	0.9	39.8
2007 Q4	12	40.4	40.8	0.60	1.0	43.0
2008 Q1	13	51.2	41.0	0.54	1.3	52.3
2008 Q2	14	31.9	41.7	0.57	0.8	31.6
2008 Q3	15	41.0	42.7	0.63	0.9	40.0
2008 Q4	16	43.8	43.0	0.58	1.0	44.6
2009 Q1	17	55.6	43.7	0.61	1.3	55.1
2009 Q2	18	33.9	44.4	0.61	0.8	33.8
2009 Q3	19	42.1	44.8	0.58	0.9	42.6
2009 Q4	20	45.6	44.9	0.52	1.0	46.6
2010 Q1	21	59.8	46.2	0.63	1.3	57.5
2010 Q2	22	35.2	46.6	0.59	0.8	35.7
2010 Q3	23	44.3	47.0	0.57	0.9	44.6
2010 Q4	24	47.9	47.2	0.51	1.0	48.9
	h					$y_{T+h|T}$
2011 Q1	1					60.3
2011 Q2	2					36.7
2011 Q3	3					46.1
2011 Q4	4					50.6
2012 Q1	5					62.8
2012 Q2	6					38.2
2012 Q3	7					48.0
2012 Q4	8					52.7

Table 7.6: Applying Holt-Winters method with multiplicative seasonality for forecasting international visitor nights (millions) in Australia. Notice the multiplicative seasonal component summing to approximately $m = 4$.

The smoothing parameters and initial estimates for the components have been estimated by minimizing SSE ($\alpha = 0$, $\beta^* = 0$ and $\gamma = 0$ and SSE= 34.6, RMSE= 1.201).

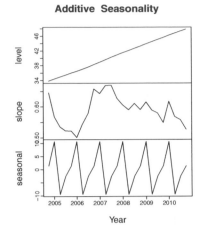
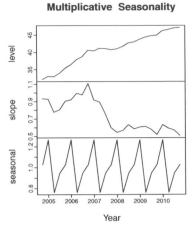

Figure 7.7: Estimated components for Holt-Winters method with additive and multiplicative seasonal components.

────────── R code ──────────

```
states <- cbind(fit1$model$states[,1:3],fit2$model$states[,1:3])
colnames(states) <- c("level","slope","seasonal","level","slope","seasonal")
plot(states, xlab="Year")
fit1$model$state[,1:3]
fitted(fit1)
fit1$mean
```

Holt-Winters damped method

A method that is often the single most accurate forecasting method for seasonal data is the Holt-Winters method with a damped trend and multiplicative seasonality:

$$\hat{y}_{t+h|t} = [\ell_t + (\phi + \phi^2 + \cdots + \phi^h)b_t]s_{t-m+h_m^+}.$$
$$\ell_t = \alpha(y_t/s_{t-m}) + (1-\alpha)(\ell_{t-1} + \phi b_{t-1})$$
$$b_t = \beta^*(\ell_t - \ell_{t-1}) + (1-\beta^*)\phi b_{t-1}$$
$$s_t = \gamma \frac{y_t}{(\ell_{t-1} + \phi b_{t-1})} + (1-\gamma)s_{t-m}$$

────────── R code ──────────

```
hw(x, damped=TRUE, seasonal="multiplicative")
```

7/6 A taxonomy of exponential smoothing methods

Exponential smoothing methods are not restricted to those we have presented so far. By considering variations in the combination of the trend and seasonal components, fifteen exponential smoothing methods are possible, listed in Table 7.7. Each method is labelled by a pair of letters (T,S) defining the type of 'Trend' and 'Seasonal' components. For example, (A,M) is the method with an additive trend and multiplicative seasonality; (M,N) is the method with multiplicative trend and no seasonality; and so on.

Trend Component	Seasonal Component		
	N (None)	A (Additive)	M (Multiplicative)
N (None)	(N,N)	(N,A)	(N,M)
A (Additive)	(A,N)	(A,A)	(A,M)
A_d (Additive damped)	(A_d,N)	(A_d,A)	(A_d,M)
M (Multiplicative)	(M,N)	(M,A)	(M,M)
M_d (Multiplicative damped)	(M_d,N)	(M_d,A)	(M_d,M)

Table 7.7: A two way classification of exponential smoothing methods.

Some of these methods we have already seen:

(N,N)	= simple exponential smoothing
(A,N)	= Holt's linear method
(M,N)	= Exponential trend method
(A_d,N)	= additive damped trend method
(M_d,N)	= multiplicative damped trend method
(A,A)	= additive Holt-Winters method
(A,M)	= multiplicative Holt-Winters method
(A_d,M)	= Holt-Winters damped method

This type of classification was proposed by Pegels (1969). It was later extended by Gardner (1985) to include methods with additive damped trend and by Taylor (2003) to include methods with multiplicative damped trend.

Table 7.8 gives the recursive formulae for applying all possible fifteen exponential smoothing methods. Each cell includes the forecast equation for generating h-step-ahead forecasts and the smoothing equations for applying the method. In Table 7.9

Trend	Seasonal		
	N	A	M
N	$\hat{y}_{t+h\|t} = \ell_t$ $\ell_t = \alpha y_t + (1-\alpha)\ell_{t-1}$	$\hat{y}_{t+h\|t} = \ell_t + s_{t-m+h_m^+}$ $\ell_t = \alpha(y_t - s_{t-m}) + (1-\alpha)\ell_{t-1}$ $s_t = \gamma(y_t - \ell_{t-1}) + (1-\gamma)s_{t-m}$	$\hat{y}_{t+h\|t} = \ell_t s_{t-m+h_m^+}$ $\ell_t = \alpha(y_t/s_{t-m}) + (1-\alpha)\ell_{t-1}$ $s_t = \gamma(y_t/\ell_{t-1}) + (1-\gamma)s_{t-m}$
A	$\hat{y}_{t+h\|t} = \ell_t + hb_t$ $\ell_t = \alpha y_t + (1-\alpha)(\ell_{t-1}+b_{t-1})$ $b_t = \beta^*(\ell_t - \ell_{t-1}) + (1-\beta^*)b_{t-1}$	$\hat{y}_{t+h\|t} = \ell_t + hb_t + s_{t-m+h_m^+}$ $\ell_t = \alpha(y_t - s_{t-m}) + (1-\alpha)(\ell_{t-1}+b_{t-1})$ $b_t = \beta^*(\ell_t - \ell_{t-1}) + (1-\beta^*)b_{t-1}$ $s_t = \gamma(y_t - \ell_{t-1} - b_{t-1}) + (1-\gamma)s_{t-m}$	$\hat{y}_{t+h\|t} = (\ell_t + hb_t)s_{t-m+h_m^+}$ $\ell_t = \alpha(y_t/s_{t-m}) + (1-\alpha)(\ell_{t-1}+b_{t-1})$ $b_t = \beta^*(\ell_t - \ell_{t-1}) + (1-\beta^*)b_{t-1}$ $s_t = \gamma(y_t/(\ell_{t-1}+b_{t-1})) + (1-\gamma)s_{t-m}$
A_d	$\hat{y}_{t+h\|t} = \ell_t + \phi_h b_t$ $\ell_t = \alpha y_t + (1-\alpha)(\ell_{t-1}+\phi b_{t-1})$ $b_t = \beta^*(\ell_t - \ell_{t-1}) + (1-\beta^*)\phi b_{t-1}$	$\hat{y}_{t+h\|t} = \ell_t + \phi_h b_t + s_{t-m+h_m^+}$ $\ell_t = \alpha(y_t - s_{t-m}) + (1-\alpha)(\ell_{t-1}+\phi b_{t-1})$ $b_t = \beta^*(\ell_t - \ell_{t-1}) + (1-\beta^*)\phi b_{t-1}$ $s_t = \gamma(y_t - \ell_{t-1} - \phi b_{t-1}) + (1-\gamma)s_{t-m}$	$\hat{y}_{t+h\|t} = (\ell_t + \phi_h b_t)s_{t-m+h_m^+}$ $\ell_t = \alpha(y_t/s_{t-m}) + (1-\alpha)(\ell_{t-1}+\phi b_{t-1})$ $b_t = \beta^*(\ell_t - \ell_{t-1}) + (1-\beta^*)\phi b_{t-1}$ $s_t = \gamma(y_t/(\ell_{t-1}+\phi b_{t-1})) + (1-\gamma)s_{t-m}$
M	$\hat{y}_{t+h\|t} = \ell_t b_t^h$ $\ell_t = \alpha y_t + (1-\alpha)\ell_{t-1}b_{t-1}$ $b_t = \beta^*(\ell_t/\ell_{t-1}) + (1-\beta^*)b_{t-1}$	$\hat{y}_{t+h\|t} = \ell_t b_t^h + s_{t-m+h_m^+}$ $\ell_t = \alpha(y_t - s_{t-m}) + (1-\alpha)\ell_{t-1}b_{t-1}$ $b_t = \beta^*(\ell_t/\ell_{t-1}) + (1-\beta^*)b_{t-1}$ $s_t = \gamma(y_t - \ell_{t-1}b_{t-1}) + (1-\gamma)s_{t-m}$	$\hat{y}_{t+h\|t} = \ell_t b_t^h s_{t-m+h_m^+}$ $\ell_t = \alpha(y_t/s_{t-m}) + (1-\alpha)\ell_{t-1}b_{t-1}$ $b_t = \beta^*(\ell_t/\ell_{t-1}) + (1-\beta^*)b_{t-1}$ $s_t = \gamma(y_t/(\ell_{t-1}b_{t-1})) + (1-\gamma)s_{t-m}$
M_d	$\hat{y}_{t+h\|t} = \ell_t b_t^{\phi_h}$ $\ell_t = \alpha y_t + (1-\alpha)\ell_{t-1}b_{t-1}^\phi$ $b_t = \beta^*(\ell_t/\ell_{t-1}) + (1-\beta^*)b_{t-1}^\phi$	$\hat{y}_{t+h\|t} = \ell_t b_t^{\phi_h} + s_{t-m+h_m^+}$ $\ell_t = \alpha(y_t - s_{t-m}) + (1-\alpha)\ell_{t-1}b_{t-1}^\phi$ $b_t = \beta^*(\ell_t/\ell_{t-1}) + (1-\beta^*)b_{t-1}^\phi$ $s_t = \gamma(y_t - \ell_{t-1}b_{t-1}^\phi) + (1-\gamma)s_{t-m}$	$\hat{y}_{t+h\|t} = \ell_t b_t^{\phi_h} s_{t-m+h_m^+}$ $\ell_t = \alpha(y_t/s_{t-m}) + (1-\alpha)\ell_{t-1}b_{t-1}^\phi$ $b_t = \beta^*(\ell_t/\ell_{t-1}) + (1-\beta^*)b_{t-1}^\phi$ $s_t = \gamma(y_t/(\ell_{t-1}b_{t-1}^\phi)) + (1-\gamma)s_{t-m}$

Table 7.8: Formulae for recursive calculations and point forecasts. In each case, ℓ_t denotes the series level at time t, b_t denotes the slope at time t, s_t denotes the seasonal component of the series at time t, and m denotes the number of seasons in a year; α, β^*, γ and ϕ are smoothing parameters, $\phi_h = \phi + \phi^2 + \cdots + \phi^h$ and $h_m^+ = \lfloor (h-1) \bmod m \rfloor + 1$.

Method	Initial values
(N,N)	$\ell_0 = y_1$
(A,N) (A_d,N)	$\ell_0 = y_1,\ b_0 = y_2 - y_1$
(M,N) (M_d,N)	$\ell_0 = y_1,\ b_0 = y_2/y_1$
(A,A) (A_d,A)	$\ell_0 = \frac{1}{m}(y_1 + \cdots + y_m)$ $b_0 = \frac{1}{m}\left[\frac{y_{m+1}-y_1}{m} + \cdots + \frac{y_{m+m}-y_m}{m}\right]$ $s_0 = y_m - \ell_0,\ s_{-1} = y_{m-1} - \ell_0,\ \ldots,\ s_{-m+1} = y_1 - \ell_0$
(A,M) (A_d,M)	$\ell_0 = \frac{1}{m}(y_1 + \cdots + y_m)$ $b_0 = \frac{1}{m}\left[\frac{y_{m+1}-y_1}{m} + \cdots + \frac{y_{m+m}-y_m}{m}\right]$ $s_0 = y_m/\ell_0,\ s_{-1} = y_{m-1}/\ell_0,\ \ldots,\ s_{-m+1} = y_1/\ell_0$

Table 7.9: Initialisation strategies for some of the more commonly used exponential smoothing methods.

we present some strategies for selecting initial values for some of the most commonly applied exponential smoothing methods. We do not recommend that these strategies be used directly; rather, they are useful in providing starting values for the optimization process.

7/7   Innovations state space models for exponential smoothing

In the rest of this chapter we study statistical models that underlie the exponential smoothing methods we have considered so far. The exponential smoothing methods presented in Table 7.8 are algorithms that generate point forecasts. The statistical models in this section generate the same point forecasts, but can also generate prediction (or forecast) intervals. A statistical model is a stochastic (or random) data generating process that can produce an entire forecast distribution. The general statistical framework we will introduce also provides a platform for using the model selection criteria introduced in Chapter 5, thus allowing the choice of model to be made in an objective manner.

Each model consists of a measurement equation that describes the observed data and some transition equations that describe how the unobserved components or states (level, trend, seasonal) change over time. Hence these are referred to as "state space models".

For each method there exist two models: one with additive errors and one with multiplicative errors. The point forecasts produced by the models are identical if they use the same smoothing parameter values. They will, however, generate different prediction intervals.

To distinguish between a model with additive errors and one with multiplicative errors (and to also distinguish the models from the methods) we add a third letter to the classification of Table 7.7. We label each state space model as ETS$(\cdot,\cdot,\cdot)$ for (Error, Trend, Seasonal). This label can also be thought of as ExponenTial Smoothing. Using the same notation as in Table 7.7, the possibilities for each component are: Error = $\{A, M\}$, Trend = $\{N, A, A_d, M, M_d\}$ and Seasonal = $\{N, A, M\}$. Therefore, in total there exist 30 such state space models: 15 with additive errors and 15 with multiplicative errors.

ETS(A,N,N): simple exponential smoothing with additive errors

As discussed in Section 7/1, the error correction form of simple exponential smoothing is given by

$$\ell_t = \ell_{t-1} + \alpha e_t,$$

where $e_t = y_t - \ell_{t-1}$ and $\hat{y}_{t|t-1} = \ell_{t-1}$. Thus, $e_t = y_t - \hat{y}_{t|t-1}$ represents a one-step forecast error and we can write $y_t = \ell_{t-1} + e_t$.

To make this into an innovations state space model, all we need to do is specify the probability distribution for e_t. For a model with additive errors, we assume that one-step forecast errors e_t are normally distributed white noise with mean 0 and variance σ^2. A short-hand notation for this is $e_t = \varepsilon_t \sim \text{NID}(0, \sigma^2)$; NID stands for "normally and independently distributed".

Then the equations of the model can be written

$$y_t = \ell_{t-1} + \varepsilon_t \tag{7.4}$$
$$\ell_t = \ell_{t-1} + \alpha \varepsilon_t. \tag{7.5}$$

We refer to (7.4) as the *measurement* (or observation) equation and (7.5) as the *state* (or transition) equation. These two equations, together with the statistical distribution of the errors, form a fully specified statistical model. Specifically, these constitute an innovations state space model underlying simple exponential smoothing.

The term "innovations" comes from the fact that all equations in this type of specification use the same random error process, ε_t. For the same reason this formulation is also referred to as a "single source of error" model in contrast to alternative multiple source of error formulations, which we do not present here.

The measurement equation shows the relationship between the observations and the unobserved states. In this case observation y_t is a linear function of the level ℓ_{t-1}, the predictable part of y_t, and the random error ε_t, the unpredictable part of y_t. For other innovations state space models, this relationship may be nonlinear.

The transition equation shows the evolution of the state through time. The influence of the smoothing parameter α is the same as for the methods discussed earlier. For example α governs the degree of change in successive levels. The higher the value of α, the more rapid the changes in the level; the lower the value of α, the smoother the changes. At the lowest extreme, where $\alpha = 0$, the level of the series does not change over time. At the other extreme, where $\alpha = 1$, the model reduces to a random walk model, $y_t = y_{t-1} + \varepsilon_t$.

ETS(M,N,N): simple exponential smoothing with multiplicative errors

In a similar fashion, we can specify models with multiplicative errors by writing the one-step random errors as relative errors:

$$\varepsilon_t = \frac{y_t - \hat{y}_{t|t-1}}{\hat{y}_{t|t-1}}$$

where $\varepsilon_t \sim \text{NID}(0, \sigma^2)$. Substituting $\hat{y}_{t|t-1} = \ell_{t-1}$ gives $y_t = \ell_{t-1} + \ell_{t-1}\varepsilon_t$ and $e_t = y_t - \hat{y}_{t|t-1} = \ell_{t-1}\varepsilon_t$.

Then we can write the multiplicative form of the state space model as

$$y_t = \ell_{t-1}(1 + \varepsilon_t)$$
$$\ell_t = \ell_{t-1}(1 + \alpha\varepsilon_t).$$

ETS(A,A,N): Holt's linear method with additive errors

For this model, we assume that one-step forecast errors are given by $\varepsilon_t = y_t - \ell_{t-1} - b_{t-1} \sim \text{NID}(0, \sigma^2)$. Substituting this into the error correction equations for Holt's linear method we obtain

$$y_t = \ell_{t-1} + b_{t-1} + \varepsilon_t$$
$$\ell_t = \ell_{t-1} + b_{t-1} + \alpha\varepsilon_t$$
$$b_t = b_{t-1} + \beta\varepsilon_t,$$

where for simplicity we have set $\beta = \alpha\beta^*$.

ETS(M,A,N): Holt's linear method with multiplicative errors

Specifying one-step forecast errors as relative errors such that

$$\varepsilon_t = \frac{y_t - (\ell_{t-1} + b_{t-1})}{(\ell_{t-1} + b_{t-1})}$$

and following a similar approach as above, the innovations state space model underlying Holt's linear method with multiplicative errors is specified as

$$y_t = (\ell_{t-1} + b_{t-1})(1 + \varepsilon_t)$$
$$\ell_t = (\ell_{t-1} + b_{t-1})(1 + \alpha\varepsilon_t)$$
$$b_t = b_{t-1} + \beta(\ell_{t-1} + b_{t-1})\varepsilon_t$$

where again $\beta = \alpha\beta^*$ and $\varepsilon_t \sim \text{NID}(0, \sigma^2)$.

Other ETS models

In a similar fashion, we can write an innovations state space model for each of the exponential smoothing methods of Table 7.8. Table 7.10 presents the equations for all of the models in the ETS framework.

Estimating ETS models

An alternative to estimating the parameters by minimizing the sum of squared errors, is to maximize the "likelihood". The likelihood is the probability of the data arising from the specified model. So a large likelihood is associated with a good model. For an additive error model, maximizing the likelihood gives the same results as minimizing the sum of squared errors. However, different results will be obtained for multiplicative error models. In this section, we will estimate the smoothing parameters α, β, γ and ϕ, and the initial states ℓ_0, b_0, $s_0, s_{-1}, \ldots, s_{-m+1}$, by maximizing the likelihood.

The possible values that the smoothing parameters can take is restricted. Traditionally the parameters have been constrained to lie between 0 and 1 so that the equations can be interpreted as weighted averages. That is, $0 < \alpha, \beta^*, \gamma^*, \phi < 1$. For the state space models, we have set $\beta = \alpha\beta^*$ and $\gamma = (1 - \alpha)\gamma^*$. Therefore the traditional restrictions translate to $0 < \alpha < 1$, $0 < \beta < \alpha$ and $0 < \gamma < 1 - \alpha$. In practice, the damping parameter ϕ is usually constrained further to prevent numerical difficulties in estimating the model. A common constraint is to set $0.8 < \phi < 0.98$.

Another way to view the parameters is through a consideration of the mathematical properties of the state space models. Then the parameters are constrained to prevent observations in

ADDITIVE ERROR MODELS

Trend	Seasonal		
	N	**A**	**M**
N	$y_t = \ell_{t-1} + \varepsilon_t$ $\ell_t = \ell_{t-1} + \alpha\varepsilon_t$	$y_t = \ell_{t-1} + s_{t-m} + \varepsilon_t$ $\ell_t = \ell_{t-1} + \alpha\varepsilon_t$ $s_t = s_{t-m} + \gamma\varepsilon_t$	$y_t = \ell_{t-1}s_{t-m} + \varepsilon_t$ $\ell_t = \ell_{t-1} + \alpha\varepsilon_t/s_{t-m}$ $s_t = s_{t-m} + \gamma\varepsilon_t/\ell_{t-1}$
A	$y_t = \ell_{t-1} + b_{t-1} + \varepsilon_t$ $\ell_t = \ell_{t-1} + b_{t-1} + \alpha\varepsilon_t$ $b_t = b_{t-1} + \beta\varepsilon_t$	$y_t = \ell_{t-1} + b_{t-1} + s_{t-m} + \varepsilon_t$ $\ell_t = \ell_{t-1} + b_{t-1} + \alpha\varepsilon_t$ $b_t = b_{t-1} + \beta\varepsilon_t$ $s_t = s_{t-m} + \gamma\varepsilon_t$	$y_t = (\ell_{t-1} + b_{t-1})s_{t-m} + \varepsilon_t$ $\ell_t = \ell_{t-1} + b_{t-1} + \alpha\varepsilon_t/s_{t-m}$ $b_t = b_{t-1} + \beta\varepsilon_t/s_{t-m}$ $s_t = s_{t-m} + \gamma\varepsilon_t/(\ell_{t-1} + b_{t-1})$
A$_d$	$y_t = \ell_{t-1} + \phi b_{t-1} + \varepsilon_t$ $\ell_t = \ell_{t-1} + \phi b_{t-1} + \alpha\varepsilon_t$ $b_t = \phi b_{t-1} + \beta\varepsilon_t$	$y_t = \ell_{t-1} + \phi b_{t-1} + s_{t-m} + \varepsilon_t$ $\ell_t = \ell_{t-1} + \phi b_{t-1} + \alpha\varepsilon_t$ $b_t = \phi b_{t-1} + \beta\varepsilon_t$ $s_t = s_{t-m} + \gamma\varepsilon_t$	$y_t = (\ell_{t-1} + \phi b_{t-1})s_{t-m} + \varepsilon_t$ $\ell_t = \ell_{t-1} + \phi b_{t-1} + \alpha\varepsilon_t/s_{t-m}$ $b_t = \phi b_{t-1} + \beta\varepsilon_t/s_{t-m}$ $s_t = s_{t-m} + \gamma\varepsilon_t/(\ell_{t-1} + \phi b_{t-1})$
M	$y_t = \ell_{t-1}b_{t-1} + \varepsilon_t$ $\ell_t = \ell_{t-1}b_{t-1} + \alpha\varepsilon_t$ $b_t = b_{t-1} + \beta\varepsilon_t/\ell_{t-1}$	$y_t = \ell_{t-1}b_{t-1} + s_{t-m} + \varepsilon_t$ $\ell_t = \ell_{t-1}b_{t-1} + \alpha\varepsilon_t$ $b_t = b_{t-1} + \beta\varepsilon_t/\ell_{t-1}$ $s_t = s_{t-m} + \gamma\varepsilon_t$	$y_t = \ell_{t-1}b_{t-1}s_{t-m} + \varepsilon_t$ $\ell_t = \ell_{t-1}b_{t-1} + \alpha\varepsilon_t/s_{t-m}$ $b_t = b_{t-1} + \beta\varepsilon_t/(s_{t-m}\ell_{t-1})$ $s_t = s_{t-m} + \gamma\varepsilon_t/(\ell_{t-1}b_{t-1})$
M$_d$	$y_t = \ell_{t-1}b_{t-1}^{\phi} + \varepsilon_t$ $\ell_t = \ell_{t-1}b_{t-1}^{\phi} + \alpha\varepsilon_t$ $b_t = b_{t-1}^{\phi} + \beta\varepsilon_t/\ell_{t-1}$	$y_t = \ell_{t-1}b_{t-1}^{\phi} + s_{t-m} + \varepsilon_t$ $\ell_t = \ell_{t-1}b_{t-1}^{\phi} + \alpha\varepsilon_t$ $b_t = b_{t-1}^{\phi} + \beta\varepsilon_t/\ell_{t-1}$ $s_t = s_{t-m} + \gamma\varepsilon_t$	$y_t = \ell_{t-1}b_{t-1}^{\phi}s_{t-m} + \varepsilon_t$ $\ell_t = \ell_{t-1}b_{t-1}^{\phi} + \alpha\varepsilon_t/s_{t-m}$ $b_t = b_{t-1}^{\phi} + \beta\varepsilon_t/(s_{t-m}\ell_{t-1})$ $s_t = s_{t-m} + \gamma\varepsilon_t/(\ell_{t-1}b_{t-1}^{\phi})$

MULTIPLICATIVE ERROR MODELS

Trend	Seasonal		
	N	**A**	**M**
N	$y_t = \ell_{t-1}(1 + \varepsilon_t)$ $\ell_t = \ell_{t-1}(1 + \alpha\varepsilon_t)$	$y_t = (\ell_{t-1} + s_{t-m})(1 + \varepsilon_t)$ $\ell_t = \ell_{t-1} + \alpha(\ell_{t-1} + s_{t-m})\varepsilon_t$ $s_t = s_{t-m} + \gamma(\ell_{t-1} + s_{t-m})\varepsilon_t$	$y_t = \ell_{t-1}s_{t-m}(1 + \varepsilon_t)$ $\ell_t = \ell_{t-1}(1 + \alpha\varepsilon_t)$ $s_t = s_{t-m}(1 + \gamma\varepsilon_t)$
A	$y_t = (\ell_{t-1} + b_{t-1})(1 + \varepsilon_t)$ $\ell_t = (\ell_{t-1} + b_{t-1})(1 + \alpha\varepsilon_t)$ $b_t = b_{t-1} + \beta(\ell_{t-1} + b_{t-1})\varepsilon_t$	$y_t = (\ell_{t-1} + b_{t-1} + s_{t-m})(1 + \varepsilon_t)$ $\ell_t = \ell_{t-1} + b_{t-1} + \alpha(\ell_{t-1} + b_{t-1} + s_{t-m})\varepsilon_t$ $b_t = b_{t-1} + \beta(\ell_{t-1} + b_{t-1} + s_{t-m})\varepsilon_t$ $s_t = s_{t-m} + \gamma(\ell_{t-1} + b_{t-1} + s_{t-m})\varepsilon_t$	$y_t = (\ell_{t-1} + b_{t-1})s_{t-m}(1 + \varepsilon_t)$ $\ell_t = (\ell_{t-1} + b_{t-1})(1 + \alpha\varepsilon_t)$ $b_t = b_{t-1} + \beta(\ell_{t-1} + b_{t-1})\varepsilon_t$ $s_t = s_{t-m}(1 + \gamma\varepsilon_t)$
A$_d$	$y_t = (\ell_{t-1} + \phi b_{t-1})(1 + \varepsilon_t)$ $\ell_t = (\ell_{t-1} + \phi b_{t-1})(1 + \alpha\varepsilon_t)$ $b_t = \phi b_{t-1} + \beta(\ell_{t-1} + \phi b_{t-1})\varepsilon_t$	$y_t = (\ell_{t-1} + \phi b_{t-1} + s_{t-m})(1 + \varepsilon_t)$ $\ell_t = \ell_{t-1} + \phi b_{t-1} + \alpha(\ell_{t-1} + \phi b_{t-1} + s_{t-m})\varepsilon_t$ $b_t = \phi b_{t-1} + \beta(\ell_{t-1} + \phi b_{t-1} + s_{t-m})\varepsilon_t$ $s_t = s_{t-m} + \gamma(\ell_{t-1} + \phi b_{t-1} + s_{t-m})\varepsilon_t$	$y_t = (\ell_{t-1} + \phi b_{t-1})s_{t-m}(1 + \varepsilon_t)$ $\ell_t = (\ell_{t-1} + \phi b_{t-1})(1 + \alpha\varepsilon_t)$ $b_t = \phi b_{t-1} + \beta(\ell_{t-1} + \phi b_{t-1})\varepsilon_t$ $s_t = s_{t-m}(1 + \gamma\varepsilon_t)$
M	$y_t = \ell_{t-1}b_{t-1}(1 + \varepsilon_t)$ $\ell_t = \ell_{t-1}b_{t-1}(1 + \alpha\varepsilon_t)$ $b_t = b_{t-1}(1 + \beta\varepsilon_t)$	$y_t = (\ell_{t-1}b_{t-1} + s_{t-m})(1 + \varepsilon_t)$ $\ell_t = \ell_{t-1}b_{t-1} + \alpha(\ell_{t-1}b_{t-1} + s_{t-m})\varepsilon_t$ $b_t = b_{t-1} + \beta(\ell_{t-1}b_{t-1} + s_{t-m})\varepsilon_t/\ell_{t-1}$ $s_t = s_{t-m} + \gamma(\ell_{t-1}b_{t-1} + s_{t-m})\varepsilon_t$	$y_t = \ell_{t-1}b_{t-1}s_{t-m}(1 + \varepsilon_t)$ $\ell_t = \ell_{t-1}b_{t-1}(1 + \alpha\varepsilon_t)$ $b_t = b_{t-1}(1 + \beta\varepsilon_t)$ $s_t = s_{t-m}(1 + \gamma\varepsilon_t)$
M$_d$	$y_t = \ell_{t-1}b_{t-1}^{\phi}(1 + \varepsilon_t)$ $\ell_t = \ell_{t-1}b_{t-1}^{\phi}(1 + \alpha\varepsilon_t)$ $b_t = b_{t-1}^{\phi}(1 + \beta\varepsilon_t)$	$y_t = (\ell_{t-1}b_{t-1}^{\phi} + s_{t-m})(1 + \varepsilon_t)$ $\ell_t = \ell_{t-1}b_{t-1}^{\phi} + \alpha(\ell_{t-1}b_{t-1}^{\phi} + s_{t-m})\varepsilon_t$ $b_t = b_{t-1}^{\phi} + \beta(\ell_{t-1}b_{t-1}^{\phi} + s_{t-m})\varepsilon_t/\ell_{t-1}$ $s_t = s_{t-m} + \gamma(\ell_{t-1}b_{t-1}^{\phi} + s_{t-m})\varepsilon_t$	$y_t = \ell_{t-1}b_{t-1}^{\phi}s_{t-m}(1 + \varepsilon_t)$ $\ell_t = \ell_{t-1}b_{t-1}^{\phi}(1 + \alpha\varepsilon_t)$ $b_t = b_{t-1}^{\phi}(1 + \beta\varepsilon_t)$ $s_t = s_{t-m}(1 + \gamma\varepsilon_t)$

Table 7.10: State space equations for each of the models in the ETS framework.

the distant past having a continuing effect on current forecasts. This leads to some *admissibility* constraints on the parameters which are usually (but not always) less restrictive than the usual region. For example for the ETS(A,N,N) model, the usual parameter region is $0 < \alpha < 1$ but the admissible region is $0 < \alpha < 2$. For the ETS(A,A,N) model, the usual parameter region is $0 < \alpha < 1$ and $0 < \beta < \alpha$ but the admissible region is $0 < \alpha < 2$ and $0 < \beta < 4 - 2\alpha$.

Model selection

A great advantage of the ETS statistical framework is that information criteria can be used for model selection. The AIC, AIC_c and BIC, introduced in Section 5/3, can be used here to determine which of the 30 ETS models is most appropriate for a given time series.

For ETS models, Akaike's Information Criterion (AIC) is defined as

$$\text{AIC} = -2\log(L) + 2k,$$

where L is the likelihood of the model and k is the total number of parameters and initial states that have been estimated.

The AIC corrected for small sample bias (AIC_c) is defined as

$$\text{AIC}_c = \text{AIC} + \frac{2(k+1)(k+2)}{T-k},$$

and the Bayesian Information Criterion (BIC) is

$$\text{BIC} = \text{AIC} + k[\log(T) - 2].$$

Some of the combinations of (Error, Trend, Seasonal) can lead to numerical difficulties. Specifically, the models that can cause such instabilities are: ETS(M,M,A), ETS(M,M$_d$,A), ETS(A,N,M), ETS(A,A,M), ETS(A,A$_d$,M), ETS(A,M,N), ETS(A,M,A), ETS(A,M,M), ETS(A,M$_d$,N), ETS(A,M$_d$,A), and ETS(A,M$_d$,M). We normally do not consider these particular combinations when selecting a model.

Models with multiplicative errors are useful when the data are strictly positive, but are not numerically stable when the data contain zeros or negative values. Therefore multiplicative errors models will not be considered if the time series is not strictly positive. In that case only the six fully additive models will be applied.

The ets() function in R

The models can be estimated in R using the ets() function in the forecast package. The R code below shows all the possible arguments this function takes, and their default values. If only the time series is specified, and all other arguments are left at their default values, then an appropriate model will be selected automatically. We explain each of the arguments below.

—————————————— R code ——————————————

```
ets(y, model="ZZZ", damped=NULL, alpha=NULL, beta=NULL,
    gamma=NULL, phi=NULL, additive.only=FALSE, lambda=NULL,
    lower=c(rep(0.0001,3), 0.8), upper=c(rep(0.9999,3),0.98),
    opt.crit=c("lik","amse","mse","sigma","mae"), nmse=3,
    bounds=c("both","usual","admissible"),
    ic=c("aicc","aic","bic"), restrict=TRUE)
```

y

   The time series to be forecast.

model

   A three-letter code indicating the model to be estimated using the ETS classification and notation. The possible inputs are "N" for none, "A" for additive, "M" for multiplicative, or "Z" for automatic selection. If any of the inputs is left as "Z" then this component is selected according to the information criterion chosen. The default value of ZZZ ensures that all components are selected using the information criterion.

damped

   If damped=TRUE, then a damped trend will be used (either A_d or M_d). If damped=FALSE, then a non-damped trend will used. If damped=NULL (the default), then either a damped or a non-damped trend will be selected according to the information criterion chosen.

alpha, beta, gamma, phi

   The values of the smoothing parameters can be specified using these arguments. If they are set to NULL (the default setting for each of them), the parameters are estimated.

additive.only

   Only models with additive components will be considered if additive.only=TRUE. Otherwise all models will be considered.

lambda

   Box-Cox transformation parameter. It will be ignored if

lambda=NULL (the default value). Otherwise, the time series will be transformed before the model is estimated. When lambda is not NULL, additive.only is set to TRUE.

lower, upper

Lower and upper bounds for the parameter estimates α, β^*, γ^* and ϕ.

opt.crit

The optimization criterion to be used for estimation. The default setting is maximum likelihood estimation, used when opt.crit=lik.

bounds

This specifies the constraints to be used on the parameters. The traditional constraints are set using bounds="usual" and the admissible constraints are set using bounds="admissible". The default (bounds="both") requires the parameters to satisfy both sets of constraints.

ic

The information criterion to be used in selecting models, set by default to aicc.

restrict

If restrict=TRUE (the default), the models that cause numerical difficulties are not considered in model selection.

Forecasting with ETS models

Point forecasts are obtained from the models by iterating the equations for $t = T + 1, \ldots, T + h$ and setting all $\varepsilon_t = 0$ for $t > T$.

For example, for model ETS(M,A,N), $y_{T+1} = (\ell_T + b_T)(1 + \varepsilon_{T+1})$. Therefore $\hat{y}_{T+1|T} = \ell_T + b_T$. Similarly,

$$y_{T+2} = (\ell_{T+1} + b_{T+1})(1 + \varepsilon_{T+1})$$
$$= [(\ell_T + b_T)(1 + \alpha \varepsilon_{T+1}) + b_T + \beta(\ell_T + b_T)\varepsilon_{T+1}](1 + \varepsilon_{T+1}).$$

Therefore, $\hat{y}_{T+2|T} = \ell_T + 2b_T$, and so on. These forecasts are identical to the forecasts from Holt's linear method and also those from model ETS(A,A,N). So the point forecasts obtained from the method and from the two models that underlie the method are identical (assuming the same parameter values are used).

A big advantage of the models is that prediction intervals can also be generated — something that cannot be done using the

methods. The prediction intervals will differ between models
with additive and multiplicative methods.

For some models, there are exact formulae that enable prediction intervals to be calculated. A more general approach that
works for all models is to simulate future sample paths, condi-
tional on the last estimate of the states, and to obtain prediction
intervals from the percentiles of these simulated future paths.
These options are available in R using the forecast function
in the forecast package. The R code below shows the all the
possible arguments this function takes when applied to an ETS
model. We explain each the arguments in what follows.

—————————————— R code ——————————————
```
forecast(object, h=ifelse(object$m>1, 2*object$m, 10),
    level=c(80,95), fan=FALSE, simulate=FALSE, bootstrap=FALSE,
    npaths=5000, PI=TRUE, lambda=object$lambda, ...)
```

object
    The object returned by the ets() function.
h
    The forecast horizon — the number of periods to be forecast.
level
    The confidence level for the prediction intervals.
fan
    If fan=TRUE, level=seq(50,99,by=1). This is suitable for
    fan plots.
simulate
    If simulate=TRUE, prediction intervals are produced by simu-
    lation rather than using algebraic formulae. Simulation will
    also be used (even if simulate=FALSE) where there are no
    algebraic formulae available for the particular model.
bootstrap
    If bootstrap=TRUE and simulate=TRUE, then the simulated
    prediction intervals use re-sampled errors rather than nor-
    mally distributed errors.
npaths
    The number of sample paths used in computing simulated
    prediction intervals.
PI
    If PI=TRUE, then prediction intervals are produced; otherwise
    only point forecasts are calculated. If PI=FALSE, then level,
    fan, simulate, bootstrap and npaths are all ignored.

lambda
The Box-Cox transformation parameter. This is ignored if
lambda=NULL. Otherwise, forecasts are back-transformed via
an inverse Box-Cox transformation.

Example 7.1   Oil production example (revisited)

Figure 7.8 shows the point forecasts and prediction intervals
from an estimated ETS(A,N,N) model. The estimates for the
smoothing parameter α and the initial level ℓ_0 are 0.89 and
447.49 respectively, identical to the estimates for the simple
exponential smoothing method estimated earlier (see beginning
of Example 7.1). The plot shows the importance of generating
prediction intervals. The intervals here are relatively wide, so
interpreting the point forecasts without accounting for the large
uncertainty can be very misleading.

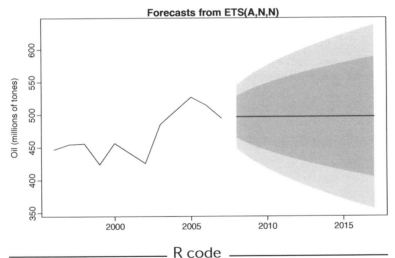

Figure 7.8: Point forecasts and 80% and 95% prediction intervals from model ETS(A,N,N).

──────────────── R code ────────────────

```
oildata <- window(oil,start=1996,end=2007)
fit <- ets(oildata, model="ANN")
plot(forecast(fit, h=3), ylab="Oil (millions of tones)")
fit$par
```

──────────────── R output ────────────────

```
alpha        l
0.892 447.489
```

Example 7.4   International tourist visitor nights in Australia (revisited)

We now employ the ETS statistical framework to forecast tourists visitor nights in Australia by international arrivals over the period 2011–2012. We let the ets() function select the model by minimizing the AICc.

———————————— R code ————————————
```
vndata <- window(austourists, start=2005)
fit <- ets(vndata)
summary(fit)
```

———————————— R output ————————————
```
ETS(M,A,M)

Call:
 ets(y = vndata)

  Smoothing parameters:
    alpha = 0.4504
    beta  = 4e-04
    gamma = 0.0046

  Initial states:
    l = 32.4349
    b = 0.6533
    s=1.0275 0.9463 0.7613 1.2648

  sigma:  0.0332

   AIC    AICc    BIC
 105.972 115.572 115.397

Training set error measures:
                   ME     RMSE     MAE       MPE     MAPE     MASE       ACF1
Training set -0.081646 1.33328 1.0647 -0.221243 2.65469 0.374361 -0.089119
```

The model selected is ETS(M,A,M):

$$y_t = (\ell_{t-1} + b_{t-1})s_{t-m}(1 + \varepsilon_t)$$
$$\ell_t = (\ell_{t-1} + b_{t-1})(1 + \alpha\varepsilon_t)$$
$$b_t = b_{t-1} + \beta(\ell_{t-1} + b_{t_1})\varepsilon_t$$
$$s_t = s_{t-m}(1 + \gamma\varepsilon_t).$$

The parameter estimates are $\alpha = 0.4504$, $\beta = 0.0004$, and $\gamma = 0.0046$. The output returns the estimates for the initial states ℓ_0, b_0, s_0, s_{-1}, s_{-2} and s_{-3}. The training RMSE for this model is slightly lower than the Holt-Winter methods with additive and multiplicative seasonality presented in Tables 7.5 and 7.6 respectively. Figure 7.9 shows the states over time while Figure 7.10 shows point forecasts and prediction intervals generated from the model. The intervals are much narrower than the prediction intervals in the oil production example.

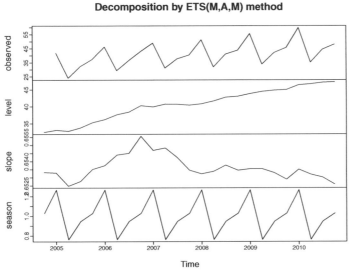

Figure 7.9: Graphical representation of the estimated states over time.

──────────── R code ────────────

```
plot(fit)
```

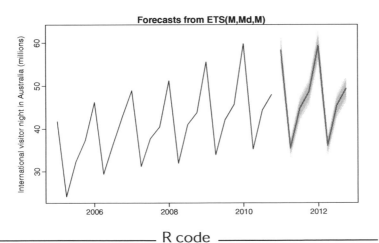

Figure 7.10: Forecasting international visitor nights in Australia from an ETS(M,M$_d$,M) model.

──────────── R code ────────────

```
plot(forecast(fit,h=8),
    ylab="International visitor night in Australia (millions)")
```

7/8   Exercises

7.1 Data set books contains the daily sales of paperback and hardcover books at the same store. The task is to forecast the next four days' sales for paperback and hardcover books (data set books).

(a) Plot the series and discuss the main features of the data.

(b) Use simple exponential smoothing with the ses function (setting initial="simple") and explore different values of α for the paperback series. Record the within-sample SSE for the one-step forecasts. Plot SSE against α and find which value of α works best. What is the effect of α on the forecasts?

(c) Now let ses select the optimal value of α. Use this value to generate forecasts for the next four days. Compare your results with (b).

(d) Repeat but with initial="optimal". How much difference does an optimal initial level make?

(e) Repeat steps (b)–(d) with the hardcover series.

7.2 (a) Apply Holt's linear method to the paperback and hardback series and compute four-day forecasts in each case.

(b) Compare the SSE measures of Holt's method for the two series to those of simple exponential smoothing in the previous question. Discuss the merits of the two forecasting methods for these data sets.

(c) Compare the forecasts for the two series using both methods. Which do you think is best?

(d) Calculate a 95% prediction interval for the first forecast for each series using both methods, assuming normal errors. Compare your forecasts with those produced by R.

7.3 For this exercise, use the price of a dozen eggs in the United States from 1900–1993 (data set eggs). Experiment with the various options in the holt() function to see how much the forecasts change with damped or exponential trend. Also try changing the parameter values for α and β to see how they affect the forecasts. Try to develop an intuition of what each parameter and argument is doing to the forecasts.

[Hint: use h=100 when calling holt() so you can clearly see the differences between the various options when plotting the forecasts.]

Which model gives the best RMSE?

7.4 For this exercise, use the quarterly UK passenger vehicle production data from 1997:1–2005:1 (data set ukcars).

(a) Plot the data and describe the main features of the series.

(b) Decompose the series using STL and obtain the seasonally adjusted data.

(c) Forecast the next two years of the series using an additive damped trend method applied to the seasonally adjusted data. Then reseasonalize the forecasts. Record the parameters of the method and report the RMSE of the one-step forecasts from your method.

(d) Forecast the next two years of the series using Holt's linear method applied to the seasonally adjusted data. Then reseasonalize the forecasts. Record the parameters of the method and report the RMSE of of the one-step forecasts from your method.

(e) Now use ets() to choose a seasonal model for the data.

(f) Compare the RMSE of the fitted model with the RMSE of the model you obtained using an STL decomposition with Holt's method. Which gives the better in-sample fits?

(g) Compare the forecasts from the two approaches? Which seems most reasonable?

7.5 For this exercise, use the monthly Australian short-term overseas visitors data, May 1985–April 2005. (Data set: visitors.)

(a) Make a time plot of your data and describe the main features of the series.

(b) Forecast the next two years using Holt-Winters' multiplicative method.

(c) Why is multiplicative seasonality necessary here?

(d) Experiment with making the trend exponential and/or damped.

(e) Compare the RMSE of the one-step forecasts from the various methods. Which do you prefer?

(f) Now fit each of the following models to the same data:

   (i) a multiplicative Holt-Winters' method;

   (ii) an ETS model;

   (iii) an additive ETS model applied to a Box-Cox transformed series;

   (iv) a seasonal naive method applied to the Box-Cox transformed series;

   (v) an STL decomposition applied to the Box-Cox transformed data followed by an ETS model applied to the seasonally adjusted (transformed) data.

(g) For each model, look at the residual diagnostics and compare the forecasts for the next two years. Which do you prefer?

7/9   Further reading

- Gardner Jr, E. S. (1985). Exponential smoothing: The state of the art. *Journal of Forecasting* **4**(1), 1–28.

- Gardner Jr, E. S. (2006). Exponential smoothing: The state of the art—Part II. *International Journal of Forecasting* **22**(4), 637–666.

- Hyndman, R. J., A. B. Koehler, J. K. Ord and R. D. Snyder (2008). *Forecasting with exponential smoothing: the state space approach.* Berlin: Springer-Verlag.

8
ARIMA models

ARIMA models provide another approach to time series forecasting. Exponential smoothing and ARIMA models are the
two most widely-used approaches to time series forecasting,
and provide complementary approaches to the problem. While
exponential smoothing models were based on a description
of trend and seasonality in the data, ARIMA models aim to
describe the autocorrelations in the data.

Before we introduce ARIMA models, we need to first discuss
the concept of stationarity and the technique of differencing
time series.

8/1 Stationarity and differencing

**A stationary time series is one whose properties do not de-
pend on the time at which the series is observed.**[1] So time
series with trends, or with seasonality, are not stationary — the
trend and seasonality will affect the value of the time series
at different times. On the other hand, a white noise series is
stationary — it does not matter when you observe it, it should
look much the same at any period of time.

Some cases can be confusing — a time series with cyclic behaviour (but with no trend or seasonality) is stationary. That is
because the cycles are not of fixed length. So before we observe
the series we cannot be sure where the peaks and troughs of the
cycles will be.

In general, a stationary time series will have no predictable
patterns in the long-term. Time plots will show the series to be

[1] More precisely, if $\{y_t\}$
is a *stationary* time
series, then for all s,
the distribution of
$(y_t, \ldots, y_{t+s})$ does not
depend on t.

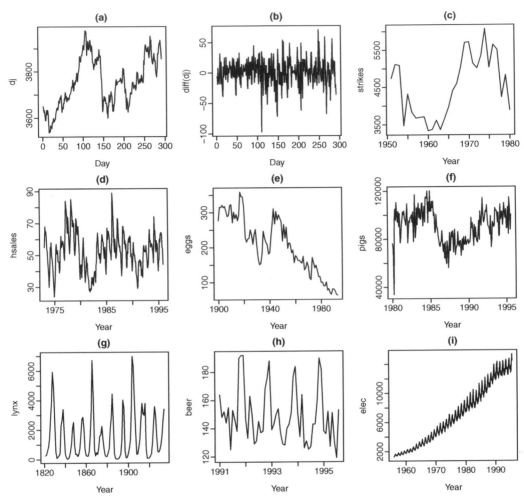

Figure 8.1: Which of these series are stationary? (a) Dow Jones index on 292 consecutive days; (b) Daily change in Dow Jones index on 292 consecutive days; (c) Annual number of strikes in the US; (d) Monthly sales of new one-family houses sold in the US; (e) Annual price of a dozen eggs in the US (constant dollars); (f) Monthly total of pigs slaughtered in Victoria, Australia; (g) Annual total of lynx trapped in the McKenzie River district of north-west Canada; (h) Monthly Australian beer production; (i) Monthly Australian electricity production.

roughly horizontal (although some cyclic behaviour is possible) with constant variance.

Consider the nine series plotted in Figure 8.1. Which of these do you think are stationary?

Obvious seasonality rules out series (d), (h) and (i). Trend rules out series (a), (c), (e), (f) and (i). Increasing variance also rules out (f). That leaves only (b) and (g) as stationary series.

At first glance, the strong cycles in series (g) might appear to make it non-stationary. But these cycles are aperiodic — they are caused when the lynx population becomes too large for the available feed, so they stop breeding and the population falls to very low numbers, then the regeneration of their food sources allows the population to grow again, and so on. In the long-term, the timing of these cycles is not predictable. Hence the series is stationary.

Differencing

In Figure 8.1, notice how the Dow Jones index data was non-stationary in panel (a), but the daily changes were stationary in panel (b). This shows one way to make a time series stationary — compute the differences between consecutive observations. This is known as **differencing**.

Transformations such as logarithms can help to stabilize the variance of a time series. Differencing can help stabilize the mean of a time series by removing changes in the level of a time series, and so eliminating (or reducing) trend and seasonality.

As well as looking at the time plot of the data, the ACF plot is also useful for identifying non-stationary time series. For a stationary time series, the ACF will drop to zero relatively quickly, while the ACF of non-stationary data decreases slowly. Also, for non-stationary data, the value of r_1 is often large and positive.

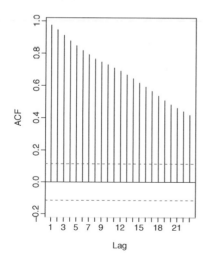
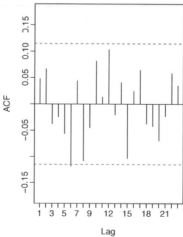

Figure 8.2: The ACF of the Dow-Jones index (left) and of the daily changes in the Dow-Jones index (right).

The ACF of the differenced Dow-Jones index looks just like that from a white noise series. There is only one autocorrelation lying just outside the 95% limits, and the Ljung-Box Q^* statistic has a p-value of 0.153 (for $h = 10$). This suggests that the *daily change* in the Dow-Jones index is essentially a random amount uncorrelated with previous days.

Random walk model

The differenced series is the *change* between consecutive observations in the original series, and can be written as

$$y'_t = y_t - y_{t-1}.$$

The differenced series will have only $T - 1$ values since it is not possible to calculate a difference y'_1 for the first observation.

When the differenced series is white noise, the model for the original series can be written as

$$y_t - y_{t-1} = e_t \quad \text{or} \quad y_t = y_{t-1} + e_t.$$

A random walk model is very widely used for non-stationary data, particularly finance and economic data. Random walks typically have:

- long periods of apparent trends up or down
- sudden and unpredictable changes in direction.

The forecasts from a random walk model are equal to the last observation, as future movements are unpredictable, and are equally likely to be up or down. Thus, the random walk model underpins naïve forecasts.

A closely related model allows the differences to have a non-zero mean. Then

$$y_t - y_{t-1} = c + e_t \quad \text{or} \quad y_t = c + y_{t-1} + e_t.$$

The value of c is the average of the changes between consecutive observations. If c is positive, then the average change is an increase in the value of y_t. Thus y_t will tend to drift upwards. But if c is negative, y_t will tend to drift downwards.

This is the model behind the drift method discussed in Section 2/3.

Second-order differencing

Occasionally the differenced data will not appear stationary and it may be necessary to difference the data a second time to obtain a stationary series:

$$
\begin{aligned}
y_t'' &= y_t' - y_{t-1}' \\
&= (y_t - y_{t-1}) - (y_{t-1} - y_{t-2}) \\
&= y_t - 2y_{t-1} + y_{t-2}.
\end{aligned}
$$

In this case, y_t'' will have $T - 2$ values. Then we would model the "change in the changes" of the original data. In practice, it is almost never necessary to go beyond second-order differences.

Seasonal differencing

A seasonal difference is the difference between an observation and the corresponding observation from the previous year. So

$$y_t' = y_t - y_{t-m} \qquad \text{where } m = \text{number of seasons.}$$

These are also called "lag-m differences" as we subtract the observation after a lag of m periods.

If seasonally differenced data appear to be white noise, then an appropriate model for the original data is

$$y_t = y_{t-m} + e_t.$$

Forecasts from this model are equal to the last observation from the relevant season. That is, this model gives seasonal naïve forecasts.

Figure 8.3 shows the seasonal differences of the logarithm of the monthly scripts for A10 (antidiabetic) drugs sold in Australia. The transformation and differencing has made the series look relatively stationary.

To distinguish seasonal differences from ordinary differences, we sometimes refer to ordinary differences as "first differences" meaning differences at lag 1.

Sometimes it is necessary to do both a seasonal difference and a first difference to obtain stationary data, as shown in Figure 8.4. Here, the data are first transformed using logarithms (second panel). Then seasonal differenced are calculated (third panel). The data still seem a little non-stationary, and so a further lot of first differences are computed (bottom panel).

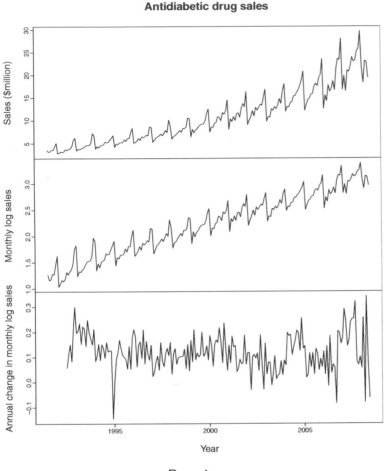

Figure 8.3: Logs and seasonal differences of the A10 (antidiabetic) sales data. The logarithms stabilize the variance, while the seasonal differences remove the seasonality and trend.

─────────── R code ───────────

```
plot(a10, xlab="Year", ylab="Sales ($million)",
  main="Antidiabetic drug sales")
plot(log(a10), xlab="Year", ylab="Monthly log sales")
plot(diff(log(a10),12), xlab="Year",
  ylab="Annual change in monthly log sales")
```

There is a degree of subjectivity in selecting what differences to apply. The seasonally differenced data in Figure 8.3 do not show substantially different behaviour from the seasonally differenced data in Figure 8.4. In the latter case, we may have decided to stop with the seasonally differenced data, and not done an extra round of differencing. In the former case, we may have decided the data were not sufficiently stationary and taken an extra round of differencing. Some formal tests

Monthly US net electricity generation

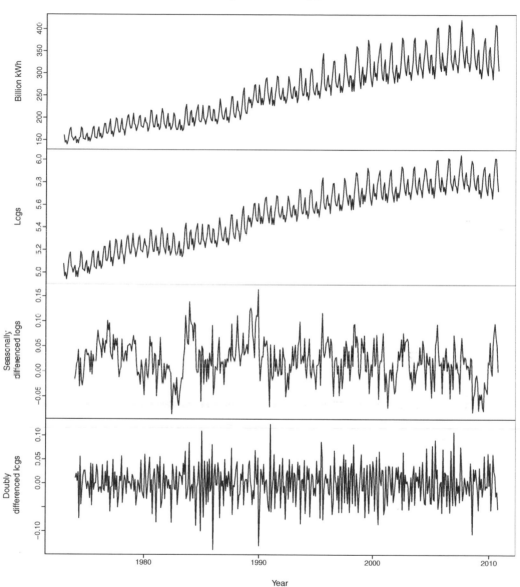

Figure 8.4: Top panel: US net electricity generation (billion kWh). Other panels show the same data after transforming and differencing.

for differencing will be discussed later, but there are always some choices to be made in the modeling process, and different analysts may make different choices.

If $y_t' = y_t - y_{t-m}$ denotes a seasonally differenced series, then the twice-differenced series is

$$
\begin{aligned}
y_t'' &= y_t' - y_{t-1}' \\
&= (y_t - y_{t-m}) - (y_{t-1} - y_{t-m-1}) \\
&= y_t - y_{t-1} - y_{t-m} + y_{t-m-1}.
\end{aligned}
$$

When both seasonal and first differences are applied, it makes no difference which is done first—the result will be the same. However, if the data have a strong seasonal pattern, we recommend that seasonal differencing be done first because sometimes the resulting series will be stationary and there will be no need for a further first difference. If first differencing is done first, there will still be seasonality present.

It is important that if differencing is used, the differences are interpretable. First differences are the change between **one observation and the next**. Seasonal differences are the change between **one year to the next**. Other lags are unlikely to make much interpretable sense and should be avoided.

Unit root tests

One way to determine more objectively if differencing is required is to use a *unit root test*. These are statistical hypothesis tests of stationarity that are designed for determining whether differencing is required.

A number of unit root tests are available, and they are based on different assumptions and may lead to conflicting answers.

One of the most popular tests is the *Augmented Dickey-Fuller (ADF) test*. For this test, the following regression model is estimated:

$$
y_t' = \phi y_{t-1} + \beta_1 y_{t-1}' + \beta_2 y_{t-2}' + \cdots + \beta_k y_{t-k}',
$$

where y_t' denotes the first-differenced series, $y_t' = y_t - y_{t-1}$ and k is the number of lags to include in the regression (often set to be about 3). If the original series, y_t, needs differencing, then the coefficient $\hat{\phi}$ should be approximately zero. If y_t is already stationary, then $\hat{\phi} < 0$. The usual hypothesis tests for regression coefficients do not work when the data are non-stationary, but the test can be carried out using the following R command.

```
———————————————— R code ————————————————
adf.test(x, alternative = "stationary")
```

In R, the default value of k is set to $\lfloor T - 1 \rfloor^{1/3}$ where T is the length of the time series and $\lfloor T - 1 \rfloor$ means the largest integer not greater than $T - 1$.

The null-hypothesis for an ADF test is that the data are non-stationary. So large p-values are indicative of non-stationarity, and small p-values suggest stationarity. Using the usual 5% threshold, differencing is required if the p-value is greater than 0.05.

Another popular unit root test is the *Kwiatkowski-Phillips Schmidt-Shin (KPSS) test*. This reverses the hypotheses, so the null-hypothesis is that the data are stationary. In this case, small p-values (e.g., less than 0.05) suggest that differencing is required.

```
———————————————— R code ————————————————
kpss.test(x)
```

A useful R function is ndiffs() which uses these tests to determine the appropriate number of first differences required for a non-seasonal time series.

More complicated tests are required for seasonal differencing and are beyond the scope of this book. A useful R function for determining whether seasonal differencing is required is nsdiffs() which uses seasonal unit root tests to determine the appropriate number of seasonal differences required.

The following code can be used to find how to make a seasonal series stationary. The resulting series stored as xstar has been differenced appropriately.

────────────────── R code ──────────────────

```
ns <- nsdiffs(x)
if(ns > 0) {
  xstar <- diff(x,lag=frequency(x),differences=ns)
} else {
  xstar <- x
}
nd <- ndiffs(xstar)
if(nd > 0) {
  xstar <- diff(xstar,differences=nd)
}
```

8/2   Backshift notation

The backward shift operator B is a useful notational device when working with time series lags:

$$By_t = y_{t-1}.$$

(Some references use L for "lag" instead of B for "backshift".) In other words, B, operating on y_t, has the effect of **shifting the data back one period**. Two applications of B to y_t **shifts the data back two periods**:

$$B(By_t) = B^2 y_t = y_{t-2}.$$

For monthly data, if we wish to consider "the same month last year," the notation is $B^{12} y_t = y_{t-12}$.

The backward shift operator is convenient for describing the process of *differencing*. A first difference can be written as

$$y_t' = y_t - y_{t-1} = y_t - By_t = (1 - B)y_t.$$

Note that a first difference is represented by $(1 - B)$. Similarly, if second-order differences have to be computed, then:

$$y_t'' = y_t - 2y_{t-1} + y_{t-2} = (1 - 2B + B^2)y_t = (1 - B)^2 y_t.$$

In general, a dth-order difference can be written as

$$(1 - B)^d y_t.$$

Backshift notation is very useful when combining differences as the operator can be treated using ordinary algebraic rules. In particular, terms involving B can be multiplied together.

For example, a seasonal difference followed by a first difference can be written as

$$(1 - B)(1 - B^m)y_t = (1 - B - B^m + B^{m+1})y_t$$
$$= y_t - y_{t-1} - y_{t-m} + y_{t-m-1},$$

the same result we obtained earlier.

8/3   Autoregressive models

In a multiple regression model, we forecast the variable of interest using a linear combination of predictors. In an autoregression model, we forecast the variable of interest using a linear combination of *past values of the variable*. The term *auto*regression indicates that it is a regression of the variable against itself.

Thus an autoregressive model of order p can be written as

$$y_t = c + \phi_1 y_{t-1} + \phi_2 y_{t-2} + \cdots + \phi_p y_{t-p} + e_t,$$

where e_t is white noise. This is like a multiple regression but with *lagged values* of y_t as predictors. We refer to this as an **AR(p) model**.

Autoregressive models are remarkably flexible at handling a wide range of different time series patterns. The two series in Figure 8.5 show series from an AR(1) model and an AR(2) model. Changing the parameters $\phi_1, \ldots, \phi_p$ results in different time series patterns. The variance of the error term e_t will only change the scale of the series, not the patterns.

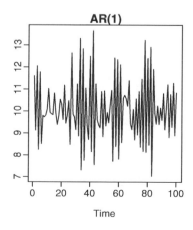
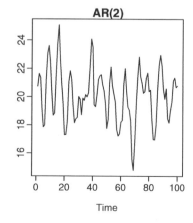

Figure 8.5: Two examples of data from autoregressive models with different parameters.

Left: AR(1) with $y_t = 18 - 0.8y_{t-1} + e_t$.

Right: AR(2) with $y_t = 8 + 1.3y_{t-1} - 0.7y_{t-2} + e_t$.

In both cases, e_t is normally distributed white noise with mean zero and variance one.

For an AR(1) model:

- when $\phi_1 = 0$, y_t is equivalent to white noise;
- when $\phi_1 = 1$ and $c = 0$, y_t is equivalent to a random walk;
- when $\phi_1 = 1$ and $c \neq 0$, y_t is equivalent to a random walk with drift;
- when $\phi_1 < 0$, y_t tends to oscillate between positive and negative values.

We normally restrict autoregressive models to stationary data, and then some constraints on the values of the parameters are required.

- For an AR(1) model: $-1 < \phi_1 < 1$.
- For an AR(2) model: $-1 < \phi_2 < 1$, $\phi_1 + \phi_2 < 1$, $\phi_2 - \phi_1 < 1$.

When $p \geq 3$ the restrictions are much more complicated. R takes care of these restrictions when estimating a model.

8/4   Moving average models

Rather than use past values of the forecast variable in a regression, a moving average model uses past forecast errors in a regression-like model.

$$y_t = c + e_t + \theta_1 e_{t-1} + \theta_2 e_{t-2} + \cdots + \theta_q e_{t-q},$$

where e_t is white noise. We refer to this as an **MA(q) model**. Of course, we do not *observe* the values of e_t, so it is not really regression in the usual sense.

Notice that each value of y_t can be thought of as a weighted moving average of the past few forecast errors. However, moving average *models* should not be confused with moving average *smoothing* we discussed in Chapter 6. A moving average model is used for forecasting future values while moving average smoothing is used for estimating the trend-cycle of past values.

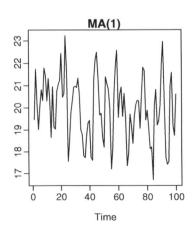

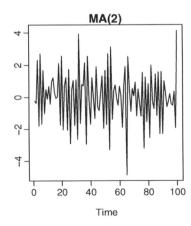

Figure 8.6: Two examples of data from moving average models with different parameters.

Left: MA(1) with $y_t = 20 + e_t + 0.8e_{t-1}$.

Right: MA(2) with $y_t = e_t - e_{t-1} + 0.8e_{t-2}$.

In both cases, e_t is normally distributed white noise with mean zero and variance one.

Figure 8.6 shows some data from an MA(1) model and an MA(2) model. Changing the parameters $\theta_1,\ldots,\theta_q$ results in different time series patterns. As with autoregressive models, the variance of the error term e_t will only change the scale of the series, not the patterns.

It is possible to write any stationary AR(p) model as an MA(∞) model. For example, using repeated substitution, we can demonstrate this for an AR(1) model:

$$
\begin{aligned}
y_t &= \phi_1 y_{t-1} + e_t \\
&= \phi_1(\phi_1 y_{t-2} + e_{t-1}) + e_t \\
&= \phi_1^2 y_{t-2} + \phi_1 e_{t-1} + e_t \\
&= \phi_1^3 y_{t-3} + \phi_1^2 e_{t-2} + \phi_1 e_{t-1} + e_t
\end{aligned}
$$

etc.

Provided $-1 < \phi_1 < 1$, the value of ϕ_1^k will get smaller as k gets larger. So eventually we obtain

$$
y_t = e_t + \phi_1 e_{t-1} + \phi_1^2 e_{t-2} + \phi_1^3 e_{t-3} + \cdots,
$$

an MA(∞) process.

The reverse result holds if we impose some constraints on the MA parameters. Then the MA model is called "invertible". That is, that we can write any invertible MA(q) process as an AR(∞) process.

Invertible models are not simply to enable us to convert from MA models to AR models. They also have some mathematical properties that make them easier to use in practice.

The invertibility constraints are similar to the stationarity constraints.

- For an MA(1) model: $-1 < \theta_1 < 1$.
- For an MA(2) model: $-1 < \theta_2 < 1$, $\theta_2 + \theta_1 > -1$, $\theta_1 - \theta_2 < 1$.

More complicated conditions hold for $q \geq 3$. Again, R will take care of these constraints when estimating the models.

8/5   Non-seasonal ARIMA models

If we combine differencing with autoregression and a moving average model, we obtain a non-seasonal ARIMA model. ARIMA is an acronym for AutoRegressive Integrated Moving

Average model ("integration" in this context is the reverse of differencing). The full model can be written as

$$y'_t = c + \phi_1 y'_{t-1} + \cdots + \phi_p y'_{t-p} + \theta_1 e_{t-1} + \cdots + \theta_q e_{t-q} + e_t, \quad (8.1)$$

where y'_t is the differenced series (it may have been differenced more than once). The "predictors" on the right hand side include both lagged values of y_t and lagged errors. We call this an **ARIMA(p,d,q) model**, where

> p = order of the autoregressive part;
> d = degree of first differencing involved;
> q = order of the moving average part.

The same stationarity and invertibility conditions that are used for autoregressive and moving average models apply to this ARIMA model.

Once we start combining components in this way to form more complicated models, it is much easier to work with the backshift notation. Then equation (8.1) can be written as

$$\underbrace{(1 - \phi_1 B - \cdots - \phi_p B^p)}_{\text{AR}(p)} \quad \underbrace{(1 - B)^d y_t}_{d \text{ differences}} = c + \underbrace{(1 + \theta_1 B + \cdots + \theta_q B^q)e_t}_{\text{MA}(q)}$$

$$\begin{array}{ccc} \uparrow & \uparrow & \uparrow \\ \text{AR}(p) & d \text{ differences} & \text{MA}(q) \end{array}$$

Selecting appropriate values for p, d and q can be difficult. The auto.arima() function in R will do it for you automatically. Later in this chapter, we will learn how the function works, and some methods for choosing these values yourself.

Many of the models we have already discussed are special cases of the ARIMA model as shown in the following table.

White noise	ARIMA(0,0,0)
Random walk	ARIMA(0,1,0) with no constant
Random walk with drift	ARIMA(0,1,0) with a constant
Autoregression	ARIMA(p,0,0)
Moving average	ARIMA(0,0,q)

Example 8.1   US personal consumption

Figure 8.7 shows quarterly percentage changes in US consumption expenditure. Although it is quarterly data, there appears to be no seasonal pattern, so we will fit a non-seasonal ARIMA model.

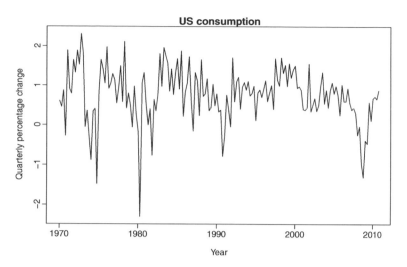

Figure 8.7: Quarterly percentage change in US consumption expenditure.

The following R code was used to automatically select a model.

```
_____ R output _____
> fit <- auto.arima(usconsumption[,1], seasonal=FALSE)

ARIMA(0,0,3) with non-zero mean
Coefficients:
         ma1      ma2      ma3   intercept
       0.2542   0.2260   0.2695    0.7562
s.e.   0.0767   0.0779   0.0692    0.0844

sigma^2 estimated as 0.3856:   log likelihood=-154.73
AIC=319.46    AICc=319.84    BIC=334.96
```

This is an ARIMA(0,0,3) or MA(3) model:

$$y_t = 0.756 + e_t + 0.254e_{t-1} + 0.226e_{t-2} + 0.269e_{t-3},$$

where e_t is white noise with standard deviation $0.62 = \sqrt{0.3856}$. Forecasts from the model are shown in Figure 8.8.

Understanding ARIMA models

The auto.arima() function is very useful, but anything automated can be a little dangerous, and it is worth understanding something of the behaviour of the models even when you rely on an automatic procedure to choose the model for you.

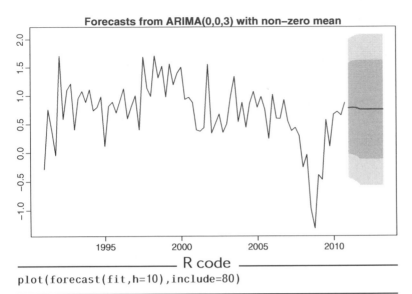

──────────── R code ────────────

```
plot(forecast(fit,h=10),include=80)
```

The constant c has an important effect on the long-term forecasts obtained from these models.

- If $c = 0$ and $d = 0$, the long-term forecasts will go to zero.
- If $c = 0$ and $d = 1$, the long-term forecasts will go to a non-zero constant.
- If $c = 0$ and $d = 2$, the long-term forecasts will follow a straight line.
- If $c \neq 0$ and $d = 0$, the long-term forecasts will go to the mean of the data.
- If $c \neq 0$ and $d = 1$, the long-term forecasts will follow a straight line.
- If $c \neq 0$ and $d = 2$, the long-term forecasts will follow a quadratic trend.

The value of d also has an effect on the prediction intervals — the higher the value of d, the more rapidly the prediction intervals increase in size. For $d = 0$, the long-term forecast standard deviation will go to the standard deviation of the historical data, so the prediction intervals will all be essentially the same.

This behaviour is seen in Figure 8.8 where $d = 0$ and $c \neq 0$. In this figure, the prediction intervals are the same for the last few forecast horizons, and the point forecasts are equal to the mean of the data.

The value of p is important if the data show cycles. To obtain cyclic forecasts, it is necessary to have $p \geq 2$ along with some additional conditions on the parameters. For an AR(2) model, cyclic behaviour occurs if $\phi_1^2 + 4\phi_2 < 0$. In that case, the average period of the cycles is[2]

$$\frac{2\pi}{\arccos(-\phi_1(1 - \phi_2)/(4\phi_2))}.$$

[2] arc cos is the inverse cosine function. You should be able to find it on your calculator. It may be labelled acos or $\cos^{-1}$.

ACF and PACF plots

It is usually not possible to tell, simply from a time plot, what values of p and q are appropriate for the data. However, it is sometimes possible to use the ACF plot, and the closely related PACF plot, to determine appropriate values for p and q.

Recall that an ACF plot shows the autocorrelations which measure the relationship between y_t and y_{t-k} for different values of k. Now if y_t and y_{t-1} are correlated, then y_{t-1} and y_{t-2} must also be correlated. But then y_t and y_{t-2} might be correlated, simply because they are both connected to y_{t-1}, rather than because of any new information contained in y_{t-2} that could be used in forecasting y_t.

To overcome this problem, we can use **partial autocorrelations**. These measure the relationship between y_t and y_{t-k} after removing the effects of other time lags — $1, 2, 3, \ldots, k-1$. So the first partial autocorrelation is identical to the first autocorrelation, because there is nothing between them to remove. The partial autocorrelations for lags 2, 3 and greater are calculated as follows:

$\alpha_k = k$th partial autocorrelation coefficient

= the estimate of ϕ_k in the autoregression model

$$y_t = c + \phi_1 y_{t-1} + \phi_2 y_{t-2} + \cdots + \phi_k y_{t-k} + e_t.$$

Varying the number of terms on the right hand side of this autoregression model gives α_k for different values of k. (In practice, there are more efficient algorithms for computing α_k than fitting all these autoregressions, but they give the same results.)

Figure 8.9 shows the ACF and PACF plots for the US consumption data shown in Figure 8.7.

The partial autocorrelations have the same critical values of $\pm 1.96/\sqrt{T}$ as for ordinary autocorrelations, and these are typically shown on the plot as in Figure 8.9.

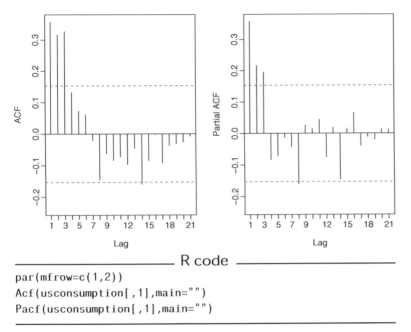

Figure 8.9: ACF and PACF of quarterly percentage change in US consumption.

A convenient way to produce a time plot, ACF plot and PACF plot in one command is to use the tsdisplay function in R.

———————— R code ————————

```
par(mfrow=c(1,2))
Acf(usconsumption[,1],main="")
Pacf(usconsumption[,1],main="")
```

If the data are from an ARIMA($p,d,0$) or ARIMA($0,d,q$) model, then the ACF and PACF plots can be helpful in determining the value of p or q. If both p and q are positive, then the plots do not help in finding suitable values of p and q.

The data may follow an ARIMA($p,d,0$) model if the ACF and PACF plots of the differenced data show the following patterns:

• the ACF is exponentially decaying or sinusoidal;
• there is a significant spike at lag p in PACF, but none beyond lag p.

The data may follow an ARIMA($0,d,q$) model if the ACF and PACF plots of the differenced data show the following patterns:

• the PACF is exponentially decaying or sinusoidal;
• there is a significant spike at lag q in ACF, but none beyond lag q.

In Figure 8.9, we see that there are three spikes in the ACF and then no significant spikes thereafter (apart from one just outside the bounds at lag 14). In the PACF, there are three spikes decreasing with the lag, and then no significant spikes thereafter (apart from one just outside the bounds at lag 8). We can ignore one significant spike in each plot if it is just outside the limits, and not in the first few lags. After all, the probability of a spike being significant by chance is about one in twenty, and we are plotting 21 spikes in each plot. The pattern in the first three spikes is what we would expect from an ARIMA(0,0,3) as the PACF tends to decay exponentially. So in this case, the ACF and PACF lead us to the same model as was obtained using the automatic procedure.

8/6   Estimation and order selection

Maximum likelihood estimation

Once the model order has been identified (i.e., the values of p, d and q), we need to estimate the parameters c, $\phi_1, \ldots, \phi_p$, $\theta_1, \ldots, \theta_q$. When R estimates the ARIMA model, it uses *maximum likelihood estimation* (MLE). This technique finds the values of the parameters which maximize the probability of obtaining the data that we have observed. For ARIMA models, MLE is very similar to the *least squares* estimates that would be obtained by minimizing

$$\sum_{t=1}^{T} e_t^2.$$

(For the regression models considered in Chapters 4 and 5, MLE gives exactly the same parameter estimates as least squares estimation.) Note that ARIMA models are much more complicated to estimate than regression models, and different software will give slightly different answers as they use different methods of estimation, or different estimation algorithms.

In practice, R will report the value of the *log likelihood* of the data; that is, the logarithm of the probability of the observed data coming from the estimated model. For given values of p, d and q, R will try to maximize the log likelihood when finding parameter estimates.

Information Criteria

Akaike's Information Criterion (AIC), which was useful in selecting predictors for regression, is also useful for determining the order of an ARIMA model. It can be written as

$$\text{AIC} = -2\log(L) + 2(p + q + k + 1),$$

where L is the likelihood of the data, $k = 1$ if $c \neq 0$ and $k = 0$ if $c = 0$. Note that the last term in parentheses is the number of parameters in the model (including σ^2, the variance of the residuals).

For ARIMA models, the corrected AIC can be written as

$$\text{AIC}_\text{c} = \text{AIC} + \frac{2(p + q + k + 1)(p + q + k + 2)}{T - p - q - k - 2}.$$

and the Bayesian Information Criterion can be written as

$$\text{BIC} = \text{AIC} + \log(T)(p + q + k - 1).$$

Good models are obtained by minimizing either the AIC, AIC_c or BIC. Our preference is to use the AIC_c.

8/7   ARIMA modelling in R

How does auto.arima() work?

The auto.arima() function in R uses a variation of the Hyndman and Khandakar algorithm[3] which combines unit root tests, minimization of the AIC_c and MLE to obtain an ARIMA model. The algorithm follows these steps.

[3] robjhyndman.com/papers/automatic

The arguments to auto.arima() provide for many variations on the algorithm. What is described here is the default behaviour.

Choosing your own model

If you want to choose the model yourself, use the Arima() function in R. For example, to fit the ARIMA(0,0,3) model to the US consumption data, the following commands can be used.

```
──────────── R code ────────────
fit <- Arima(usconsumption[,1], order=c(0,0,3))
```

Hyndman-Khandakar algorithm
for automatic ARIMA modelling

---

1. The number of differences d is determined using repeated KPSS tests.

2. The values of p and q are then chosen by minimizing the AIC_c after differencing the data d times. Rather than considering every possible combination of p and q, the algorithm uses a stepwise search to traverse the model space.

   (a) The best initial model (with smallest AIC_c) is selected from the following four:

   $ARIMA(2,d,2)$,
   $ARIMA(0,d,0)$,
   $ARIMA(1,d,0)$,
   $ARIMA(0,d,1)$.

   If $d = 0$ then the constant c is included; if $d \geq 1$ then the constant c is set to zero. This is called the "current model".

   (b) Variations on the current model are considered:
   - vary p and/or q from the current model by ± 1;
   - include/exclude c from the current model.

   The best model considered so far (either the current model, or one of these variations) becomes the new current model.

   (c) Repeat Step 2(b) until no lower AIC_c can be found.

There is another function arima() in R which also fits an ARIMA model. However, it does not allow for the constant c unless $d = 0$, and it does not return everything required for the forecast() function. Finally, it does not allow the estimated model to be applied to new data (which is useful for checking forecast accuracy). Consequently, it is recommended that you use Arima() instead.

Modelling procedure

When fitting an ARIMA model to a set of time series data, the following procedure provides a useful general approach.

1. Plot the data. Identify any unusual observations.
2. If necessary, transform the data (using a Box-Cox transformation) to stabilize the variance.
3. If the data are non-stationary: take first differences of the data until the data are stationary.
4. Examine the ACF/PACF: Is an AR(p) or MA(q) model appropriate?
5. Try your chosen model(s), and use the AIC_c to search for a better model.
6. Check the residuals from your chosen model by plotting the ACF of the residuals, and doing a portmanteau test of the residuals. If they do not look like white noise, try a modified model.
7. Once the residuals look like white noise, calculate forecasts.

The automated algorithm only takes care of steps 3–5. So even if you use it, you will still need to take care of the other steps yourself.

The process is summarized in Figure 8.10.

Example 8.2   Seasonally adjusted electrical equipment orders

We will apply this procedure to the seasonally adjusted electrical equipment orders data shown in Figure 8.11.

1. The time plot shows some sudden changes, particularly the big drop in 2008/2009. These changes are due to the global economic environment. Otherwise there is nothing unusual about the time plot and there appears to be no need to do any data adjustments.
2. There is no evidence of changing variance, so we will not do a Box-Cox transformation.
3. The data are clearly non-stationary as the series wanders up and down for long periods. Consequently, we will take a first difference of the data. The differenced data are shown in Figure 8.12. These look stationary, and so we will not consider further differences.

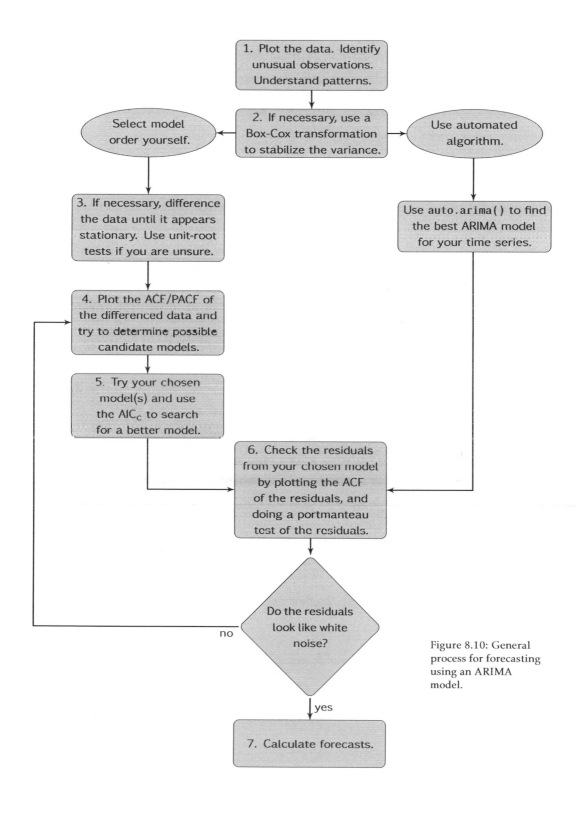

Figure 8.10: General process for forecasting using an ARIMA model.

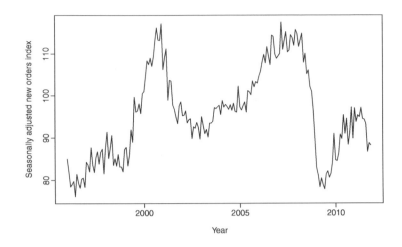

Figure 8.11: Seasonally adjusted electrical equipment orders index in the Euro area.

―――――――――― R code ――――――――――
```
eeadj <- seasadj(stl(elecequip, s.window="periodic"))
plot(eeadj)
```

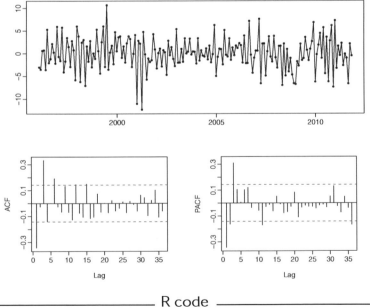

Figure 8.12: Time plot and ACF and PACF plots for differenced seasonally adjusted electrical equipment data.

―――――――――― R code ――――――――――
```
tsdisplay(diff(eeadj), main="")
```

4. The PACF shown in Figure 8.12 is suggestive of an AR(3) model. So an initial candidate model is an ARIMA(3,1,0). There are no other obvious candidate models.

5. We fit an ARIMA(3,1,0) model along with variations including ARIMA(4,1,0), ARIMA(2,1,0), ARIMA(3,1,1), etc. Of these, the ARIMA(3,1,1) has a slightly smaller AIC$_c$ value.

───────────────── R output ─────────────────
```
> fit <- Arima(eeadj, order=c(3,1,1))
> summary(fit)
Series: eeadj
ARIMA(3,1,1)

Coefficients:
          ar1      ar2      ar3      ma1
       0.0519   0.1191   0.3730   0.4542
s.e.   0.1840   0.0888   0.0679   0.1993

sigma^2 estimated as 9.532:  log likelihood=-484.08
AIC=978.17   AICc=978.49   BIC=994.4
```
───

6. The ACF plot of the residuals from the ARIMA(3,1,1) model shows all correlations within the threshold limits indicating that the residuals are behaving like white noise. A portmanteau test returns a large p-value, also suggesting the residuals are white noise.

───────────────── R code ─────────────────
```
Acf(residuals(fit))
Box.test(residuals(fit), lag=24, fitdf=4, type="Ljung")
```
───

7. Forecasts from the chosen model are shown in Figure 8.13.

If we had used the automated algorithm instead, we would have obtained exactly the same model in this example.

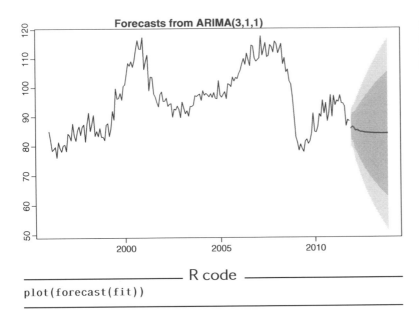

Figure 8.13: Forecasts for the seasonally adjusted electrical orders index.

———————— R code ————————

```
plot(forecast(fit))
```

Understanding constants in R

A non-seasonal ARIMA model can be written as

$$(1 - \phi_1 B - \cdots - \phi_p B^p)(1 - B)^d y_t = c + (1 + \theta_1 B + \cdots + \theta_q B^q)e_t$$

or equivalently as

$$(1 - \phi_1 B - \cdots - \phi_p B^p)(1 - B)^d (y_t - \mu t^d/d!) = (1 + \theta_1 B + \cdots + \theta_q B^q)e_t,$$

$$(8.2)$$

where $c = \mu(1 - \phi_1 - \cdots - \phi_p)$ and μ is the mean of $(1 - B)^d y_t$. R uses the parametrization of equation (8.2).

Thus, the inclusion of a constant in a non-stationary ARIMA model is equivalent to inducing a polynomial trend of order d in the forecast function. (If the constant is omitted, the forecast function includes a polynomial trend of order $d - 1$.) When $d = 0$, we have the special case that μ is the mean of y_t.

arima() By default, the arima() command in R sets $c = \mu = 0$ when $d > 0$ and provides an estimate of μ when $d = 0$. The parameter μ is called the "intercept" in the R output. It will be close to the sample mean of the time series, but usually not identical to it as the sample mean is not the maximum likelihood estimate when $p + q > 0$.

The arima() command has an argument include.mean which only has an effect when $d = 0$ and is TRUE by default. Setting include.mean=FALSE will force $\mu = 0$.

Arima() The Arima() command from the forecast package provides more flexibility on the inclusion of a constant. It has an argument include.mean which has identical functionality to the corresponding argument for arima(). It also has an argument include.drift which allows $\mu \neq 0$ when $d = 1$. For $d > 1$, no constant is allowed as a quadratic or higher order trend is particularly dangerous when forecasting. The parameter μ is called the "drift" in the R output when $d = 1$.

There is also an argument include.constant which, if TRUE, will set include.mean=TRUE if $d = 0$ and include.drift=TRUE when $d = 1$. If include.constant=FALSE, both include.mean and include.drift will be set to FALSE. If include.constant is used, the values of include.mean=TRUE and include.drift=TRUE are ignored.

auto.arima() The auto.arima() function automates the inclusion of a constant. By default, for $d = 0$ or $d = 1$, a constant will be included if it improves the AIC_c value; for $d > 1$ the constant is always omitted. If allowdrift=FALSE is specified, then the constant is only allowed when $d = 0$.

8/8   Forecasting

Point forecasts

Although we have calculated forecasts from the ARIMA models in our examples, we have not yet explained how they are obtained. Point forecasts can be calculated using the following three steps.

1. Expand the ARIMA equation so that y_t is on the left hand side and all other terms are on the right.
2. Rewrite the equation by replacing t by $T + h$.
3. On the right hand side of the equation, replace future observations by their forecasts, future errors by zero, and past errors by the corresponding residuals.

Beginning with $h = 1$, these steps are then repeated for $h = 2, 3, \ldots$ until all forecasts have been calculated.

The procedure is most easily understood via an example. We will illustrate it using the ARIMA(3,1,1) model fitted in the previous section. The model can be written as follows

$$(1 - \hat{\phi}_1 B - \hat{\phi}_2 B^2 - \hat{\phi}_3 B^3)(1 - B)y_t = (1 + \hat{\theta}_1 B)e_t,$$

where $\hat{\phi}_1 = 0.0519$, $\hat{\phi}_2 = 0.1191$, $\hat{\phi}_3 = 0.3730$ and $\hat{\theta}_1 = -0.4542$. Then we expand the left hand side to obtain

$$\left[1 - (1 + \hat{\phi}_1)B + (\hat{\phi}_1 - \hat{\phi}_2)B^2 + (\hat{\phi}_2 - \hat{\phi}_3)B^3 + \hat{\phi}_3 B^4\right]y_t = (1 + \hat{\theta}_1 B)e_t,$$

and applying the backshift operator gives

$$y_t - (1 + \hat{\phi}_1)y_{t-1} + (\hat{\phi}_1 - \hat{\phi}_2)y_{t-2} + (\hat{\phi}_2 - \hat{\phi}_3)y_{t-3} + \hat{\phi}_3 y_{t-4} = e_t + \hat{\theta}_1 e_{t-1}.$$

Finally, we move all terms other than y_t to the right hand side:

$$y_t = (1 + \hat{\phi}_1)y_{t-1} - (\hat{\phi}_1 - \hat{\phi}_2)y_{t-2} - (\hat{\phi}_2 - \hat{\phi}_3)y_{t-3} - \hat{\phi}_3 y_{t-4} + e_t + \hat{\theta}_1 e_{t-1}.$$
$$(8.3)$$

This completes the first step. While the equation now looks like an ARIMA(4,0,1), it is still the same ARIMA(3,1,1) model we started with. It cannot be considered an ARIMA(4,0,1) because the coefficients do not satisfy the stationarity conditions.

For the second step, we replace t by $T + 1$ in (8.3):

$$y_{T+1} = (1 + \hat{\phi}_1)y_T - (\hat{\phi}_1 - \hat{\phi}_2)y_{T-1} - (\hat{\phi}_2 - \hat{\phi}_3)y_{T-2} - \hat{\phi}_3 y_{T-3} + e_{T+1} + \hat{\theta}_1 e_T.$$

Assuming we have observations up to time T, all values on the right hand side are known except for e_{T+1} which we replace by zero and e_T which we replace by the last observed residual $\hat{e}_T$:

$$\hat{y}_{T+1|T} = (1 + \hat{\phi}_1)y_T - (\hat{\phi}_1 - \hat{\phi}_2)y_{T-1} - (\hat{\phi}_2 - \hat{\phi}_3)y_{T-2} - \hat{\phi}_3 y_{T-3} + \hat{\theta}_1 \hat{e}_T.$$

A forecast of y_{T+2} is obtained by replacing t by $T + 2$ in (8.3). All values on the right hand side will be known at time T except y_{T+1} which we replace by $\hat{y}_{T+1|T}$, and e_{T+2} and e_{T+1}, both of which we replace by zero:

$$\hat{y}_{T+2|T} = (1 + \hat{\phi}_1)\hat{y}_{T+1|T} - (\hat{\phi}_1 - \hat{\phi}_2)y_T - (\hat{\phi}_2 - \hat{\phi}_3)y_{T-1} - \hat{\phi}_3 y_{T-2}.$$

The process continues in this manner for all future time periods. In this way, any number of point forecasts can be obtained.

Forecast intervals

The calculation of ARIMA forecast intervals is much more difficult, and the details are largely beyond the scope of this book. We will just give some simple examples.

The first forecast interval is easily calculated. If $\hat{\sigma}$ is the standard deviation of the residuals, then a 95% forecast interval is given by $\hat{y}_{T+1|T} \pm 1.96\hat{\sigma}$. This result is true for all ARIMA models regardless of their parameters and orders.

Multi-step forecast intervals for ARIMA$(0,0,q)$ models are relatively easy to calculate. We can write the model as

$$y_t = e_t + \sum_{i=1}^{q} \theta_i e_{t-i}.$$

Then the estimated forecast variance can be written as

$$v_{T+h|T} = \hat{\sigma}^2 \left[1 + \sum_{i=1}^{h-1} \hat{\theta}_i^2 \right], \qquad \text{for } h = 2, 3, \ldots,$$

and a 95% forecast interval is given by $\hat{y}_{T+h|T} \pm 1.96\sqrt{v_{T+h|T}}$.

On page 225, we showed that an AR(1) model can be written as an MA(∞) model. Using this equivalence, the above result for MA(q) models can also be used to obtain forecast intervals for AR(1) models.

More general results, and other special cases of multi-step forecast intervals for an ARIMA(p,d,q) model, are given in more advanced textbooks such as Brockwell and Davis (1991, Section 9.5).

The forecast intervals for ARIMA models are based on assumptions that the residuals are uncorrelated and normally distributed. If either of these are assumptions do not hold, then the forecast intervals may be incorrect. For this reason, always plot the ACF and histogram of the residuals to check the assumptions before producing forecast intervals.

In general, forecast intervals from ARIMA models will increase as the forecast horizon increases. For stationary models (i.e., with $d = 0$), they will converge so forecast intervals for long horizons are all essentially the same. For $d > 1$, the forecast intervals will continue to grow into the future.

As with most forecast interval calculations, ARIMA-based intervals tend to be too narrow. This occurs because only the variation in the errors has been accounted for. There is also variation in the parameter estimates, and in the model order, that has not been included in the calculation. In addition, the calculation assumes that the historical patterns that have been modelled will continue into the forecast period.

8/9 Seasonal ARIMA models

So far, we have restricted our attention to non-seasonal data and non-seasonal ARIMA models. However, ARIMA models are also capable of modelling a wide range of seasonal data.

A seasonal ARIMA model is formed by including additional seasonal terms in the ARIMA models we have seen so far. It is written as follows:

$$\text{ARIMA} \underbrace{(p,d,q)}_{\uparrow} \underbrace{(P,D,Q)_m}_{\uparrow}$$

$$\left(\begin{array}{c} \text{Non-seasonal part} \\ \text{of the model} \end{array} \right) \left(\begin{array}{c} \text{Seasonal part} \\ \text{of the model} \end{array} \right)$$

where m = number of observations per year. We use uppercase notation for the seasonal parts of the model, and lowercase notation for the non-seasonal parts of the model.

The seasonal part of the model consists of terms that are very similar to the non-seasonal components of the model, but they involve backshifts of the seasonal period. For example, an ARIMA$(1,1,1)(1,1,1)_4$ model (without a constant) is for quarterly data ($m = 4$) and can be written as

$$(1 - \phi_1 B)(1 - \Phi_1 B^4)(1 - B)(1 - B^4)y_t = (1 + \theta_1 B)(1 + \Theta_1 B^4)e_t.$$

$$\left(\begin{array}{c} \text{Non-seasonal} \\ \text{AR(1)} \end{array} \right) \quad \left(\begin{array}{c} \text{Non-seasonal} \\ \text{difference} \end{array} \right) \quad \left(\begin{array}{c} \text{Non-seasonal} \\ \text{MA(1)} \end{array} \right)$$

$$\left(\begin{array}{c} \text{Seasonal} \\ \text{AR(1)} \end{array} \right) \quad \left(\begin{array}{c} \text{Seasonal} \\ \text{difference} \end{array} \right) \quad \left(\begin{array}{c} \text{Seasonal} \\ \text{MA(1)} \end{array} \right)$$

The additional seasonal terms are simply multiplied with the non-seasonal terms.

ACF/PACF

The seasonal part of an AR or MA model will be seen in the seasonal lags of the PACF and ACF. For example, an ARIMA$(0,0,0)(0,0,1)_{12}$ model will show:

- a spike at lag 12 in the ACF but no other significant spikes.
- The PACF will show exponential decay in the seasonal lags; that is, at lags 12, 24, 36, ...

Similarly, an ARIMA$(0,0,0)(1,0,0)_{12}$ model will show:

- exponential decay in the seasonal lags of the ACF
- a single significant spike at lag 12 in the PACF.

In considering the appropriate seasonal orders for an ARIMA model, restrict attention to the seasonal lags.

The modelling procedure is almost the same as for non-seasonal data, except that we need to select seasonal AR and MA terms as well as the non-seasonal components of the model. The process is best illustrated via examples.

Example 8.3 *European quarterly retail trade*

We will describe the seasonal ARIMA modelling procedure using quarterly European retail trade data from 1996 to 2011. The data are plotted in Figure 8.14.

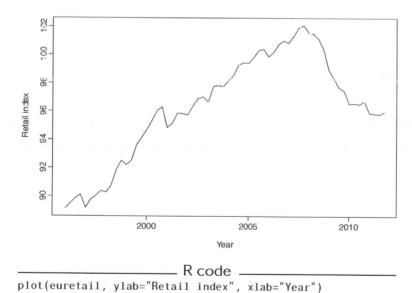

Figure 8.14: Quarterly retail trade index in the Euro area (17 countries), 1996–2011, covering wholesale and retail trade, and repair of motor vehicles and motorcycles. (Index: 2005 = 100).

——————— R code ———————
```
plot(euretail, ylab="Retail index", xlab="Year")
```

The data are clearly non-stationary, with some seasonality, so we will first take a seasonal difference. The seasonally differenced data are shown in Figure 8.15. These also appear to be non-stationary, and so we take an additional first difference, shown in Figure 8.16.

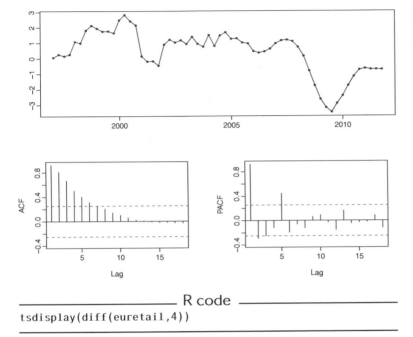

Figure 8.15: Seasonally differenced European retail trade index.

──────────────── R code ────────────────

```
tsdisplay(diff(euretail,4))
```

Our aim now is to find an appropriate ARIMA model based on the ACF and PACF shown in Figure 8.16. The significant spike at lag 1 in the ACF suggests a non-seasonal MA(1) component, and the significant spike at lag 4 in the ACF suggests a seasonal MA(1) component. Consequently, we begin with an ARIMA(0,1,1)(0,1,1)$_4$ model, indicating a first and seasonal difference, and non-seasonal and seasonal MA(1) components. The residuals for the fitted model are shown in Figure 8.17. (By analogous logic applied to the PACF, we could also have started with an ARIMA(1,1,0)(1,1,0)$_4$ model.)

Both the ACF and PACF show significant spikes at lag 2, and almost significant spikes at lag 3, indicating some additional non-seasonal terms need to be included in the model. The AIC$_c$ of the ARIMA(0,1,2)(0,1,1)$_4$ model is 74.36, while that for the ARIMA(0,1,3)(0,1,1)$_4$ model is 68.53. We tried other models with AR terms as well, but none that gave a smaller AIC$_c$ value. Consequently, we choose the ARIMA(0,1,3)(0,1,1)$_4$ model. Its residuals are plotted in Figure 8.18. All the spikes are now within the significance limits, and so the residuals appear to be

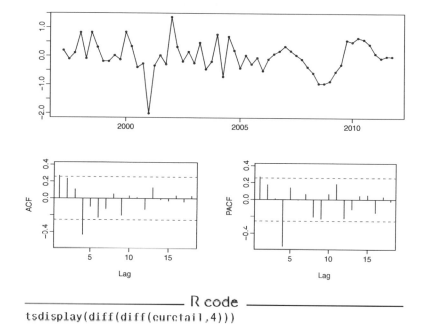

Figure 8.16: Double differenced European retail trade index.

_____ R code _____

```
tsdisplay(diff(diff(euretail,4)))
```

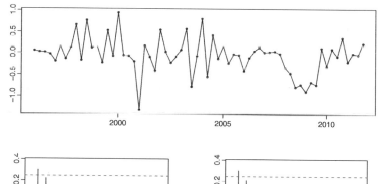

Figure 8.17: Residuals from the fitted ARIMA$(0,1,3)(0,1,1)_4$ model for the European retail trade index data.

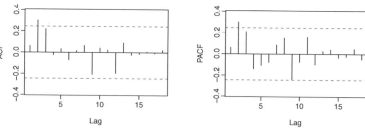

_____ R code _____

```
fit <- Arima(euretail, order=c(0,1,1), seasonal=c(0,1,1))
tsdisplay(residuals(fit))
```

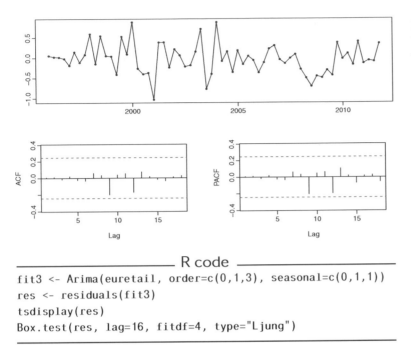

Figure 8.18: Residuals from the fitted ARIMA$(0,1,3)(0,1,1)_4$ model for the European retail trade index data.

R code

```
fit3 <- Arima(euretail, order=c(0,1,3), seasonal=c(0,1,1))
res <- residuals(fit3)
tsdisplay(res)
Box.test(res, lag=16, fitdf=4, type="Ljung")
```

white noise. A Ljung-Box test also shows that the residuals have no remaining autocorrelations.

So we now have a seasonal ARIMA model that passes the required checks and is ready for forecasting. Forecasts from the model for the next three years are shown in Figure 8.19. Notice how the forecasts follow the recent trend in the data (this occurs because of the double differencing). The large and rapidly increasing prediction intervals show that the retail trade index could start increasing or decreasing at any time — while the point forecasts trend downwards, the prediction intervals allow for the data to trend upwards during the forecast period.

We could have used auto.arima() to do most of this work for us. It would have given the following result.

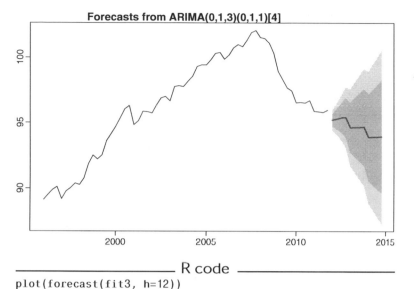

Figure 8.19: Forecasts of the European retail trade index data using the ARIMA$(0,1,3)(0,1,1)_4$ model. 80% and 95% prediction intervals are shown.

―――――――――― R code ――――――――――

```
plot(forecast(fit3, h=12))
```

―――――――――― R output ――――――――――

```
> auto.arima(euretail)
ARIMA(1,1,1)(0,1,1)[4]

Coefficients:
          ar1       ma1      sma1
        0.8828   -0.5208   -0.9704
s.e.    0.1424    0.1755    0.6792

sigma^2 estimated as 0.1411:   log likelihood=-30.19
AIC=68.37    AICc=69.11    BIC=76.68
```

Notice that it has selected a different model (with a larger AIC_c value). auto.arima() takes some short-cuts in order to speed up the computation and will not always give the best model. You can turn the short-cuts off and then it will sometimes return a different model.

—————————————— R output ——————————————

```
> auto.arima(euretail, stepwise=FALSE, approximation=FALSE)
ARIMA(0,1,3)(0,1,1)[4]

Coefficients:
         ma1     ma2     ma3    sma1
      0.2625  0.3697  0.4194  -0.6615
s.e.  0.1239  0.1260  0.1296   0.1555

sigma^2 estimated as 0.1451:  log likelihood=-28.7
AIC=67.4    AICc=68.53    BIC=77.78
```

This time it returned the same model we had identified.

Example 8.4 Cortecosteroid drug sales in Australia

Our second example is more difficult. We will try to forecast monthly cortecosteroid drug sales in Australia. These are known as H02 drugs under the Anatomical Therapeutical Chemical classification scheme.

Data from July 1991 to June 2008 are plotted in Figure 8.20. There is a small increase in the variance with the level, and so we take logarithms to stabilize the variance.

The data are strongly seasonal and obviously non-stationary, and so seasonal differencing will be used. The seasonally differenced data are shown in Figure 8.21. It is not clear at this point whether we should do another difference or not. We decide not to, but the choice is not obvious.

The last few observations appear to be different (more variable) from the earlier data. This may be due to the fact that data are sometimes revised as earlier sales are reported late.

In the plots of the seasonally differenced data, there are spikes in the PACF at lags 12 and 24, but nothing at seasonal lags in the ACF. This may be suggestive of a seasonal AR(2) term. In the non-seasonal lags, there are three significant spikes in the PACF suggesting a possible AR(3) term. The pattern in the ACF is not indicative of any simple model.

Consequently, this initial analysis suggests that a possible model for these data is an $ARIMA(3,0,0)(2,1,0)_{12}$. We fit this model, along with some variations on it, and compute their AIC_c values which are shown in the following table.

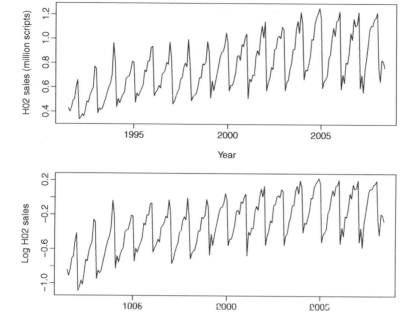

Figure 8.20: Cortecos-
teroid drug sales in
Australia (in millions
of scripts per month).
Logged data shown in
bottom panel.

—————————————— R code ——————————————

```
lh02 <- log(h02)
par(mfrow=c(2,1))
plot(h02, ylab="H02 sales (million scripts)", xlab="Year")
plot(lh02, ylab="Log H02 sales", xlab="Year")
```

Model	AIC_c
$ARIMA(3,0,0)(2,1,0)_{12}$	-475.12
$ARIMA(3,0,1)(2,1,0)_{12}$	-476.31
$ARIMA(3,0,2)(2,1,0)_{12}$	-474.88
$ARIMA(3,0,1)(1,1,0)_{12}$	-463.40
$ARIMA(3,0,1)(0,1,1)_{12}$	-483.67
$ARIMA(3,0,1)(0,1,2)_{12}$	-485.48
$ARIMA(3,0,1)(1,1,1)_{12}$	-484.25

Of these models, the best is the $ARIMA(3,0,1)(0,1,2)_{12}$ model
(i.e., it has the smallest AIC_c value).

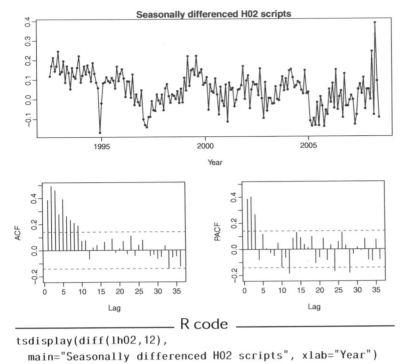

Figure 8.21: Seasonally differenced cortecosteroid drug sales in Australia (in millions of scripts per month).

─────────── R code ───────────

```
tsdisplay(diff(lh02,12),
    main="Seasonally differenced H02 scripts", xlab="Year")
```

─────────── R output ───────────

```
> fit <- Arima(h02, order=c(3,0,1), seasonal=c(0,1,2), lambda=0)

ARIMA(3,0,1)(0,1,2)[12]
Box Cox transformation: lambda= 0

Coefficients:
          ar1      ar2     ar3     ma1     sma1     sma2
      -0.1603   0.5481  0.5678  0.3827  -0.5222  -0.1768
s.e.   0.1636   0.0878  0.0942  0.1895   0.0861   0.0872

sigma^2 estimated as 0.004145:   log likelihood=250.04
AIC=-486.08   AICc=-485.48   BIC=-463.28
```

The residuals from this model are shown in Figure 8.22. There are significant spikes in both the ACF and PACF, and the model fails a Ljung-Box test. The model can still be used for forecasting, but the prediction intervals may not be accurate due to the correlated residuals.

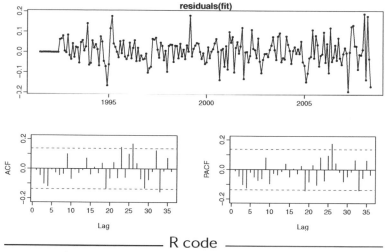

Figure 8.22: Residuals from the ARIMA$(3,0,1)(0,1,2)_{12}$ model applied to the H02 monthly script sales data.

```
———————————— R code ————————————
tsdisplay(residuals(fit))
Box.test(residuals(fit), lag=36, fitdf=6, type="Ljung")
```

Next we will try using the automatic ARIMA algorithm. Running auto.arima() with arguments left at their default values led to an ARIMA$(2,1,3)(0,1,1)_{12}$ model. However, the model still fails a Ljung-Box test. Sometimes it is just not possible to find a model that passes all the tests.

Finally, we tried running auto.arima() with differencing specified to be $d = 0$ and $D = 1$, and allowing larger models than usual. This led to an ARIMA$(4,0,3)(0,1,1)_{12}$ model, which did pass all the tests.

```
———————————— R code ————————————
fit <- auto.arima(h02, lambda=0, d=0,D=1,max.order=9,
                  stepwise=FALSE, approximation=FALSE)
tsdisplay(residuals(fit))
Box.test(residuals(fit), lag=36, fitdf=8, type="Ljung")
```

Test set evaluation: We will compare some of the models fitted so far using a test set consisting of the last two years of data. Thus, we fit the models using data from July 1991 to June 2006, and forecast the script sales for July 2006 – June 2008. The results are summarised in the following table.

Model	RMSE
ARIMA(3,0,0)(2,1,0)$_{12}$	0.0661
ARIMA(3,0,1)(2,1,0)$_{12}$	0.0646
ARIMA(3,0,2)(2,1,0)$_{12}$	0.0645
ARIMA(3,0,1)(1,1,0)$_{12}$	0.0679
ARIMA(3,0,1)(0,1,1)$_{12}$	0.0644
ARIMA(3,0,1)(0,1,2)$_{12}$	0.0622
ARIMA(3,0,1)(1,1,1)$_{12}$	0.0630
ARIMA(4,0,3)(0,1,1)$_{12}$	0.0648
ARIMA(3,0,3)(0,1,1)$_{12}$	0.0640
ARIMA(4,0,2)(0,1,1)$_{12}$	0.0648
ARIMA(3,0,2)(0,1,1)$_{12}$	0.0644
ARIMA(2,1,3)(0,1,1)$_{12}$	0.0634
ARIMA(2,1,4)(0,1,1)$_{12}$	0.0632
ARIMA(2,1,5)(0,1,1)$_{12}$	0.0640

——————————————————— R code ———————————————————

```
getrmse <- function(x,h,...)
{
    train.end <- time(x)[length(x)-h]
    test.start <- time(x)[length(x)-h+1]
    train <- window(x,end=train.end)
    test <- window(x,start=test.start)
    fit <- Arima(train,...)
    fc <- forecast(fit,h=h)
    return(accuracy(fc,test)[2,"RMSE"])
}

getrmse(h02,h=24,order=c(3,0,0),seasonal=c(2,1,0),lambda=0)
getrmse(h02,h=24,order=c(3,0,1),seasonal=c(2,1,0),lambda=0)
getrmse(h02,h=24,order=c(3,0,2),seasonal=c(2,1,0),lambda=0)
getrmse(h02,h=24,order=c(3,0,1),seasonal=c(1,1,0),lambda=0)
getrmse(h02,h=24,order=c(3,0,1),seasonal=c(0,1,1),lambda=0)
getrmse(h02,h=24,order=c(3,0,1),seasonal=c(0,1,2),lambda=0)
getrmse(h02,h=24,order=c(3,0,1),seasonal=c(1,1,1),lambda=0)
getrmse(h02,h=24,order=c(4,0,3),seasonal=c(0,1,1),lambda=0)
getrmse(h02,h=24,order=c(3,0,3),seasonal=c(0,1,1),lambda=0)
getrmse(h02,h=24,order=c(4,0,2),seasonal=c(0,1,1),lambda=0)
getrmse(h02,h=24,order=c(3,0,2),seasonal=c(0,1,1),lambda=0)
getrmse(h02,h=24,order=c(2,1,3),seasonal=c(0,1,1),lambda=0)
getrmse(h02,h=24,order=c(2,1,4),seasonal=c(0,1,1),lambda=0)
getrmse(h02,h=24,order=c(2,1,5),seasonal=c(0,1,1),lambda=0)
```

The models that have the lowest AIC_c values tend to give slightly better results than the other models, but there is not a large difference. Also, the only model that passed the residual tests did not give the best test set RMSE values.

When models are compared using AIC_c values, it is important that all models have the same orders of differencing. However, when comparing models using a test set, it does not matter how the forecasts were produced — the comparisons are always valid. Consequently, in the table above, we can include some models with only seasonal differencing and some models with both first and seasonal differencing. But in the earlier table containing AIC_c values, we compared models with only seasonal differencing.

None of the models considered here pass all the residual tests. In practice, we would normally use the best model we could find, even if it did not pass all tests.

Forecasts from the ARIMA(3,0,1)(0,1,2)$_{12}$ model (which has the lowest RMSE value on the test set, and the best AICc value amongst models with only seasonal differencing and fewer than six parameters) are shown in the figure below.

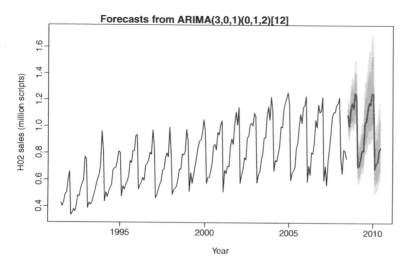

Figure 8.23: Forecasts from the ARIMA$(3,0,1)(0,1,2)_{12}$ model applied to the H02 monthly script sales data.

```
————————— R code —————————
fit <- Arima(h02, order-c(3,0,1), seasonal=c(0,1,2), lambda=0)
plot(forecast(fit), ylab-"H02 sales (million scripts)", xlab="Year")
```

8/10 ARIMA vs ETS

It is a commonly held myth that ARIMA models are more general than exponential smoothing. While linear exponential smoothing models are all special cases of ARIMA models, the non-linear exponential smoothing models have no equivalent ARIMA counterparts. There are also many ARIMA models that have no exponential smoothing counterparts. In particular, every ETS model is non-stationary, while ARIMA models can be stationary.

The ETS models with seasonality or non-damped trend or both have two unit roots (i.e., they need two levels of differencing to make them stationary). All other ETS models have one unit root (they need one level of differencing to make them stationary).

The following table gives the equivalence relationships for the two classes of models.

ETS model	ARIMA model	Parameters
ETS(A,N,N)	ARIMA(0,1,1)	$\theta_1 = \alpha - 1$
ETS(A,A,N)	ARIMA(0,2,2)	$\theta_1 = \alpha + \beta - 2$ $\theta_2 = 1 - \alpha$
ETS(A,A$_d$,N)	ARIMA(1,1,2)	$\phi_1 = \phi$ $\theta_1 = \alpha + \phi\beta - 2$ $\theta_2 = (1 - \alpha)\phi$
ETS(A,N,A)	ARIMA(0,0,m)(0,1,0)$_m$	
ETS(A,A,A)	ARIMA(0,1,$m+1$)(0,1,0)$_m$	
ETS(A,A$_d$,A)	ARIMA(1,0,$m+1$)(0,1,0)$_m$	

For the seasonal models, there are a large number of restrictions on the ARIMA parameters

8/11   Exercises

8.1 Figure 8.24 shows the ACFs for 36 random numbers, 360 random numbers and for 1,000 random numbers.

(a) Explain the differences among these figures. Do they all indicate the data are white noise?

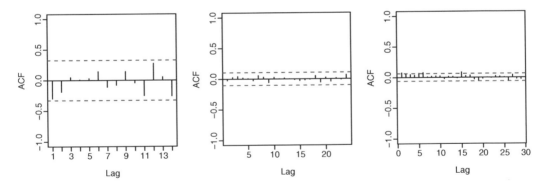

(b) Why are the critical values at different distances from the mean of zero? Why are the autocorrelations different in each figure when they each refer to white noise?

Figure 8.24: Left: ACF for a white noise series of 36 numbers. Middle: ACF for a white noise series of 360 numbers. Right: ACF for a white noise series of 1,000 numbers.

8.2 A classic example of a non-stationary series is the daily closing IBM stock prices (data set ibmclose). Use R to plot the daily closing prices for IBM stock and the ACF and PACF. Explain how each plot shows the series is non-stationary and should be differenced.

8.3 For the following series, find an appropriate Box-Cox transformation and order of differencing in order to obtain stationary data.

   (a) usnetelec
   (b) usgdp
   (c) mcopper
   (d) enplanements
   (e) visitors

8.4 For the enplanements data, write down the differences you chose above using backshift operator notation.

8.5 Use R to simulate and plot some data from simple ARIMA models.

   (a) Generate data from an AR(1) model with $\phi_1 = 0.6$ and $\sigma^2 = 1$. Start with $y_0 = 0$.
   (b) Produce a time plot for the series. How does the plot change as you change ϕ_1?
   (c) Generate data from an MA(1) model with $\theta_1 = 0.6$ and $\sigma^2 = 1$. Start with $e_0 = 0$.
   (d) Produce a time plot for the series. How does the plot change as you change θ_1?
   (e) Generate data from an ARMA(1,1) model with $\phi_1 = 0.6$ and $\theta_1 = 0.6$ and $\sigma^2 = 1$. Start with $y_0 = 0$ and $e_0 = 0$.
   (f) Generate data from an AR(2) model with $\phi_1 = -0.8$ and $\phi_2 = 0.3$ and $\sigma^2 = 1$. Start with $y_0 = y_{-1} = 0$.
   (g) Graph the latter two series and compare them.

8.6 Consider the number of women murdered each year (per 100,000 standard population) in the United States (data set wmurders).

   (a) By studying appropriate graphs of the series in R, find an appropriate ARIMA(p, d, q) model for these data.

(b) Should you include a constant in the model? Explain.

(c) Write this model in terms of the backshift operator.

(d) Fit the model using R and examine the residuals. Is the model satisfactory?

(e) Forecast three times ahead. Check your forecasts by hand to make sure you know how they have been calculated.

(f) Create a plot of the series with forecasts and prediction intervals for the next three periods shown.

(g) Does auto.arima give the same model you have chosen? If not, which model do you think is better?

(h) Find the latest data from http://data.is/ XKa24F and compare with your forecasts.

8.7 Consider the quarterly number of international tourists to Australia for the period 1999–2010. (Data set austourists.)

(a) Describe the time plot.

(b) What can you learn from the ACF graph?

(c) What can you learn from the PACF graph?

(d) Produce plots of the seasonally differenced data $(1 - B^4)Y_t$. What model do these graphs suggest?

(e) Does auto.arima give the same model that you chose? If not, which model do you think is better?

(f) Write the model in terms of the backshift operator, and then without using the backshift operator.

8.8 Consider the total net generation of electricity (in billion kilowatt hours) by the U.S. electric industry (monthly for the period 1985–1996). (Data set usmelec.) In general there are two peaks per year: in mid-summer and mid-winter.

(a) Examine the 12-month moving average of this series to see what kind of trend is involved.

(b) Do the data need transforming? If so, find a suitable transformation.

(c) Are the data stationary? If not, find an appropriate differencing which yields stationary data.

(d) Identify a couple of ARIMA models that might be useful in describing the time series. Which of your models is the best according to their AIC values?

(e) Estimate the parameters of your best model and do diagnostic testing on the residuals. Do the residuals resemble white noise? If not, try to find another ARIMA model which fits better.

(f) Forecast the next 15 years of generation of electricity by the U.S. electric industry. Get the latest figures from http://data.is/zgRWCO to check on the accuracy of your forecasts.

(g) How many years of forecasts do you think are sufficiently accurate to be usable?

8.9 For the mcopper data:

(a) if necessary, find a suitable Box-Cox transformation for the data;

(b) fit a suitable ARIMA model to the transformed data using auto.arima();

(c) try some other plausible models by experimenting with the orders chosen;

(d) choose what you think is the best model and check the residual diagnostics;

(e) produce forecasts of your fitted model. Do the forecasts look reasonable?

(f) compare the results with what you would obtain using ets() (with no transformation).

8.10 Choose one of the following seasonal time series: condmilk, hsales, uselec

(a) Do the data need transforming? If so, find a suitable transformation.

(b) Are the data stationary? If not, find an appropriate differencing which yields stationary data.

(c) Identify a couple of ARIMA models that might be useful in describing the time series. Which of your models is the best according to their AIC values?

(d) Estimate the parameters of your best model and do diagnostic testing on the residuals. Do the residuals resemble white noise? If not, try to find another ARIMA model which fits better.

(e) Forecast the next 24 months of data using your preferred model.

(f) Compare the forecasts obtained using ets().

8.11 For the same time series you used in **8.10**, try using a non-seasonal model applied to the seasonally adjusted data obtained from STL. The stlf() function will make the calculations easy (with method="arima"). Compare the forecasts with those obtained in **8.10**. Which do you think is the best approach?

8/12   Further reading

- Box, G. E. P., G. M. Jenkins and G. C. Reinsel (2008). *Time series analysis: forecasting and control*. 4th. Hoboken, NJ: John Wiley & Sons.

- Brockwell, P. J. and R. A. Davis (2002). *Introduction to Time Series and Forecasting*. 2nd ed. New York: Springer.

- Chatfield, C. (2000). *Time-series forecasting*. Boca Raton: Chapman & Hall/CRC.

- Peña, D., G. C. Tiao and R. S. Tsay, eds. (2001). *A course in time series analysis*. New York: John Wiley & Sons.

- Shumway, R. H. and D. S. Stoffer (2011). *Time series analysis and its applications: with R examples*. 3rd ed. New York: Springer.

9
Advanced forecasting methods

In this chapter, we briefly discuss four more advanced forecasting methods that build on the models discussed in earlier chapters.

9/1 *Dynamic regression models*

The time series models in the previous two chapters allow for the inclusion of information from the past observations of a series, but not for the inclusion of other information that may be relevant. For example, the effects of holidays, competitor activity, changes in the law, the wider economy, or some other external variables may explain some of the historical variation and allow more accurate forecasts. On the other hand, the regression models in Chapter 5 allow for the inclusion of a lot of relevant information from predictor variables, but do not allow for the subtle time series dynamics that can be handled with ARIMA models.

In this section, we consider how to extend ARIMA models to allow other information to be included in the models. We begin by simply combining regression models and ARIMA models to give regression with ARIMA errors. These are then extended into the general class of dynamic regression models.

In Chapter 5 we considered regression models of the form

$$y_t = \beta_0 + \beta_1 x_{1,t} + \cdots + \beta_k x_{k,t} + e_t,$$

where y_t is a linear function of the k predictor variables $(x_{1,t}, \ldots, x_{k,t})$, and e_t is usually assumed to be an uncorrelated error term (i.e., it is white noise). We considered tests such as the Durbin-Watson test for assessing whether e_t was significantly correlated.

In this chapter, we will allow the errors from a regression to contain autocorrelation. To emphasise this change in perspective, we will replace e_t by n_t in the equation. The error series n_t is assumed to follow an ARIMA model. For example, if n_t follows an ARIMA(1,1,1) model, we can write

$$y_t = \beta_0 + \beta_1 x_{1,t} + \cdots + \beta_k x_{k,t} + n_t,$$
$$(1 - \phi_1 B)(1 - B)n_t = (1 + \theta_1 B)e_t,$$

where e_t is a white noise series.

Notice that the model has two error terms here — the error from the regression model that we denote by n_t and the error from the ARIMA model that we denote by e_t. Only the ARIMA model errors are assumed to be white noise.

Estimation

When we estimate the parameters from the model, we need to minimise the sum of squared e_t values. If, instead, we minimised the sum of squared n_t values (which is what would happen if we estimated the regression model ignoring the autocorrelations in the errors), then several problems arise.

1. The estimated coefficients $\hat{\beta}_0, \ldots, \hat{\beta}_k$ are no longer the best estimates as some information has been ignored in the calculation;
2. Statistical tests associated with the model (e.g., t-tests on the coefficients) are incorrect.
3. The AIC of the fitted models are not a good guide as to which is the best model for forecasting.

In most cases, the p-values associated with the coefficients will be too small, and so some predictor variables appear to be important when they are not. This is known as "spurious regression".

Minimising the sum of squared e_t values avoids these problems. Alternatively, maximum likelihood estimation can be used; this will give very similar estimates for the coefficients.

An important consideration in estimating a regression with ARMA errors is that all variables in the model must first be stationary. So we first have to check that y_t and all the predictors $(x_{1,t}, \ldots, x_{k,t})$ appear to be stationary. If we estimate the model while any of these are non-stationary, the estimated coefficients can be incorrect.

One exception to this is the case where non-stationary variables are co-integrated. If there exists a linear combination between the non-stationary y_t and predictors that is stationary, then the estimated coefficients are correct.[1]

So we first difference the non-stationary variables in the model. It is often desirable to maintain the form of the relationship between y_t and the predictors, and consequently it is common to difference all variables if any of them need differencing. The resulting model is then called a "model in differences" as distinct from a "model in levels" which is what is obtained when the original data are used without differencing.

If all the variables in the model are stationary, then we only need to consider ARMA errors for the residuals. It is easy to see that a regression model with ARIMA errors is equivalent to a regression model in differences with ARMA errors. For example, if the above regression model with ARIMA(1,1,1) errors is differenced we obtain the model

$$y_t' = \beta_1 x_{1,t}' + \cdots + \beta_k x_{k,t}' + n_t',$$
$$(1 - \phi_1 B)n_t' = (1 + \theta_1 B)e_t,$$

where $y_t' = y_t - y_{t-1}$, $x_{t,i}' = x_{t,i} - x_{t-1,i}$ and $n_t' = n_t - n_{t-1}$, which is a regression model in differences with ARMA errors.

Model selection

To determine the appropriate ARIMA error structure, we first need to calculate n_t. But we cannot get n_t without knowing the coefficients, $\beta_0, \ldots, \beta_k$. To estimate these coefficients, we first need to specify the ARIMA error structure. So we are stuck in an infinite loop where each part of the model needs to be specified before we can estimate the other parts of the models.

A solution is to begin with a proxy model for the ARIMA errors. A common approach with non-seasonal data is to start with an AR(2) model for the errors, or an ARIMA(2,0,0)(1,0,0)$_m$ model for seasonal data. While it is unlikely that these will be the best error models, they will allow most of the autocorrelation to be included in the model, and so the resulting β coefficients should not be too far wrong.

Once we have a proxy model for the ARIMA errors, we estimate the regression coefficients, calculate the preliminary

[1] Forecasting with cointegrated models is discussed in R. Harris and R. Sollis (2003). *Applied Time Series Modelling and Forecasting*. Chichester, UK: John Wiley & Sons.

values of n_t, and then select a more appropriate ARMA model for n_t before re-estimating the entire model.

The full modelling procedure is outlined below. We assume that you have already chosen the predictor variables (this assumption will be removed shortly). We also assume that any Box-Cox transformations have already been applied if required.

1. Check that the forecast variable and all predictors are stationary. If not, apply differencing until all variables are stationary. Where appropriate, use the same differencing for all variables to preserve interpretability.

2. Fit the regression model with AR(2) errors for non-seasonal data or ARIMA(2,0,0)(1,0,0)$_m$ errors for seasonal data.

3. Calculate the errors (n_t) from the fitted regression model and identify an appropriate ARMA model for them.

4. Re-fit the entire model using the new ARMA model for the errors.

5. Check that the e_t series looks like white noise.

The AIC can be calculated for the final model, and this value can be used to determine the best predictors. That is, the procedure should be repeated for all subsets of predictors to be considered, and the model with the lowest AIC value selected.

The procedure is illustrated in the following example.

Example 9.1   US Personal Consumption and Income

Figure 9.1 shows quarterly changes in personal consumption expenditure and personal disposable income from 1970 to 2010. We would like to forecast changes in expenditure based on changes in income. An increase in income does not necessarily translate into an instant increase in consumption (e.g., after the loss of a job, it may take a few months for expenses to be reduced to allow for the new circumstances). However, we will ignore this complexity in this example and try to measure the instantaneous effect of the average change of income on the average change of consumption expenditure.

The data are clearly already stationary (as we are considering percentage changes rather than raw expenditure and income),

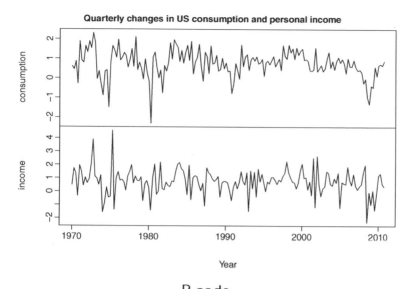

Figure 9.1: Percentage changes in quarterly personal consumption expenditure and personal disposable income for the USA, 1970 to 2010.

───────────── R code ─────────────

```
plot(usconsumption, xlab="Year",
   main="Quarterly changes in US consumption and personal income")
```

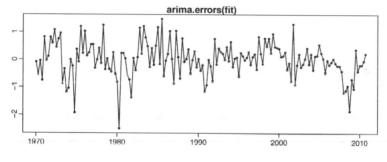

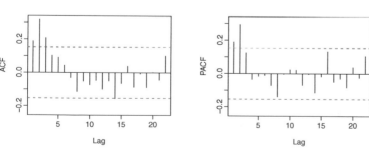

Figure 9.2: Errors (n_t) obtained from regression change in consumption expenditure on change in disposable income, assuming a proxy AR(2) error model.

───────────── R code ─────────────

```
fit <- Arima(usconsumption[,1], xreg=usconsumption[,2],
         order=c(2,0,0))
tsdisplay(arima.errors(fit), main="ARIMA errors")
```

so there is no need for any differencing. So we first regress consumption on income assuming AR(2) errors. The resulting n_t values are shown in Figure 9.2. Possible candidate ARIMA models include an MA(3) and AR(2). However, further exploration reveals that an ARIMA(1,0,2) has the lowest AIC_c value. We refit the model with ARIMA(1,0,2) errors to obtain the following results.

——————————— R output ———————————

```
> (fit2 <- Arima(usconsumption[,1], xreg=usconsumption[,2],
            order=c(1,0,2)))
Series: usconsumption[, 1]
ARIMA(1,0,2) with non-zero mean

Coefficients:
         ar1      ma1     ma2   intercept   usconsumption[, 2]
      0.6516  -0.5440  0.2187     0.5750               0.2420
s.e.  0.1468   0.1576  0.0790     0.0951               0.0513

sigma^2 estimated as 0.3396:  log likelihood=-144.27
AIC=300.54   AICc=301.08   BIC=319.14
```

A Ljung-Box test shows the residuals are uncorrelated.

——————————— R output ———————————

```
> Box.test(residuals(fit2), fitdf=5, lag=10, type="Ljung")
        Box-Ljung test
data:  residuals(fit2)
X-squared = 4.5948, df = 5, p-value = 0.4673
```

Forecasts are, of course, only possible if we have future values of changes in personal disposable income. Here we will calculate forecasts assuming that for the next 8 quarters, the percentage change in personal disposable income is equal to the mean percentage change from the last forty years.

The prediction intervals for this model are narrower than those for the model developed in Section 8.1 (p. 8.8) because we are now able to explain some of the variation in the data using the income predictor.

Regression with ARIMA errors in R

The R function Arima() will fit a regression model with ARIMA errors if the argument xreg is used. The order argument specifies the order of the ARIMA error model. If differencing is

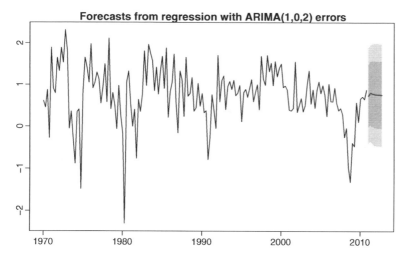

Figure 9.3: Forecasts obtained from regressing the percentage change in consumption expenditure on the percentage change in disposable income, with an ARIMA(1,0,2) error model.

```
―――――――――――――――――― R code ――――――――――――――――――
fcast <- forecast(fit2, xreg=rep(mean(usconsumption[,2]),8), h=8)
plot(fcast,
  main="Forecasts from regression with ARIMA(1,0,2) errors")
```

specified, then the differencing is applied to all variables in the regression model before the model is estimated. For example, suppose we issue the following R command.

```
―――――――――――――――――― R code ――――――――――――――――――
fit <- Arima(y, xreg=x, order=c(1,1,0))
```

This will fit the model $y'_t = \beta_1 x'_t + n'_t$ where $n'_t = \phi_1 n'_{t-1} + e_t$ is an AR(1) error. This is equivalent to the model

$$y_t = \beta_0 + \beta_1 x_t + n_t$$

where n_t is an ARIMA(1,1,0) error. Notice that the constant term disappears due to the differencing. If you want to include a constant in the differenced model, specify include.drift=TRUE.

The auto.arima() function will also handle regression terms. For example, the following command will give the same model as that obtained in the preceding analysis.

```
―――――――――――――――――― R code ――――――――――――――――――
fit <- auto.arima(usconsumption[,1], xreg=usconsumption[,2])
```

Forecasting

To forecast a regression model with ARIMA errors, we need to forecast the regression part of the model and the ARIMA part of the model, and combine the results. As with ordinary regression models, to obtain forecasts, we need to first forecast the predictors. When the predictors are known into the future (e.g., calendar-related variables such as time, day-of-week, etc.), this is straightforward. But when the predictors are themselves unknown, we must either model them separately, or use assumed future values for each predictor.

It is important to realise that the prediction intervals from regression models (with or without ARIMA errors) do not take account of the uncertainty in the forecasts of the predictors.

Stochastic and deterministic trends

We have considered two different ways of modelling a trend. A *deterministic trend* is obtained using the regression model

$$y_t = \beta_0 + \beta_1 t + n_t,$$

where n_t is an ARMA process. A *stochastic trend* is obtained using the model

$$y_t = \beta_0 + \beta_1 t + n_t,$$

where n_t is an ARIMA process with $d = 1$. In that case, we can difference both sides so that $y'_t = \beta_1 + n'_t$ where n'_t is an ARMA process. In other words,

$$y_t = y_{t-1} + \beta_1 + n'_t.$$

So this is very similar to a random walk with drift, but here the error term is an ARMA process rather than simply white noise.

Although these models appear quite similar (they only differ in the number of differences that need to be applied to n_t), their forecasting characteristics are quite different.

Example 9.2   International visitors to Australia

Figure 9.4 shows the total number of international visitors to Australia each year from 1980 to 2010. We will fit both a deterministic and a stochastic trend model to these data.

The deterministic trend model is obtained as follows:

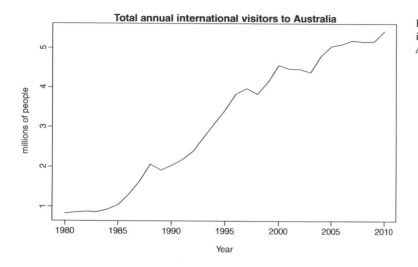

Figure 9.4: Annual international visitors to Australia, 1980–2010.

———————————— R output ————————————
```
> auto.arima(austa, d=0, xreg=1:length(austa))
ARIMA(2,0,0) with non-zero mean

Coefficients:
          ar1       ar2   intercept   1:length(austa)
       1.0371   -0.3379      0.4173            0.1715
s.e.   0.1675    0.1797      0.1866            0.0102

sigma^2 estimated as 0.02486:   log likelihood=12.7
```

This model can be written as

$$y_t = 0.42 + 0.17t + n_t$$
$$n_t = 1.04n_{t-1} - 0.34n_{t-2} + e_t$$
$$e_t \sim \mathrm{NID}(0, 0.025).$$

The estimated growth in visitor numbers is 0.17 million people per year.

Alternatively, the stochastic trend model can be estimated.

――――――――――――――― R output ―――――――――――――――

```
> auto.arima(austa, d=1)
Series: austa
ARIMA(0,1,0) with drift

Coefficients:
      drift
      0.154
s.e.  0.033

sigma^2 estimated as 0.0324:  log likelihood=9.07
AIC=-14.14   AICc=-13.69   BIC=-11.34
```

This model can be written as $y_t - y_{t-1} = 0.15 + e_t$, or equivalently

$$y_t = y_0 + 0.15t + n_t$$
$$n_t = n_{t-1} + e_t$$
$$e_t \sim \text{NID}(0, 0.032).$$

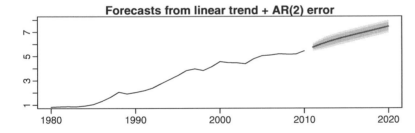

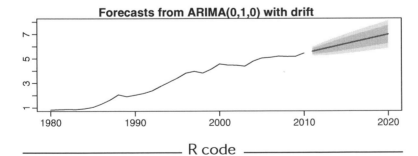

Figure 9.5: Forecasts of annual international visitors to Australia using a deterministic trend model and a stochastic trend model.

――――――――――――――― R code ―――――――――――――――

```
fit1 <- Arima(austa, order=c(0,1,0), include.drift=TRUE)
fit2 <- Arima(austa, order=c(2,0,0), include.drift=TRUE)
par(mfrow=c(2,1))
plot(forecast(fit2), main="Forecasts from linear trend + AR(2) error",
  ylim=c(1,8))
plot(forecast(fit1), ylim=c(1,8))
```

In this case, the estimated growth in visitor numbers is 0.15 million people per year.

Although the growth estimates are similar, the prediction intervals are not, as shown in Figure 9.5. In particular, stochastic trends have much wider prediction intervals because the errors are non-stationary.

There is an implicit assumption with a deterministic trend that the slope of the trend is not going to change over time. On the other hand, stochastic trends can change and the estimated growth is only assumed to be the average growth over the historical period, not necessarily the rate of growth that will be observed into the future. Consequently, it is safer to forecast with stochastic trends, especially for longer forecast horizons, as the prediction intervals allow for greater uncertainty in future growth.

Lagged predictors

Sometimes, the impact of a predictor included in a regression model will not be simple and immediate. For example, an advertising campaign may impact sales for some time beyond the end of the campaign, and sales in one month will depend on advertising expenditure in each of the past few months. Similarly, a change in a company safety policy may reduce accidents immediately, but have a diminishing effect over time as employees take less care as they become familiar with the new working conditions.

In these situations, we need to allow for lagged effects of the predictor. Suppose we have only one predictor in our model. Then a model that allows for lagged effects can be written as

$$y_t = \beta_0 + \gamma_0 x_t + \gamma_1 x_{t-1} + \cdots + \gamma_k x_{t-k} + n_t,$$

where n_t is an ARIMA process. The value of k can be selected using the AIC along with the values of p and q for the ARIMA error.

Example 9.3   TV advertising and insurance quotations

A US insurance company advertises on national television in an attempt to increase the number of insurance quotations provided (and consequently the number of new policies). Figure 9.6 shows the number of quotations and the expenditure

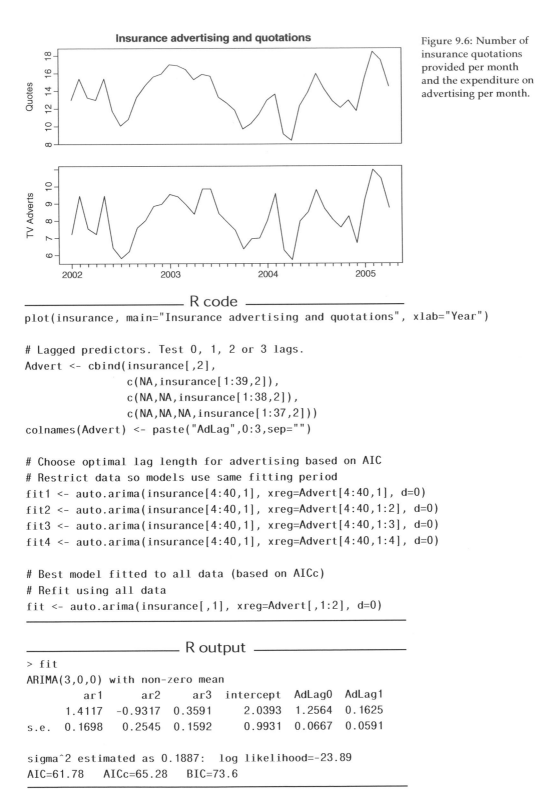

Figure 9.6: Number of insurance quotations provided per month and the expenditure on advertising per month.

─────────────── R code ───────────────

```
plot(insurance, main="Insurance advertising and quotations", xlab="Year")


# Lagged predictors. Test 0, 1, 2 or 3 lags.
Advert <- cbind(insurance[,2],
                c(NA,insurance[1:39,2]),
                c(NA,NA,insurance[1:38,2]),
                c(NA,NA,NA,insurance[1:37,2]))
colnames(Advert) <- paste("AdLag",0:3,sep="")


# Choose optimal lag length for advertising based on AIC
# Restrict data so models use same fitting period
fit1 <- auto.arima(insurance[4:40,1], xreg=Advert[4:40,1], d=0)
fit2 <- auto.arima(insurance[4:40,1], xreg=Advert[4:40,1:2], d=0)
fit3 <- auto.arima(insurance[4:40,1], xreg=Advert[4:40,1:3], d=0)
fit4 <- auto.arima(insurance[4:40,1], xreg=Advert[4:40,1:4], d=0)


# Best model fitted to all data (based on AICc)
# Refit using all data
fit <- auto.arima(insurance[,1], xreg=Advert[,1:2], d=0)
```

─────────────── R output ───────────────

```
> fit
ARIMA(3,0,0) with non-zero mean
          ar1       ar2      ar3   intercept   AdLag0   AdLag1
       1.4117   -0.9317   0.3591      2.0393   1.2564   0.1625
s.e.   0.1698    0.2545   0.1592      0.9931   0.0667   0.0591

sigma^2 estimated as 0.1887:   log likelihood=-23.89
AIC=61.78    AICc=65.28    BIC=73.6
```

on television advertising for the company each month from January 2002 to April 2005.

We will consider including advertising expenditure for up to four months; that is, the model may include advertising expenditure in the current month, and the three months before that. It is important when comparing models that they are all using the same training set. So in the following code, we exclude the first three months in order to make fair comparisons. The best model is the one with the smallest AIC_c value.

The chosen model includes advertising only in the current month and the previous month, and has AR(3) errors. The model can be written as

$$y_t = \beta_0 + \gamma_0 x_t + \gamma_1 x_{t-1} + n_t,$$

where y_t is the number of quotations provided in month t, x_t is the advertising expenditure in month t,

$$n_t = \phi_1 n_{t-1} + \phi_2 n_{t-2} + \phi_3 n_{t-3} + e_t,$$

and e_t is white noise.

We can calculate forecasts using this model if we assume future values for the advertising variable. If we set future monthly advertising to 8 units, we get the following forecasts.

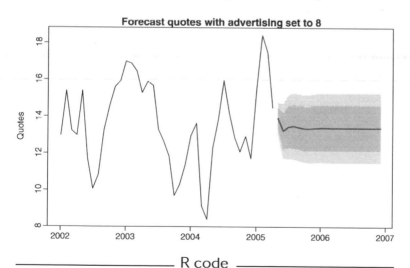

Figure 9.7: Forecasts of monthly insurance quotes assuming future advertising is 8 units in each future month.

―――――――――――― R code ――――――――――――
```
fc8 <- forecast(fit, xreg=cbind(c(Advert[40,1],rep(8,19)),rep(8,20)), h=20)
plot(fc8, main="Forecast quotes with advertising set to 8", ylab="Quotes")
```

9/2 Vector autoregressions

One limitation with the models we have considered so far is that they impose a unidirectional relationship — the forecast variable is influenced by the predictor variables, but not vice versa. However, there are many cases where the reverse should also be allowed for — where all variables affect each other. Consider the series in Example 9.1. The changes in personal consumption expenditure (C_t) are forecast based on the changes in personal disposable income (I_t). In this case a bi-directional relationship may be more suitable: an increase in I_t will lead to an increase in C_t and vice versa.

An example of such a situation occurred in Australia during the Global Financial Crisis of 2008–2009. The Australian government issued stimulus packages that included cash payments in December 2008, just in time for Christmas spending. As a result, retailers reported strong sales and the economy was stimulated. Consequently, incomes increased.

Such feedback relationships are allowed for in the vector autoregressive (VAR) framework. In this framework, all variables are treated symmetrically. They are all modelled as if they influence each other equally. In more formal terminology, all variables are now treated as "endogenous". To signify this we now change the notation and write all variables as ys: $y_{1,t}$ denotes the tth observation of variable y_1, $y_{2,t}$ denotes the tth observation of variable y_2, and so on.

A VAR model is a generalisation of the univariate autoregressive model for forecasting a collection of variables; that is, a vector of time series.[2] It comprises one equation per variable considered in the system. The right hand side of each equation includes a constant and lags of all the variables in the system. To keep it simple, we will consider a two variable VAR with one lag. We write a 2-dimensional VAR(1) as

$$y_{1,t} = c_1 + \phi_{11,1} y_{1,t-1} + \phi_{12,1} y_{2,t-1} + e_{1,t} \qquad (9.1a)$$

$$y_{2,t} = c_2 + \phi_{21,1} y_{1,t-1} + \phi_{22,1} y_{2,t-1} + e_{2,t} \qquad (9.1b)$$

where $e_{1,t}$ and $e_{2,t}$ are white noise processes that may be contemporaneously correlated. Coefficient $\phi_{ii,\ell}$ captures the influence of the ℓth lag of variable y_i on itself, while coefficient $\phi_{ij,\ell}$ captures the influence of the ℓth lag of variable y_j on y_i.

[2] A more flexible generalisation would be a Vector ARMA process. However, the relative simplicity of VARs has led to their dominance in forecasting. Interested readers may refer to G. Athanasopoulos, D. S. Poskitt and F. Vahid (2012). Two Canonical VARMA Forms: Scalar Component Models Vis-à-Vis the Echelon Form. *Econometric Reviews* **31**(1), 60–83.

If the series modelled are stationary we forecast them by directly fitting a VAR to the data (known as a "VAR in levels"). If the series are non-stationary we take differences to make them stationary and then we fit a VAR model (known as a "VAR in differences"). In both cases, the models are estimated equation by equation using the principle of least squares. For each equation, the parameters are estimated by minimising the sum of squared $e_{i,t}$ values.

The other possibility which is beyond the scope of this book and therefore we do not explore here, is that series may be non-stationary but they are cointegrated, which means that there exists a linear combination of them that is stationary. In this case a VAR specification that includes an error correction mechanism (usually referred to as a vector error correction model) should be included and alternative estimation methods to least squares estimation should be used.[3]

Forecasts are generated from a VAR in a recursive manner. The VAR generates forecasts for each variable included in the system. To illustrate the process, assume that we have fitted the 2-dimensional VAR(1) described in equations (9.1a)–(9.1b) for all observations up to time T. Then the one-step-ahead forecasts are generated by

$$\hat{y}_{1,T+1|T} = \hat{c}_1 + \hat{\phi}_{11,1}y_{1,T} + \hat{\phi}_{12,1}y_{2,T}$$
$$\hat{y}_{2,T+1|T} = \hat{c}_2 + \hat{\phi}_{21,1}y_{1,T} + \hat{\phi}_{22,1}y_{2,T}.$$

This is the same form as (9.1a)–(9.1b) except that the errors have been set to zero and parameters have been replaced with their estimates. For $h = 2$, the forecasts are given by

$$\hat{y}_{1,T+2|T} = \hat{c}_1 + \hat{\phi}_{11,1}\hat{y}_{1,T+1} + \hat{\phi}_{12,1}\hat{y}_{2,T+1}$$
$$\hat{y}_{2,T+2|T} = \hat{c}_2 + \hat{\phi}_{21,1}\hat{y}_{1,T+1} + \hat{\phi}_{22,1}\hat{y}_{2,T+1}.$$

Again, this is the same form as (9.1a)–(9.1b) except that the errors have been set to zero, parameters have been replaced with their estimates, and the unknown values of y_1 and y_2 have been replaced with their forecasts. The process can be iterated in this manner for all future time periods.

There are two decisions one has to make when using a VAR to forecast. They are, how many variables (denoted by K) and how many lags (denoted by p) should be included in the system. The number of coefficients to be estimated in a VAR is equal

[3] Interested readers should refer to J. D. Hamilton (1994). *Time Series Analysis*. Princeton University Press, Princeton, and H. Lütkepohl (2007). General-to-specific or specific-to-general modelling? An opinion on current econometric terminology. *Journal of Econometrics* **136**, 234–319.

to $K + pK^2$ (or $1 + pK$ per equation). For example, for a VAR with $K = 5$ variables and $p = 3$ lags, there are 16 coefficients per equation making for a total of 80 coefficients to be estimated. The more coefficients to be estimated the larger the estimation error entering the forecast.

In practice it is usual to keep K small and include only variables that are correlated to each other and therefore useful in forecasting each other. Information criteria are commonly used to select the number of lags to be included.

VARs are implemented in the **vars** package in R. It contains a function VARselect to choose the number of lags p using four different information criteria: AIC, HQ, SC and FPE. We have met the AIC before, and SC is simply another name for the BIC (SC stands for Schwarz Criterion after Gideon Schwarz who proposed it). HQ is the Hannan-Quinn criterion and FPE is the "Final Prediction Error" criterion.[4] Care should be taken using the AIC as it tends to choose large numbers of lags. Instead, for VAR models, we prefer to use the BIC.

A criticism VARs face is that they are atheoretical. They are not built on some economic theory that imposes a theoretical structure to the equations. Every variable is assumed to influence every other variable in the system, which makes direct interpretation of the estimated coefficients very difficult. Despite this, VARs are useful in several contexts:

1. forecasting a collection of related variables where no explicit interpretation is required;
2. testing whether one variable is useful in forecasting another (the basis of Granger causality tests);
3. impulse response analysis, where the response of one variable to a sudden but temporary change in another variable is analysed;
4. forecast error variance decomposition, where the proportion of the forecast variance of one variable is attributed to the effect of other variables.

Example 9.4   A VAR model for forecasting US consumption

The R output on the following page shows the lag length selected by each of the information criteria available in the **vars** package. There is a large discrepancy between a VAR(5) selected by the AIC and a VAR(1) selected by the BIC. This is

[4] For a detailed comparison of these criteria, see Chapter 4.3 of H. Lütkepohl (2005). *New introduction to multiple time series analysis*. Berlin: Springer-Verlag.

————————————— R output —————————————

```
> library(vars)
> VARselect(usconsumption, lag.max=8, type="const")$selection
AIC(n)  HQ(n)  SC(n) FPE(n)
     5      1      1      5
> var <- VAR(usconsumption, p=3, type="const")
> serial.test(var, lags.pt=10, type="PT.asymptotic")
Portmanteau Test (asymptotic)
data:  Residuals of VAR object var
Chi-squared = 33.3837, df = 28, p-value = 0.2219


> summary(var)
VAR Estimation Results:
=========================

Endogenous variables: consumption, income
Deterministic variables: const
Sample size: 161


Estimation results for equation consumption:
=============================================
               Estimate Std. Error t value Pr(>|t|)
consumption.l1  0.22280    0.08580   2.597 0.010326 *
income.l1       0.04037    0.06230   0.648 0.518003
consumption.l2  0.20142    0.09000   2.238 0.026650 *
income.l2      -0.09830    0.06411  -1.533 0.127267
consumption.l3  0.23512    0.08824   2.665 0.008530 **
income.l3       0.02416    0.06130   0.394 0.694427
const           0.31972    0.09119   3.506 0.000596 ***

Estimation results for equation income:
=========================================
               Estimate Std. Error t value Pr(>|t|)
consumption.l1  0.48705    0.11637   4.186 4.77e-05 ***
income.l1      -0.24881    0.08450  -2.945 0.003736 **
consumption.l2  0.03222    0.12206   0.264 0.792135
income.l2      -0.11112    0.08695  -1.278 0.203170
consumption.l3  0.40297    0.11967   3.367 0.000959 ***
income.l3      -0.09150    0.08326  -1.099 0.273484
const           0.36280    0.12368   2.933 0.003865 **
---
Signif. codes:  0 `***' 0.001 `**' 0.01 `*' 0.05 `.' 0.1 ` ' 1

Correlation matrix of residuals:
           consumption income
consumption     1.0000 0.3639
income          0.3639 1.0000
```

not unusual. As a result we first fit a VAR(1), selected by the BIC. In similar fashion to the univariate ARIMA methodology we test that the residuals are uncorrelated using a Portmanteau test[5] The null hypothesis of no serial correlation in the residuals is rejected for both a VAR(1) and a VAR(2) and therefore we fit a VAR(3) as now the null is not rejected. The forecasts generated by the VAR(3) are plotted in Figure 9.8.

[5] The tests for serial correlation in the "vars" package are multivariate generalisations of the tests presented in Section 2/6.

Figure 9.8: Forecasts for US consumption and income generated from a VAR(3).

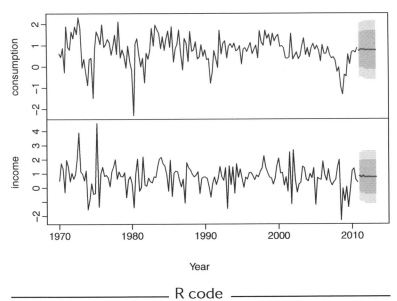

Forecasts from VAR(3)

```
fcst <- forecast(var)
plot(fcst, xlab="Year")
```

9/3   Neural network models

Artificial neural networks are forecasting methods that are based on simple mathematical models of the brain. They allow complex nonlinear relationships between the response variable and its predictors.

Neural network architecture

A neural network can be thought of as a network of "neurons" organised in layers. The predictors (or inputs) form the bottom layer, and the forecasts (or outputs) form the top layer. There may be intermediate layers containing "hidden neurons".

The very simplest networks contain no hidden layers and are equivalent to linear regression. Figure 9.9 shows the neural network version of a linear regression with four predictors. The coefficients attached to these predictors are called "weights". The forecasts are obtained by a linear combination of the inputs. The weights are selected in the neural network framework using a "learning algorithm" that minimises a "cost function" such as MSE. Of course, in this simple example, we can use linear regression which is a much more efficient method for training the model.

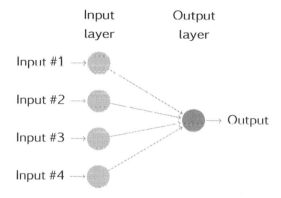

Figure 9.9: A simple neural network equivalent to a linear regression.

Once we add an intermediate layer with hidden neurons, the neural network becomes non-linear. A simple example is shown in Figure 9.10.

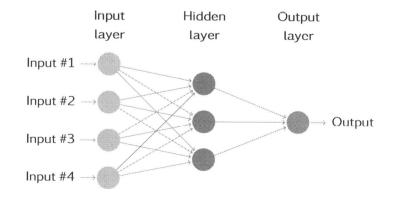

Figure 9.10: A neural network with four inputs and one hidden layer with three hidden neurons.

This is known as a *multilayer feed-forward network* where each layer of nodes receives inputs from the previous layers.

The outputs of nodes in one layer are inputs to the next layer.
The inputs to each node are combined using a weighted linear
combination. The result is then modified by a nonlinear function before being output. For example, the inputs into hidden
neuron j in Figure 9.10 are linearly combined to give

$$z_j = b_j + \sum_{i=1}^{4} w_{i,j} x_i.$$

In the hidden layer, this is then modified using a nonlinear
function such as a sigmoid,

$$s(z) = \frac{1}{1 + e^{-z}},$$

to give the input for the next layer. This tends to reduce the
effect of extreme input values, thus making the network somewhat robust to outliers.

The parameters b_1, b_2, b_3 and $w_{1,1}, \ldots, w_{4,3}$ are "learned"
from the data. The values of the weights are often restricted to
prevent them becoming too large. The parameter that restricts
the weights is known as the "decay parameter" and is often set
to be equal to 0.1.

The weights take random values to begin with, which are
then updated using the observed data. Consequently, there
is an element of randomness in the predictions produced by
a neural network. Therefore, the network is usually trained
several times using different random starting points, and the
results are averaged.

The number of hidden layers, and the number of nodes
in each hidden layer, must be specified in advance. We will
consider how these can be chosen using cross-validation later in
this chapter.

Example 9.5   Credit scoring

To illustrate neural network forecasting, we will use the credit
scoring example that was discussed in Chapter 5. There we
fitted the following linear regression model:

$$y = \beta_0 + \beta_1 x_1 + \beta_2 x_2 + \beta_3 x_3 + \beta_4 x_4 + e,$$

where

y = credit score,

x_1 = log savings,

x_2 = log income,

x_3 = log time at current address,

x_4 = log time in current job,

e = error.

Here "log" means the transformation $\log(x + 1)$. This could be represented by the network shown in Figure 9.9 where the inputs are $x_1, \ldots, x_4$ and the output is y. The more sophisticated neural network shown in Figure 9.10 could be fitted as follows.

────────────────── R code ──────────────────

```
library(caret)
creditlog <- data.frame(score=credit$score,
  log.savings=log(credit$savings+1),
  log.income=log(credit$income+1),
  log.address=log(credit$time.address+1),
  log.employed=log(credit$time.employed+1),
  fte=credit$fte, single=credit$single)
fit <- avNNet(score ~ log.savings + log.income + log.address +
  log.employed, data=creditlog, repeats=25, size=3, decay=0.1,
  linout=TRUE)
```

The avNNet function from the **caret** package fits a feed-forward neural network with one hidden layer. The network specified here contains three nodes (size=3) in the hidden layer. The decay parameter has been set to 0.1. The argument repeats=25 indicates that 25 networks were trained and their predictions are to be averaged. The argument linout=TRUE indicates that the output is obtained using a linear function. In this book, we will always specify linout=TRUE.

Neural network autoregression

With time series data, lagged values of the time series can be used as inputs to a neural network. Just as we used lagged values in a linear autoregression model (Chapter 8), we can use lagged values in a neural network autoregression.

In this book, we only consider feed-forward networks with one hidden layer, and use the notation NNAR(p, k) to indicate there are p lagged inputs and k nodes in the hidden layer. For example, a NNAR(9,5) model is a neural network with the last nine observations $(y_{t-1}, y_{t-2}, \ldots, y_{t-9})$ used as inputs to forecast the output y_t, and with five neurons in the hidden layer. A NNAR$(p, 0)$ model is equivalent to an ARIMA$(p, 0, 0)$ model but without the restrictions on the parameters to ensure stationarity.

With seasonal data, it is useful to also add the last observed values from the same season as inputs. For example, an NNAR$(3, 1, 2)_{12}$ model has inputs y_{t-1}, y_{t-2}, y_{t-3} and y_{t-12}, and two neurons in the hidden layer. More generally, an NNAR$(p, P, k)_m$ model has inputs $(y_{t-1}, y_{t-2}, \ldots, y_{t-p}, y_{t-m}, y_{t-2m}, y_{t-Pm})$ and k neurons in the hidden layer. A NNAR$(p, P, 0)_m$ model is equivalent to an ARIMA$(p, 0, 0)(P, 0, 0)_m$ model but without the restrictions on the parameters to ensure stationarity.

The nnetar() function fits an NNAR$(p, P, k)_m$ model. If the values of p and P are not specified, they are automatically selected. For non-seasonal time series, the default is the optimal number of lags (according to the AIC) for a linear AR(p) model. For seasonal time series, the default values are $P = 1$ and p is chosen from the optimal linear model fitted to the seasonally adjusted data. If k is not specified, it is set to $k = (p + P + 1)/2$ (rounded to the nearest integer).

Example 9.6 Sunspots

The surface of the sun contains magnetic regions that appear as dark spots. These affect the propagation of radio waves and so telecommunication companies like to predict sunspot activity in order to plan for any future difficulties. Sunspots follow a cycle of length between 9 and 14 years. In Figure 9.11, forecasts from an NNAR(9) are shown for the next 20 years.

──────────────── R code ────────────────

```
fit <- nnetar(sunspotarea)
plot(forecast(fit,h=20))
```

The forecasts actually go slightly negative, which is of course impossible. If we wanted to restrict the forecasts to remain positive, we could use a log transformation (specified by the Box-Cox parameter $\lambda = 0$):

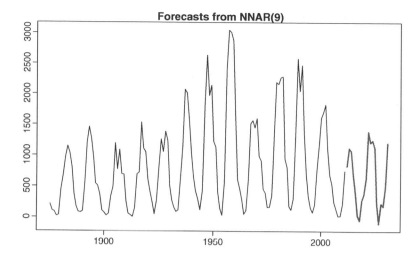

Figure 9.11: Forecasts from a neural network with nine lagged inputs and one hidden layer containing five neurons.

R code

```
fit <- nnetar(sunspotarea,lambda=0)
plot(forecast(fit,h=20))
```

9/4   *Forecasting hierarchical or grouped time series*

Warning: this is a more advanced section and assumes knowledge of matrix algebra.

Time series can often be naturally disaggregated in a hierarchical structure using attributes such as geographical location, product type, etc. For example, the total number of bicycles sold by a cycling warehouse can be disaggregated into a hierarchy of bicycle types. Such a warehouse will sell road bikes, mountain bikes, children bikes or hybrids. Each of these can be disaggregated into finer categories. Children's bikes can be divided into balance bikes for children under 4 years old, single speed bikes for children between 4 and 6 and bikes for children over the age of 6. Hybrid bikes can be divided into city, commuting, comfort, and trekking bikes; and so on. Such disaggregation imposes a hierarchical structure. We refer to these as hierarchical time series.

Another possibility is that series can be naturally grouped together based on attributes without necessarily imposing a hierarchical structure. For example the bicycles sold by the warehouse can be for males, females or unisex. They can be used for racing, commuting or recreational purposes. They can be single speed or have multiple gears. Frames can be carbon, aluminium or steel. Grouped time series can be thought of as hierarchical time series that do not impose a unique hierarchical structure in the sense that the order by which the series can be grouped is not unique.

In this section we present alternative approaches for forecasting time series data that possess hierarchical structures. Figure 9.12 shows a $K = 2$-level hierarchy.[6] At the top of the hierarchy, level 0, is the "Total", the most aggregate level of the data. We denote as y_t the tth observation of the "Total" series for $t = 1, \ldots, T$. Below this level we denote as $y_{j,t}$ the tth observation of the series which corresponds to node j of the hierarchical tree. The "Total" is disaggregated into 2 series at level 1 and each of these into 3 and 2 series respectively at the bottom level of the hierarchy, level 2. The total number of series in a hierarchy is given by $n = 1 + n_1 + \cdots + n_K$ where n_i is the number of series at level i of the hierarchy. In this case $n = 1 + 2 + 5 = 8$.

[6] We will use this hierarchical structure in order to introduce the methods for forecasting hierarchical time series that follow.

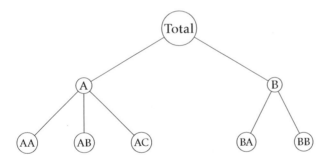

Figure 9.12: A two level hierarchical tree diagram.

For any time t, the observations of the bottom level series will aggregate to the observations of the series above. This can be effectively represented using matrix notation. We construct an $n \times n_K$ matrix referred to as the "summing" matrix S which dictates how the bottom level series are aggregated, consistent with the hierarchical structure. For the hierarchy in Figure 9.12

we can write

$$
\begin{bmatrix}
y_t \\
y_{A,t} \\
y_{B,t} \\
y_{AA,t} \\
y_{AB,t} \\
y_{AC,t} \\
y_{BA,t} \\
y_{BB,t}
\end{bmatrix}
=
\begin{bmatrix}
1 & 1 & 1 & 1 & 1 \\
1 & 1 & 1 & 0 & 0 \\
0 & 0 & 0 & 1 & 1 \\
1 & 0 & 0 & 0 & 0 \\
0 & 1 & 0 & 0 & 0 \\
0 & 0 & 1 & 0 & 0 \\
0 & 0 & 0 & 1 & 0 \\
0 & 0 & 0 & 0 & 1
\end{bmatrix}
\begin{bmatrix}
y_{AA,t} \\
y_{AB,t} \\
y_{AC,t} \\
y_{BA,t} \\
y_{BB,t}
\end{bmatrix}
$$

or in more compact notation

$$y_t = S y_{K,t},$$

where y_t is a vector of all the observations in the hierarchy at time t, S is the summing matrix as defined above, and $y_{K,t}$ is a vector of all the observation in the bottom level of the hierarchy at time t.

We are interested in generating forecasts for each series in the hierarchy. We denote as $\hat{y}_{j,h}$ the h-step-ahead forecast generated for the series at node j having observed the time series up to observation T and as $\hat{y}_h$ the h-step-ahead forecast generated for the "Total" series.[7] We refer to these as "base" forecasts. They are independent forecasts generated for each series in the hierarchy using a suitable forecasting method presented in earlier sections of this book. These base forecasts are then combined to produce final forecasts for the whole hierarchy that aggregate in a manner that is consistent with the structure of the hierarchy. We refer to these as revised forecasts and denote them as $\tilde{y}_{j,h}$ and $\tilde{y}_h$ respectively.

There are a number of ways of combining the base forecasts in order to obtain revised forecasts. The following sections discuss some of the possible combining approaches.

[7] We have simplified the previously used notation of $\hat{y}_{T+h|T}$ for brevity

The bottom-up approach

A commonly applied method for hierarchical forecasting is the bottom-up approach. This approach involves first generating base independent forecasts for each series at the bottom level of the hierarchy and then aggregating these upwards to produce revised forecasts for the whole hierarchy.

For example, for the hierarchy of Figure 9.12 we first generate h-step-ahead base forecasts for the bottom level series:

$\hat{y}_{AA,h}, \hat{y}_{AB,h}, \hat{y}_{AC,h}, \hat{y}_{BA,h}$ and $\hat{y}_{BB,h}$. Aggregating these up the hierarchy we get h-step-ahead forecasts for the rest of the series: $\tilde{y}_{A,h} = \hat{y}_{AA,h} + \hat{y}_{AB,h} + \hat{y}_{AC,h}, \tilde{y}_{B,h} = \hat{y}_{BA,h} + \hat{y}_{BB,h}$ and $\tilde{y}_h = \tilde{y}_{A,h} + \tilde{y}_{B,h}$. Note that for the bottom-up approach the revised forecasts for the bottom level series are equal to the base forecasts.

Using matrix notation we can again employ the summing matrix and write

$$\tilde{y}_h = S\hat{y}_{K,h}.$$

The greatest advantage of this approach is that no information is lost due to aggregation. On the other hand bottom level data can be quite noisy and more challenging to model and forecast.

Top-down approaches

Top-down approaches involve first generating base forecasts for the "Total" series y_t on the top of the hierarchy and then disaggregating these downwards. We let $p_1, \ldots, p_{m_K}$ be a set of proportions which dictate how the base forecasts of the "Total" series are to be distributed to revised forecasts for each series at the bottom level of the hierarchy. Once the bottom level forecasts have been generated we can use the summing matrix to generate forecasts for the rest of the series in the hierarchy. Note that for top-down approaches the top level revised forecasts are equal to the top level base forecasts, i.e., $\tilde{y}_h = \hat{y}_h$.

The most common top-down approaches specify proportions based on the historical proportions of the data. The two most common versions follow.

Average historical proportions

$$p_j = \frac{1}{T} \sum_{t=1}^{T} \frac{y_{j,t}}{y_t}$$

for $j = 1, \ldots, m_K$. Each proportion p_j reflects the average of the historical proportions of the bottom level series $y_{j,t}$ over the period $t = 1, \ldots, T$ relative to the total aggregate y_t.

Proportions of the historical averages

$$p_j = \sum_{t=1}^{T} \frac{y_{j,t}}{T} \bigg/ \sum_{t=1}^{T} \frac{y_t}{T}$$

for $j = 1,\ldots,m_K$. Each proportion p_j captures the average historical value of the bottom level series $y_{j,t}$ relative to the average value of the total aggregate y_t.

The greatest attribute of such top-down approaches is their simplicity to apply. One only needs to model and generate forecasts for the most aggregated top level series. In general these approaches seem to produce quite reliable forecasts for the aggregate levels and they are very useful with low count data. On the other hand, their greatest disadvantage is the loss of information due to aggregation. With these top-down approaches, we are unable to capture and take advantage of individual series characteristics such as time dynamics, special events, etc.

In the example on forecasting Australian domestic tourism demand that follows, the data are highly seasonal. The seasonal pattern of tourist arrivals may vary across series depending on the tourism destination. An area with beaches as its main tourist attractions will have a very different seasonal pattern to an area with skiing as its main tourist attraction. This will not be captured by disaggregating the total of these destinations based on historical proportions. Finally, with these methods the disaggregation of the "Total" series forecasts depends on historical and static proportions, and these proportions may be distorted by trends in the data.

Forecasted proportions   An alternative approach that improves on the historical and static nature of the proportions specified above is to use forecasted proportions.

To demonstrate the intuition of this method, consider a one level hierarchy. We first generate h-step-ahead base forecasts for all the series independently. At level 1 we calculate the proportion of each h-step-ahead base forecast to the aggregate of all the h-step-ahead base forecasts at this level. We refer to these as the forecasted proportions and we use these to disaggregate the top level forecast and generate revised forecasts for the whole of the hierarchy.

For a K-level hierarchy this process is repeated for each node going from the top to the very bottom level. Applying this process leads to the following general rule for obtaining the forecasted proportions

$$p_j = \prod_{\ell=0}^{K-1} \frac{\hat{y}_{j,h}^{(\ell)}}{\hat{S}_{j,h}^{(\ell+1)}}$$

for $j = 1, 2, \ldots, m_K$. These forecasted proportions disaggregate the h-step-ahead base forecast of the "Total" series to h-step-ahead revised forecasts of the bottom level series. $\hat{y}_{j,h}^{(\ell)}$ is the h-step-ahead base forecast of the series that corresponds to the node which is ℓ levels above j. $\hat{S}_{j,h}^{(\ell)}$ is the sum of the h-step-ahead base forecasts below the node that is ℓ levels above node j and are directly connected to that node.

We will use the hierarchy of Figure 9.12 to explain this notation and to demonstrate how this general rule is reached. Assume we have generated independent base forecasts for each series in the hierarchy. Remember that for the top level "Total" series, $\tilde{y}_h = \hat{y}_h$. Here are some example using the above notation:

- $\hat{y}_{A,h}^{(1)} = \hat{y}_{B,h}^{(1)} = \tilde{y}_h$

- $\hat{y}_{BA,h}^{(1)} = \hat{y}_{BB,h}^{(1)} = \hat{y}_{B,h}$

- $\hat{y}_{AA,h}^{(2)} = \hat{y}_{AB,h}^{(2)} = \hat{y}_{AC,h}^{(2)} = \hat{y}_{BA,h}^{(2)} = \hat{y}_{BB,h}^{(2)} = \tilde{y}_h$

- $\hat{S}_{BA,h}^{(1)} = \hat{S}_{BB,h}^{(1)} = \hat{y}_{BA,h} + \hat{y}_{BB,h}$

- $\hat{S}_{BA,h}^{(2)} = \hat{S}_{BB,h}^{(2)} = \hat{S}_{A,h}^{(1)} = \hat{S}_{B,h}^{(1)} = \hat{S}_h = \hat{y}_{A,h} + \hat{y}_{B,h}$

Moving down the farthest left branch of the hierarchy the final revised forecasts are

$$\tilde{y}_{A,h} = \left(\frac{\hat{y}_{A,h}}{\hat{S}_{A,h}^{(1)}} \right) \tilde{y}_h = \left(\frac{\hat{y}_{AA,h}^{(1)}}{\hat{S}_{AA,h}^{(2)}} \right) \tilde{y}_h$$

and

$$\tilde{y}_{AA,h} = \left(\frac{\hat{y}_{AA,h}}{\hat{S}_{AA,h}^{(1)}} \right) \tilde{y}_{A,h} = \left(\frac{\hat{y}_{AA,h}}{\hat{S}_{AA,h}^{(1)}} \right) \left(\frac{\hat{y}_{AA,h}^{(1)}}{\hat{S}_{AA,h}^{(2)}} \right) \tilde{y}_h.$$

Consequently,

$$p_1 = \left(\frac{\hat{y}_{AA,h}}{\hat{S}_{AA,h}^{(1)}} \right) \left(\frac{\hat{y}_{AA,h}^{(1)}}{\hat{S}_{AA,h}^{(2)}} \right) \tilde{y}_h$$

The other proportions can be similarly obtained. The greatest disadvantage of the top-down forecasted proportions approach, which is a disadvantage of any top-down approach, is that they do not produce unbiased revised forecasts even if the base forecasts are unbiased.

Middle-out approach

The middle-out approach combines bottom-up and top-down approaches. First the "middle level" is chosen and base forecasts are generated for all the series of this level and the ones below. For the series above the middle level, revised forecasts are generated using the bottom-up approach by aggregating the "middle-level" base forecasts upwards. For the series below the "middle level", revised forecasts are generated using a top-down approach by disaggregating the "middle level" base forecasts downwards.

The optimal combination approach

This approach involves first generating independent base forecast for each series in the hierarchy. As these base forecasts are independently generated they will not be "aggregate consistent" (i.e., they will not add up according to the hierarchical structure). The optimal combination approach optimally combines the independent base forecasts and generates a set of revised forecasts that are as close as possible to the univariate forecasts but also aggregate consistently with the hierarchical structure.

   Unlike any other existing method, this approach uses all the information available within a hierarchy. It allows for correlations and interactions between series at each level of the hierarchy, it accounts for ad hoc adjustments of forecasts at any level, and, provided the base forecasts are unbiased, it produces unbiased revised forecasts.

   The general idea is derived from the representation of the h-step-ahead base forecasts for the whole of the hierarchy by the linear regression model. We write

$$\hat{y}_h = S\beta_h + \varepsilon_h$$

where $\hat{y}_h$ is a vector of the h-step-ahead base forecasts for the whole hierarchy, β_h is the unknown mean of the future values of the bottom level K, and ε_h has zero mean and covariance matrix Σ_h. Note that ε_h represents the error in the above regression and should not be confused with the h-step-ahead forecast error.

In general Σ_h in unknown. However, if we assume that the errors approximately satisfy the same aggregation structure as the original data, (i.e., $\varepsilon_h \approx S\varepsilon_{K,h}$ where $\varepsilon_{K,h}$ contains the forecast errors in the bottom level), then the best linear unbiased estimator for β_h is $\hat{\beta}_h = (S'S)^{-1}S'\hat{y}_n(h)$. This leads to a set of revised forecasts given by

$$\tilde{y}_h = S(S'S)^{-1}S'\hat{y}_h.$$

Assuming that the errors approximately satisfy the hierarchical aggregation structure will be true provided that the base forecasts also approximately satisfy this aggregation structure, which should occur for any reasonable set of forecasts.

The hts package

Hierarchical time series forecasting is implemented in the **hts** package in R.

The hts function creates a hierarchical time series. The required inputs are the bottom level time series obsverations, and information about the hierarchical structure. For example, the structure shown in Figure 9.12 is specified as follows:

——————————— R code ———————————
```
# bts is a time series matrix containing the bottom level series
# The first three series belong to one group, and the last two series
# belong to a different group
y <- hts(bts, nodes=list(2, c(3,2)))
```

For a grouped but non-hierarchical time series, the gts function can be used. If there are more levels, the g argument should be a matrix where each row contains the grouping structure for each level.

Forecasts are obtained, as usual, with the forecast function. By default it produces forecasts using the optimal combination approach with ETS models used for the base forecasts. But other models and methods can be specified via the following arguments.

fmethod The forecasting model to be used for the base forecasts. Possible values are "ets", "arima" and "rw".

method The method used for reconciling the base forecasts. It can take the following values:

comb Optimal combination forecasts;

bu Bottom-up forecasts;

mo Middle-out forecasts where the level used is specified by the level argument'

tdgsa Top-down forecasts based on the average historical proportions (Gross-Sohl method A);[8]

tdgsf Top-down forecasts based on the proportion of historical averages (Gross-Sohl method F);

tdfp Top-down forecasts using forecast proportions.

[8] C. W. Gross and J. E. Sohl (1990). Disaggregation methods to expedite product line forecasting. *Journal of Forecasting* **9**, 233–254.

Example 9.7   *Australian tourism hierarchy*

Australia is divided into eight geographical areas (some referred to as states and others as territories) with each one having its own government and some economic and administrative autonomy. Business planners and tourism authorities are interested in forecasts for the whole of Australia, the states and the territories, and also smaller regions. In this example we concentrate on quarterly domestic tourism demand, measured as the number of visitor nights Australians spend away from home, for the three largest states of Australia, namely Victoria (VIC), New South Wales (NSW), Queensland (QLD) and other. For each of these we consider visitor nights for each respective capital city, namely, Melbourne (MEL), Sydney (SYD) and Brisbane (BGC).[9] The hierarchical structure is shown in Figure 9.13. The CAP category in the bottom level includes visitor nights in all other five capital cities of the remaining states and territories.

[9] For the purpose of this example we include with Brisbane, visitor nights at the Gold Coast, a coastal city and a major tourism attraction near Brisbane.

Figure 9.13: Australian tourism hierarchy.

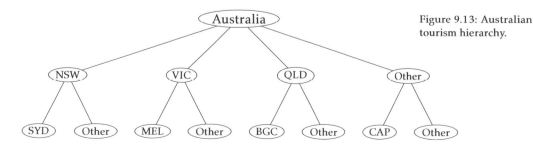

Figure 9.14 shows all the times series in the hierarchy which span the period 1998:Q1 to 2011:Q4. The dotted lines show the revised forecasts generated by the optimal combination approach. The base forecasts for each series are generated using the ETS methodology of Chapter 7.

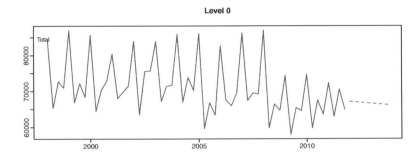

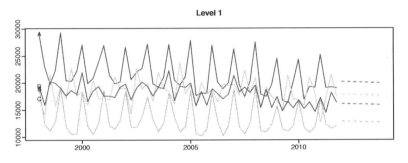

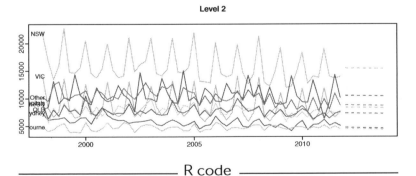

Figure 9.14: Hierarchical time series and 8-step-ahead revised forecasts for Australian domestic tourism generated by the optimal combination approach. The base forecasts for each series were generated using the ETS methodology of Chapter 7.

―――――― R code ――――――

```
require(hts)
y <- hts(vn, nodes=list(4,c(2,2,2,2)))
allf <- forecast(y, h=8)
plot(allf)
```